SECRETARIAL ENGLISH

by

DONALD A. SHEFF

PRENTICE HALL REGENTS, Englewood Cliffs, NJ 07632

SECRETARIAL ENGLISH

This book has been adapted from
BUSINESS ENGLISH – COLLEGE LEVEL

Printed in the United States of America

10 9 8 7 6 5 4

ISBN 0-13-797770-0 01

Prentice-Hall International (UK) Limited, *London*
Prentice-Hall of Australia Pty. Limited, *Sydney*
Prentice-Hall Canada Inc., *Toronto*
Prentice-Hall Hispanoamericana, S.A., *Mexico*
Prentice-Hall of India Private Limited, *New Delhi*
Prentice-Hall of Japan, Inc., *Tokyo*
Simon & Schuster Asia Pte. Ltd., *Singapore*
Editora Prentice-Hall do Brasil, Ltda., *Rio de Janeiro*

PREFACE

A socially-minded citizen has suggested that we ought to publicly acknowledge the modern secretary, whose services in today's complex world are so necessary and important.

We heartily agree with this suggestion and accept it by dedicating and addressing this book to all those who are employed as secretaries or who are planning secretarial careers.

Because of the title of this book do you, at this point, feel like asking if there is a difference between secretarial English and just good English? In all honesty, we must admit that there isn't any difference. Good English is good English, no matter where, or when or by whom it is used.

There are, however, differences in the way books present and treat a subject. This book offers all the English that the secretary in particular needs to know. It is a thoroughly reliable text in which all problems and difficulties are foreseen, presented, dealt with and explained by means of examples, suggestions, hints and memory guides.

Every rule, every point of grammar, punctuation or idiomatic or common usage, has its appropriate exercise. Each of these exercises is preceded by easy-to-follow instructions that state the purpose of the exercise and tell how and what to do with it. These exercises form the continuing link that will help you learn and make unimpeded progress in the use of good English.

Of all the skills that the modern secretary possesses — and she must possess quite a number in a high degree of excellence — the ability to understand, interpret and use good English is probably the most important. Indeed, if the modern secretary is to achieve a position that offers interesting work and challenging opportunities for advancement, she must be able to use English correctly and fluently. It is the very cornerstone of a satisfying career.

Now that you have read the Preface, it is suggested that you riffle through the pages of this book to get a quick, overall view of its appearance and contents. It *looks* inviting, doesn't it? You are invited to study it and keep it handy for reference and guidance in your career.

CONTENTS

LESSON 1

THE SENTENCE

1. what is a sentence **2. sentence fragments**

3. run-on sentences **4. agreement of subject and predicate**

Zoologists tell us that almost all animals communicate – the jungles offer a symphony of meaningful grunts, whistles, howls, and clicks. Even the seas are filled with the soggy sounds of fish communicating with one another. Why, then, is man considered unique in his ability to communicate? Because the communication of all these other animals is limited to disconnected instinctive signals – a shriek of alarm . . . a mating call . . . a triumphal cry of "Food!" Man's uniqueness lies in his ability to go beyond these isolated instinctive signals and to weld them in the crucible of his mind into complex *abstract ideas.* Man's genius lies in his ability to communicate these complex ideas through the medium of *language.*

Language is simply the audible expression of thought. It is not an artificial creation, but rather a natural expression that follows the natural flow of ideas in the mind. The man who thinks clearly, writes clearly. The man who thinks fuzzily and lazily, writes the same way. In other words, your language reflects your mind.

The rules of language that we call *grammar* are not the creation of some bearded philosophers. Rather they are a *description* of the natural pattern of language that civilized man has evolved over hundreds of centuries. A rule of grammar does not say, "This is so because we say it's so." It says, in effect, "This is so because this is the way the mind thinks. Anything else is less clear, less meaningful, less logical."

The objective of language is to communicate thoughts completely and clearly. To achieve this objective, the *sentence* is the basic unit since it is the "lowest form" that expresses a *complete thought.* A word or phrase by itself is merely a fragment of thought – the cry of an animal in the jungle. A sentence is the full expression of thought.

So let's start with the *sentence* in our study of Secretarial English – our study of grammar as it relates to the business world – for it is with the sentence that the art of language begins.

1. what is a SENTENCE?

Since the sentence is the basic unit of language that expresses a *complete thought,* every sentence must contain two essential parts:

1. *A subject,* which tells us whom or what we are talking about.
2. *A predicate,* which tells us what the subject does.

John speaks. This is a sentence. It expresses a complete thought by telling us:

a. Who? *John.* (The subject)
b. Does what? *Speaks.* (The predicate)

Tall, handsome John speaks. This, too, is a complete sentence. We have merely added some words that *describe* our subject. *They do not change the subject.* The subject is still *John* and the predicate is still *speaks.*

Tall, handsome John speaks with fluency and persuasion. Again, this is a complete sentence. *Tall, handsome* describes *John. With fluency and persuasion* describes *speaks.* The subject remains *John.* The predicate remains *speaks.*

Use this approach whenever you want to find the subject and the predicate of a sentence. Just ask yourself two simple questions:

a. Who or what is the doer of the action? (The subject)
b. What does the subject do? (The predicate)

For the moment, disregard all other words that merely describe the subject or the predicate.

1 The manager works with diligence and initiative.

a. Who? *Manager.* (The subject)
b. Does what? *Works.* (The predicate)
c. Disregard *with diligence and initiative.*

2 On Wednesday evening after the banquet, the executives will meet.

a. Who? *Executives.* (The subject)
b. Do what? *Will meet.* (The predicate)
c. Disregard *on Wednesday evening, after the banquet....*

In this sentence the predicate consists of more than one word, *will meet.* The word *will* is what we call an *auxiliary verb.* You'll learn more about these in a later lesson. For now, be alert to recognize an auxiliary verb whenever it is part of the predicate. You'll see it in a number of the following examples.

3 The secretary, after taking dictation, transcribed her notes.

a. Who? *Secretary* (The subject)
b. Did what? *Transcribed.* (The predicate)
c. Disregard *after taking dictation ... her notes.*

4 No one in all this confusion can decide upon a course of action.

a. Who? *(No) one.* (The subject)
b. Does what? *Can decide.* (The predicate)
c. Disregard all other words.

5 Eye-catching and appealing are our new package designs.

a. What? *Designs.* (In this sentence the subject comes *after* the predicate.)
b. Do what? *Are.* (The predicate)
c. Disregard all other words.

Would you have located the subject and predicate more easily if the sentence had been written in the more usual subject-before-predicate order, as follows: *Our new package designs are eye-catching and appealing.*

Don't let the predicate-before-subject order fool you. Simply rearrange the sentence mentally into the usual subject-before-predicate order.

6 Can you mail me the invoice by Friday? By rearranging this question into an affirmative statement, you can quickly locate the subject and predicate: *You can mail me the invoice by Friday.*

a. Who? *You.* (The subject)
b. Do what? *Can mail.* (The predicate)
c. Disregard all other words.

7 There are two men to see you. Here again a little rearrangement will make it much easier for you to locate the subject and the predicate: *Two men are there to see you.*

a. Who? *Men.* (The subject)
b. Do what? *Are.* (The predicate)
c. Disregard all other words.

8 Uranium and plutonium are fissionable materials.

a. What? *Uranium (and) plutonium.* (The subject in this case consists of more than one item.)
b. Do what? *Are.* (The predicate)
c. Disregard all other words.

When, as in this example, the subject is composed of two or more items, it is called a *compound subject.* You may remember that in chemistry a compound is a substance that is composed of two or more elements. So too in grammar, where the word *compound* is used in a number of different instances to indicate that something is made up of *more than one* part. In this example, you see a compound *subject.* Why is it compound?

9 Sales last year rose in May and fell in June.

a. What? *Sales.* (The subject)
b. Did what? *Rose . . . fell.* (The predicate in this case consists of more than one action.)
c. Disregard all other words.

As you probably guessed, the predicate in this example is called a *compound predicate.* Why?

10 Stand still!

a. Who? *You.* (Understood)
b. Do what? *Stand.*
c. Disregard *still.*

What do we mean by *understood?* This is a particular type of sentence—a command. Most commands are given quickly and curtly. The subject of the command is understood to mean *you.* Remember, though, in all other types of sentences the subject must be specifically stated. *Only* in commands can the subject be left to the imagination.

2. sentence FRAGMENTS

Is this a sentence: *John.* Obviously not. It names a subject, *John,* but does not tell us what the subject *does.* In other words, it is not a sentence because it contains no predicate and does not express a complete thought. It is only a piece or *fragment* of a sentence.

Is this a sentence: *Tall, handsome John.* Again, the answer is *No.* Our subject is described to us, but we are still not told what he does. We still have no predicate and no complete thought. Remember, a sentence must contain both a subject and a predicate and also must express a complete thought. A frequent mistake that some careless people make is to write only part of a sentence as though it were a complete sentence. For example: *Wrong: John Smith, president of our firm. Was invited to the banquet.*

Is either of these parts a complete sentence?

1 John Smith, president of our firm.

2 Was invited to the banquet.

No. Neither part is a complete sentence. Part 1 contains a subject, but no predicate. Part 2 contains a predicate, but no subject. Alone, each part is merely a *fragment* of a sentence. *Guard against sentence fragments!* To correct sentence fragments like 1 and 2, above, is simple. **Right: John Smith, president of our firm, was invited to the banquet.** We now have one sentence that includes a subject and predicate and expresses a complete thought.

EXAMPLES

1 Right: Our book, the latest, most authoritative word on the subject, has just been put on the market.

Wrong: Our book, the latest most authoritative word on the subject. Has just been put on the market.

2 Right: The course that we are offering you is the finest you can get anywhere.

Wrong: The course that we are offering you. Is the finest you can get anywhere.

3 Right: The committee of which you are a member met in secret session.

Wrong: The committee of which you are a member. Met in secret session.

There is another type of sentence fragment of which you should be wary on the job. This is the fragment that *apparently* contains both a subject and a predicate, but does not express a complete thought. For example, is this a sentence: *John, running at full speed.* Let's test it:

a. Who? *John.* (The subject)

b. Doing what? *Running.* (The apparent predicate)

c. Complete thought? NO! It leaves us with the question: *John running at full speed,* did what? This sentence fragment may be completed as follows: *John, running at full speed, fell.*

Remember, a sentence must express a complete thought! If it does not express a complete thought, it is not a sentence; it is merely a fragment of a sentence. Beware of sentence fragments.

Now let's turn to the final type of sentence fragment. Is this a complete sentence: *Since the order arrived.* Answer: NO! The word *since* limits our thought in such a manner that it does not express a complete thought although it contains a subject, *order,* and a predicate, *arrived.* The expression *since the order arrived* leaves you up in the air. You want to know: *Since the order arrived,* what happened? You must add something to complete the thought. For example, you might say: *Since the order arrived, we have made headway.*

In the sentence *Since the order arrived, we have made headway* there are clearly two distinct parts, each of which contains a subject and a predicate. *Since the order arrived* contains the subject *order* and the predicate *arrived. We have made headway* contains the subject *we* and the predicate *have made.* When a sentence contains two or more parts, each of which contains a subject and a predicate, we call each such part a *clause* of the sentence. In the above example, *Since the order arrived* is a clause; *we have made headway* is a clause.

A quick inspection of these two clauses shows you that there is an obvious difference between them. Do you see it? That's right. The clause *We have made headway* expresses a complete thought; it could stand as a sentence by itself: *We have made headway.* For this reason it is called an *independent clause.* An independent clause is simply a clause that expresses a complete thought and, therefore, could stand by itself as a sentence.

What about the clause *Since the order arrived?* Can it stand by itself as a sentence? Obviously not. The word *since* makes it *dependent* upon the rest of the sentence. For this reason it is called a *dependent* clause. What does it depend upon to complete it? That's right. It depends upon the *independent* clause, *we have made headway.*

There are many words like *since* that limit a thought, render it incomplete by itself, and make it *dependent* upon a main thought. Here are some other examples:

1 **Though we received your order, we could not fill it.** The word *though* makes *Though we received your order* incomplete by itself. It makes it *dependent* upon the main thought, *we could not fill it. Though we received your order* is the dependent clause; *we could not fill it* is the independent clause.

2 **As soon as we heard the news, we ran to congratulate you.** *As soon as* makes *As soon as we heard the news* dependent upon *we ran to congratulate you. As soon as we heard the news* is the dependent clause. What is the independent clause? Why is it independent?

3 **We left the theater because we failed to get the part.** Here, the dependent part comes last. *Because* makes *because we failed to get the part* dependent upon *we left the theater.* What is the dependent clause? The independent clause?

4 **We kept trying until it was too late.** *Until* makes *until it was too late* dependent upon *We kept trying.*

When you have a sentence like any of the above examples that is composed of a dependent clause linked to an independent clause, that sentence is called a *complex sentence.* What is a *complex* sentence? That's right. It's a sentence composed of an independent clause and a dependent clause. For the moment the important thing to remember is that you must never write one of these dependent clauses by itself as though it were a complete sentence.

Wrong: *Since the order arrived.* This is not a complete sentence. It is merely a fragment of a sentence. Guard against sentence fragments! Be sure to connect a dependent clause with an independent clause to form a complex sentence.

EXAMPLES

1 **Right: Though the weather was cloudy, we went sailing.**

Wrong: Though the weather was cloudy. We went sailing.

2 **Right: Although we received your last shipment, we feel it is of such inferior quality that we should get a rebate.**

Wrong: Although we received your last shipment. We feel it is of such inferior quality that we should get a rebate.

3 **Right: He won because he was the fastest.**

Wrong: He won. Because he was the fastest.

4 **Right: Because he was fastest, he won.**

Wrong: Because he was fastest. He won.

3. RUN-ON sentences

Look at these two sentences:

1. We hope to attend the banquet.

2. We may be detained by business.

You could combine these two sentences into one thought, as follows:

3. We hope to attend the banquet, but we may be detained by business.

Don't you agree that Sentence 3 better expresses the relationship between the ideas of Sentences 1 and 2?

Very often you will have two sentences that are so closely related that you may want to combine them into one. Don't think, however, that you can throw them together in a haphazard fashion. A sentence is like a building block. To connect two building blocks, you would use a good strong glue. To attach one sentence to another, you also need a strong *glue* to hold them together. This *glue* is supplied in Sentence 3 by the comma and the word *but:* **We hope to attend the banquet, but we may be detained by business.**

As you will learn in Lesson 9, the word *but* is called a *conjunction.* Two other conjunctions that can be used as *glue* to hold sentences together are *and* and *or.* For example: **Mr. Jackson took the 5:15 train, and he should be here any minute. You must accept our offer, or you will suffer the consequences.**

One great mistake that you should always avoid is trying to attach two sentences without using a *strong enough* glue. Here are two examples of the use of *glue* that is too weak to do the job:

❶ **Wrong: We hope to attend the banquet we may be detained by business.** Here no glue is used at all. There is nothing to hold the two sentences together. They fall apart.

❷ **Wrong: We hope to attend the banquet, we may be detained by business.** Here a comma is used to hold the two sentences together, but a comma by itself is not a strong enough glue to do the job. The two sentences again fall apart.

These two sentences are examples of an error that we call the *run-on sentence.* When two sentences are thrown together without a strong enough glue to hold them, the result is a run-on sentence. To correct such run-on sentences, either separate the two parts into individual sentences or use a strong glue like *but, and,* or *or* preceded by a comma.

Right: We hope to attend the banquet, but we may be detained by business.

One other type of glue that is strong enough to hold two sentences together is the *semicolon* (;). This mark of punctuation should be used only when the two thoughts are very closely related.

Right: Thank you for your note; it was most timely.

Right: We cannot send the dies; they are not yet in stock.

You have probably guessed that the run-on sentence is the opposite of the sentence fragment. The run-on sentence contains too much while the sentence fragment does not contain enough. Both are equally undesirable.

Remember these points, then:

1. To connect two sentences, you must use a *strong* glue such as a semicolon, or one

of the conjunctions *and, but, or* preceded by a comma.

2. You cannot hold two sentences together by using no glue at all; by using only a comma by itself as *glue;* or by using the conjunction *(and, but, or)* by itself without a comma (except in very short sentences, as will be explained later).

EXAMPLES

1 Right: Here is your order. We look forward to your reply.

Right: Here is your order, and we look forward to your reply.

Right: Here is your order; we look forward to your reply.

Wrong: Here is your order we look forward to your reply.

Wrong: Here is your order, we look forward to your reply.

2 Right: We are new in this field. Our clocks are unmatched in quality.

Right: We are new in this field, but our clocks are unmatched in quality.

Wrong: We are new in this field our clocks are unmatched in quality.

Wrong: We are new in this field, our clocks are unmatched in quality.

3 Right: We must change our advertising appeal. We may lose a large part of our market.

Right: We must change our advertising appeal, or we may lose a large part of our market.

4. AGREEMENT of SUBJECT and PREDICATE

When you answer your employer's phone, you would never say, *"Mr. Smith are here."* You wince just to think of it. When sentences are more complicated, however, you may fall into just such an error; and this is where knowing the subject and predicate can help you on the job.

For your sentence to be grammatically correct, *its predicate must agree with its subject in number.* This means that if the subject is singular you use a singular predicate. If the subject is plural, you use a plural predicate. For example, what would you do with a sentence like this: **One man in the firm of hundreds (is, are) to be honored.**

To solve this problem merely ask yourself: What is the subject of this sentence? Who is to be honored? *One man* is to be honored, not *this firm of hundreds.* Since the predicate must agree with the subject in number, use the singular predicate *is.* The sentence now reads: **One man in this firm of hundreds is to be honored.**

Below is a series of hints to help you determine whether to use a singular or a plural predicate.

HINTS on AGREEMENT of SUBJECT and PREDICATE

HINT 1.

Jack and Jill (is, are) going up a hill. This problem-sentence is easy. It contains two subjects (Jack, Jill) connected by *and.* The sentence means that both of them are going up a hill so it calls for the plural predicate *are.* **Jack and Jill are going up a hill.**

This illustrates the general rule: Whenever a sentence contains two or more subjects connected by *and*, use a plural predicate. Usually this is obvious and natural. **The Acme Company and the Omega Company are merging. Good bookkeepers and good stenographers are hard to find.**

There is one exception to this rule. When both subjects really refer to one person or one thing, use a singular predicate. For example: **The treasurer and secretary is here.** One man holds both positions. *He* is here. If the positions are held by two different men, however, then the general rule applies: **The president and the secretary are here.**

BUT: Bread and butter is my favorite snack. *Bread* and *Butter* are so closely identified in this sentence as to be considered one unit; therefore, use the singular predicate **is.**

BUT: Bread and butter are on my shopping list.

HINT 2.

❶ **Jack or Jill (is, are) going up the hill.** In this problem, notice first that there are two subjects connected by *or – Jack or Jill.* Here's a little trick that will help you with sentences like this. Whenever two or more subjects are connected by *or* or *nor,* make the predicate agree with the subject *closest* to it.

Jack or Jill (is, are) going up the hill. *Jill* is closer to the predicate. *Jill* is singular. Therefore, use the singular predicate *is going*. **Jack or Jill is going up the hill.**

❷ **Either Mr. Jones or Mr. Smith is going to the meeting.** *Mr. Smith* is closer to the predicate. *Mr. Smith* is singular. Therefore, use the singular predicate *is going.*

❸ **Neither the chair nor the table has arrived.** Remember, the same rule applies to two or more subjects connected by *nor. Table* is closer to the predicate. *Table* is singular. Therefore, use *has.*

❹ **The boys or the girls are going to win.** *Girls* is closer to the predicate. *Girls* is plural. Therefore, use the plural predicate *are.*

❺ **Neither the chairs nor the tables have arrived.** *Tables* is closer to the predicate. *Tables* is plural. Therefore, use *have.*

❻ **Either the secretaries or their bosses are to blame.** *Bosses* is closer to the predicate. *Bosses* is plural. Therefore, use *are.*

❼ **Mr. Sawyer or his sons (has, have) studied your problem.** This sentence is a little more complicated. One of the subjects is singular, *Mr. Sawyer*. The other subject is plural, *sons.* By applying our general rule, we can easily determine the proper predicate. *Sons* is closer to the predicate. *Sons* is plural. Therefore, we use the plural word *have:* **Mr. Sawyer or his sons have studied your problem.**

❽ **The boys or Mr. Sawyer has studied your problem.** Here *Mr. Sawyer* is closer to the predicate. Therefore, use *has.* It should be noted, however, that as a general rule of business usage, it is better to place the plural subject closer to the predicate. Thus Sentence No. 7 is a better sentence than Sentence No. 8. Read these sentences aloud. Don't you agree that Sentence No. 7 sounds better?

9 Neither the table nor the chairs have arrived. *Chairs* is plural. Therefore, use *have.*

10 Mr. Smith, Mr. Jones, or their aides have completed the report. In this sentence there are three subjects connected by *or*. This is no problem for our general rule. *Aides* is closest to the predicate. Therefore, we use the plural word *have.*

HINT 3.

Words such as *each, anybody,* and *nobody* are tricky. You can save yourself a great deal of grief on the job if you remember that when any one of the following words is the subject of a sentence, you use a *singular* predicate.

1 Each. Each of the officers in the firm is a future chairman. The subject is *each*, not *officers. Each* means *each one.* Therefore, use the singular predicate *is.*

2 Anyone. Anyone is qualified for the job. *Anyone* means *any one person,* and is therefore singular.

3 Anybody. Anybody is capable of filling this position. *Anybody* is the same as *anyone,* and is therefore singular.

4 Someone. Someone is going to suffer for this. *Someone* means *some one person.*

5 Somebody. Somebody has missed the point. *Somebody* is the same as *someone.*

6 Everyone. Everyone in town was sad when the Mets lost.

7 Everybody. Everybody here wants to go to the meeting.

HINT 4.

When determining the subject, disregard expressions beginning with words such as *of, in, at.* These small words are called *prepositions.* In Lesson 7 we will discuss prepositions at length. For now, just remember that you disregard an expression that begins with a word such as *of, in,* or *at* when looking for the subject of a sentence. Look at these examples:

1 Each of the soldiers is a potential leader. Disregard *of the soldiers. Each . . . is a potential leader.*

2 Nobody in the whole army is capable of doing a better job. Disregard *in the whole army. Nobody . . . is capable of doing a better job.*

3 Everyone at headquarters has his job outlined. Disregard *at headquarters. Everyone . . . has his job outlined.*

HINT 5.

Always disregard expressions beginning with *as well as, together with, in addition to, accompanied by,* etc. These expressions give supplementary, incidental information which could be omitted. They do not change the subject.

1 The book, as well as the papers, has been received. The subject is *book.* Disregard *as well as the papers.*

2 My employer, in addition to his associates, was pleased. The subject is *employer.* Disregard *in addition to his associates.*

3 Mr. Smith, together with his secretary, is scheduled to arrive at noon. The subject is *Mr. Smith.* Disregard *together with his secretary.*

4 **The salesman, accompanied by his family, takes the plane tonight.** The subject is *salesman.* Disregard *accompanied by his family.*

HINT 6.

In determining whether a subject is singular or plural, always look to the *meaning* of the word rather than to its form. For example, take the word *news.* Though *news* ends in *s,* it is singular in meaning. Therefore, it calls for a singular predicate. **No news is good news. The news is encouraging.**

Similarly, though the word *series* ends in *s,* it too is singular. **The series of revisions is completed. A series of changes has been made.**

Finally, the names of some school subjects and some diseases end in **s,** but are singular in meaning. For example: *economics, politics, civics, physics, mathematics, measles, and mumps.* **Economics is a required subject, as is civics. Measles is a mild disease. Physics is a basic tool of modern industry. Mumps is a dangerous illness if not treated properly.**

HINT 7.

When a quantity is measured in *one lump sum,* it should be treated as though it were one item. For example:

1 **Five tons is a lot of coal.** We are really referring to one large amount of coal.

2 **Eighty miles per hour is too fast.** Eighty miles per hour is one speed.

3 **Two hundred dollars is a fair amount.** We are referring to one sum of money.

On the other hand, when a quantity is measured in *piece-by-piece* units, use a plural predicate.

There are five men waiting.

In this box are 80 shirts.

Two hundred units have been produced.

You may have trouble when the word *number* is the subject of a sentence. Remember this rule-of-thumb: When *number* is preceded by *the,* use a singular predicate. When any other word, including *a,* precedes *number,* use a plural predicate.

The number of failures is low.

A number of people have failed.

HINT 8.

Beware of titles of books and articles that sound plural. For example:

1 **Right: "Business Letters" is a fine book.** You are referring to one book, though its title sounds plural.

2 **Right: "Notes on Fashions" is in this issue of Jones Magazine.** This is one article; therefore, use the singular predicate.

HINT 9.

Certain words refer to a number of people or things that comprise one group – words such as *committee, jury, class, faculty, crowd,* and *mob.* These words may be either singular or plural depending upon their *meaning* in a sentence. When the entire group to which they refer acts as a *single unit,* use a *singular* predicate.

The committee is scheduled to meet at one o'clock.

The class was led in the procession by the principal.

The jury has rendered its verdict.

When, however, you refer to the *individuals* that make the groups, use a plural predicate.

The committee are violently debating the merits of the proposed system.

The class were arguing with one another.

..ave been embroiled in major dis-..ment for three hours.

Although the latter three sentences are grammatically correct, there is no denying that they sound extremely awkward. They just don't *sound* right! For this reason, you would be well-advised to rewrite these sentences as follows:

The members of the committee are violently debating the merits of the proposed system.

The students in the class were arguing with one another.

The men and women of the jury have been embroiled in major disagreement for three hours.

These sentences sound better, don't they?

HINT 10.

The name of a firm frequently includes the names of more than one person, and it often includes the word *company.* Again, you must decide whether the company name is being used in a particular sentence in a singular or in a plural sense.

Merrill Lynch, Pierce, Fenner and Smith is America's largest brokerage house.

The American Steel Company has its main offices in Pittsburgh.

In both of the preceding sentences, we have treated the firm as a *single* unit and have therefore used a *singular* predicate. In actual business practice, however, it has become common for the representative of a firm to refer to his company as *we* rather than *it.* Compare these two sentences.

American Steel is pleased to announce that it has developed a new type of alloy especially designed to solve your problem.

American Steel is pleased to announce that we have developed a new type of alloy especially designed to solve your problem.

The use of *it* in the first sentence is cold and impersonal. The use of *we* in the second sentence adds a slight dash of warmth to the statement; it conjures up an image of the many hard-working men and women who have toiled to create this new alloy. This *human* company image may be just the subtle touch that creates a sale for one firm rather than for another. For this reason, the use of a firm name in the plural sense has become an extremely common and accepted practice in American business today.

HINT 11.

You have already been introduced to the type of sentence in which the predicate appears *before* the subject. You learned that you can easily recognize the parts of this type of sentence if you mentally rearrange the sentence into the usual subject-before-predicate order. For example, try this sentence: **Listed among those men suggested for promotion (was, were) George Shultz.** By reversing the order for the sentence, you easily find the solution: **Reverse: George Shultz was listed among those men suggested for promotion.**

Many predicate-before-subject sentences begin with the word *there:* **There (is, are) three new designs that have been selected.** This problem can be solved the same way – by mentally reversing the elements. **Reverse: Three new designs that have been selected are there.**

See how this procedure works with the following sentence: **There (is, are) a large area of disagreement between the factions. Reverse: A large area of disagreement between**

the factions is there.

How about this sentence?

There (is, are) a man and his child to see you, Doctor. Just reverse the order of the sentence, and the answer becomes obvious. **Reverse: A man and his child are there to see you, Doctor.**

HINT 12.

The word *none* can be either singular or plural depending upon its reference in a sentence. Most often it is considered plural and requires a plural predicate.

None of the orders have been processed yet, is preferred. **None of the orders has been processed yet,** is also correct since *none* can mean *not one;* therefore: **Not one . . . has been processed yet.**

HINT 13.

The word *some* may be singular or plural depending upon its meaning in a particular sentence. Here's an easy way to tell the difference in most sentences containing this word. Generally, *some* is followed by a phrase beginning with *of.* If the noun or pronoun in such a phrase is plural, treat *some* as plural. **Some of the men have returned to work.**

If the noun or pronoun in the phrase is singular, treat *some* as singular. **Some of the work is considered satisfactory. Some of the firm's capital is being ear-marked for expansion.**

HINT 14.

Frequently a fraction or percentage is used as the subject of a sentence. **Three-fifths of the men have arrived. Sixty per cent of our quota has been met.**

The same rule-of-thumb that we used with *some* applies to these fractions and percentages:

Half of the farms in this area are for sale.
Fifty per cent of this farm is lying fallow.
One quarter of the order has been shipped.
Twenty-five per cent of the orders have been shipped.

EXERCISE 1 — Identifying the Subject and Predicate

This problem deals with identifying the subject and the predicate of a sentence. In each of the following sentences, underline the subject with one line; underline the predicate with two lines. Remember, ask yourself two questions: 1. Who or what? (The subject) 2. Does what? (The predicate). Disregard all other words.

1. I like this book.
2. This book has been sold to over 200,000 readers.
3. These readers have uniformly expressed their delight with this book.
4. Did you enjoy it?
5. I certainly did enjoy it.
6. George and Harry are co-owners of the restaurant.
7. Mr. Roberts and Mr. Jones are in their offices.
8. At the stroke of noon the President and his cabinet met in the East Wing.
9. Have you seen the President and his cabinet in session?
10. Neither Mr. Black nor Mr. Green has sent in his reply.
11. We wish to see either Miss White or Miss Brown.
12. Neither of them is here.
13. She can type and file expertly.
14. The secretary has transcribed and mailed the letter.
15. Has the letter been typed and mailed?
16. There is a simple solution to the problem of unfulfilled obligations.
17. A free and strong America is the objective of our government policies.
18. The men will rise early and depart for the camp at the appointed hour.
19. Before him stood New York—big and beautiful—with its towering buildings, shimmering rivers, and ribbon-like bridges.
20. Give it to me this minute.
21. Ready to greet the new supervisor was his staff of assistants.
22. Waiting at the airport were the accountant and the lawyer.
23. There are more than 50 percent of the offices rented.
24. Near him sat the two partners of the firm.
25. Needed more than economy is efficiency.

EXERCISE 2 — Sentence Fragments

A. **This problem deals with recognizing incomplete thoughts. As you know, a sentence must express a complete thought. Below is a list of expressions. Some of them express complete thoughts. In the space provided, mark C next to these sentences to indicate that they are <u>complete</u> sentences. The rest of these expressions do not express complete thoughts. Mark F next to these to indicate that these expressions are sentence <u>fragments</u>.**

1. Running down the street at full speed. 1. ____________
2. Despite his lack of experience and maturity. 2. ____________
3. We agree. 3. ____________
4. Night after night, day after day, till he could hardly speak anymore. 4. ____________
5. Mr. Roberts, the most noted authority on aerodynamics in recent years. 5. ____________
6. Furtively looking up and down the street, then darting to safety in the shadows, he escaped. 6. ____________
7. Where are we going? 7. ____________
8. Despite all his protestations to the contrary and his insistence that he was innocent, he was convicted. 8. ____________
9. Although we were certain that he was a fine leader and were willing to follow him wherever he would lead. 9. ____________
10. When the order arrives and is processed by the receiving department. 10. ____________
11. Despite explicit orders to the contrary. 11. ____________
12. Nearing the attainment of the production goals set at our last meeting. 12. ____________
13. Nearly everyone present, including the President and his aides. 13. ____________
14. Nearly everyone was present, including the President and his aides. 14. ____________
15. There is no time for further discussion. 15. ____________
16. Delivery of one table, four chairs, two desks, and three lamps. 16. ____________
17. Your order was received. 17. ____________
18. Forgetting all the instructions the foreman had given him in the morning. 18. ____________
19. Don't send the letter. 19. ____________
20. Where in this entire office? 20. ____________

EXERCISE 2 Recognition of Clauses DEPENDENT AND INDEPENDENT

B. **The problem here is to recognize a clause (a group of words with a subject and predicate) and to label it dependent if it cannot stand alone as a sentence, or independent if it can stand alone. In each sentence below a group of words is *italicized*. In the space to the right, write D if it is a dependent clause; write I if it is an independent clause; write N if it is not a clause.**

1.	I prefer the typewriter *on the table.*	1. ________
2.	*When a letter is typed,* it represents the firm.	2. ________
3.	He led his sales force *because of his ambition.*	3. ________
4.	*Because he was ambitious,* he soon impressed his employers.	4. ________
5.	*We can offer this guarantee* because of our high quality control.	5. ________
6.	*Standing behind each man* is a woman who prods him into action.	6. ________
7.	*She is a fine bookkeeper* because she is quick with figures.	7. ________
8.	*Although we have worked hard,* the end is not yet in sight.	8. ________
9.	*Your order was received in time* despite an unexpected delay.	9. ________
10.	Because we have years of experience, *we can do the best job.*	10. ________

EXERCISE 2 Simple and Complex Sentences

C. **A simple sentence is a sentence composed of one independent clause. A complex sentence is a sentence composed of an independent clause and a dependent clause. In the space to the right of each example, write S if it is a <u>simple</u> sentence; write X if it is a <u>complex</u> sentence; write F if it is a sentence <u>fragment</u>.**

1.	On the last day in April we will hold our meeting.	1. ________
2.	Despite our protests, he entered the primary race for the Senate.	2. ________
3.	We will expect delivery as soon as possible.	3. ________
4.	After they deliver the goods, we will bill them.	4. ________
5.	If anything ever sounded as though it were unwise.	5. ________
6.	Please try to arrive before 10 o'clock to avoid any delay.	6. ________
7.	Though you have a prior engagement, won't you try to attend?	7. ________
8.	There are several good reasons for our decision and for our unwillingness to participate.	8. ________
9.	The merchandise arrived in damaged condition despite the warnings we sent you.	9. ________
10.	Don't you agree with the Commission's report on unemployment?	10. ________

EXERCISE 2 — Proofreading for Sentence Fragments

D. **In creating copy for advertising, copywriters occasionally take liberties with the strict rules of grammar in order to emphasize a point. Sometimes, however, they go "overboard" in violating these rules, and any emphasis they hoped for is buried in a morass of misapplied English. We think that this has happened in the advertising copy presented below which is filled with a stream of sentence fragments. Circle any marks of punctuation and capital letters that should be changed.**

MIRACLE IN THE MEADOW

There's a 12-story miracle in Flushing Meadow Park called Unisphere. It's the largest replica of the world ever built. And the symbol of the 1964-1965 New York World's Fair.

Before Unisphere was completed, it confronted U. S. Steel with unbelievable engineering and construction problems. Since it's an open sculpture, with virtually every part exposed, Unisphere had to be built to withstand the rain and ice. And the salt-laden gales that sweep across Long Island.

But all these problems were solved. Without sacrificing beauty for strength, or strength for beauty. And defying predictions that Unisphere was "impossible," it was completed a full five months ahead of schedule. And when the last section of the stainless-steel globe was put into place, all the pieces fit perfectly. They had to. There wasn't a replacement part on earth, because nothing like Unisphere had ever been attempted before.

Unisphere towers 140 feet over a reflecting pool. Has 500 separate parts. Weighs 900 thousand pounds. And has a diameter of 120 feet.

It will remain as a permanent reminder of man's aspirations for peace through mutual understanding, and a symbol of his achievements in an expanding universe. Unisphere is truly the miracle in the meadow.

EXERCISE 3 — Run-on Sentences

This problem deals with recognizing run-on sentences. Some of the following sentences are correct; others are run-on sentences. Wherever there is an error in punctuation or capitalization, cross out the error and write your correction in the space above. If a sentence is entirely correct, mark C in the left-hand margin.

1. Have your representative call, a definite appointment should be made in advance.

2. Maybe later on we will be willing to do as your order man writes, just now, however, we do not wish to change.

3. Are the letters and articles graded according to difficulty, in our book they are.

4. Mr. James Quinn, a man with considerable experience in office planning, will be ready to help you on March 4.

5. At this time, however, we do not wish to change, we are sure you will understand.

6. But read the booklet, yours will bear your imprint on the front and back covers.

7. She learns all the good points and fortifies herself with facts and evidence about the superiority of York silk and the weak points of others so that when she is ready to buy silk she will want York and no other brand.

8. Won't you please take a few moments of your time to tell us the details of the improper shipment, armed with this information, we will be in a position to ship you the correct items.

9. We are making our plans for next summer, we are interested in your booklet concerning York silk.

10. Try Smilo toothpaste, it will give you the smile of contentedness.

EXERCISE 4 Sentence Fragments and Run-on Sentences

A. **This problem deals with distinguishing a complete sentence from a sentence fragment or a run-on sentence. In the space provided, mark C if the expression is a complete sentence; mark F if it is a sentence fragment; and mark R if it is a run-on sentence.**

1. Whenever the attorney had a chance to speak. 1. ______
2. Ship the books, w. will remit within 30 days. 2. ______
3. Lessons by day, study at night. 3. ______
4. Because of his initiative, and because he had the proper connections. 4. ______
5. What will happen next? 5. ______
6. Continue with your college course, you will graduate at the head of your class. 6. ______
7. Looking around, sizing up the situation, and foretelling all its ramifications. 7. ______
8. Oil, steel, and coal in the right proportions. 8. ______
9. Expect only big things of yourself, and never waver or doubt that they will come true. 9. ______
10. Though Miss Blake is young, she is not immature, so I am convinced she can handle the job. 10. ______
11. Speaking of telephone prices. A new low rate for evening calls is now in practice. 11. ______
12. Carbon copies are important for checking data, especially in business correspondence. 12. ______
13. Stay late tonight, you will be paid for overtime. 13. ______
14. Please check your accuracy, however speed is essential too. 14. ______
15. Of course we are interested, you would be too. 15. ______
16. We have written twice, please reply at once. 16. ______
17. As soon as the incident was reported, rumors started flying; accordingly, the President rushed to clarify the issues to the nation. ______
18. Courtesy is contagious, therefore smile often. 18. ______
19. Help! 19. ______
20. We followed the directions, but we couldn't assemble the instrument no matter how many different ways we attempted to arrange the elements. 20. ______

EXERCISE 4 Sentence Fragments and Run-on Sentences

B. **This letter contains a number of sentence fragments and run-on sentences. Proofread this letter, crossing out all mistakes and making all necessary changes.**

Dear Mr. White:

No two men are alike, one man jumps to a conclusion without careful consideration of all available information. Another man examines each fact. Checks every claim. And profits from the experience of others, then he makes his decision.

We believe you are the latter type of purchaser. The man who has to see for himself before he buys. For this reason we are delighted to offer you a Slick Electric Razor on a free-home-trial basis. Although you may have used another razor all your life. After seven days with the Slick you will never again want to switch back to your old-type razor.

So mail the enclosed card today, we will ship your sample Slick Razor by return post.

Sincerely,

EXERCISE 5 — The Subject of a Sentence

A. **This problem deals with identifying the subject of a sentence and determining if it is singular or plural. In the column headed Subject, write the subject of each sentence. In the column headed Number write S if the subject is singular and P if the subject is plural.**

		SUBJECT	NUMBER
1.	A man called at your office.	1. ______	______
2.	A tall, dark, handsome, cultured man called at your office.	2. ______	______
3.	Frank and Mary are staying overtime today.	3. ______	______
4.	Macy's and Gimbel's are friendly competitors.	4. ______	______
5.	Efficient supervisors and executives have always been at a premium.	5. ______	______
6.	Both the designer and the engineer seem competent workers.	6. ______	______
7.	Peaches and cream is my favorite breakfast dish.	7. ______	______
8.	A supervisor for all receptionists must be picked today.	8. ______	______
9.	Bread and butter is a staple in the American diet.	9. ______	______
10.	Office machinery must be covered and carefully protected.	10. ______	______

EXERCISE 5 — The Predicate of a Sentence

B. **This problem deals with identifying the predicate. In the column headed Predicate, write the predicate of the sentence. In the column headed Subject Number, write S if the subject is singular and P if the subject is plural.**

		PREDICATE	SUBJECT NUMBER
1.	Mr. Smith and his partner will speak at the meeting today.	1. ______	______
2.	Either Mary or her friend will be the best model for the new uniform.	2. ______	______
3.	Neither time nor effort should be spared in practicing typing.	3. ______	______
4.	Neither the desk nor the chairs have arrived at the office.	4. ______	______
5.	Each of the applicants has to fill out a questionnaire.	5. ______	______
6.	Anyone of the export firms is able to handle the shipment.	6. ______	______
7.	Everybody in the sales force is asked to use the suggestion box.	7. ______	______
8.	Somebody in the executive office is responsible for time studies.	8. ______	______
9.	The news of the sales losses is coming over the ticker tape.	9. ______	______
10.	Each male and each female has equal opportunity for promotion.	10. ______	______

EXERCISE 5 — Identifying Subject and Predicate

C. **This problem deals with your ability to pick out subjects and predicates found in a business letter. Underline each subject once and each predicate twice.**

Gentlemen:

In your recent letter you ordered several items for immediate delivery. Our production manager and our consulting engineer have informed me of some delays in retooling machines for your order. We shall expedite this adjustment and put your order into work quickly. The shipping department will, of course, inform you of the shipping date, and Mr. Jones will visit you personally if necessary. Please understand our problems in retooling and accept our assurance of careful attention. Both Mr. Jones and I shall look forward to serving you.

Sincerely,

EXERCISE 6 — Agreement of Subject and Predicate

A. **This problem deals with agreement of subject and predicate. In the space provided, write the correct predicate. Remember, first find the subject; then choose its predicate. If you have any trouble, review the Hints on Agreement of Subject and Predicate.**

1. Each order (has, have) been received. 1. ____________
2. Each of the orders (has, have) been received. 2. ____________
3. Nobody among the secretaries (seem, seems) capable of supervising tests. 3. ____________
4. My boss, together with his assistant, (was, were) able to attend the convention. 4. ____________
5. Mr. Jones, together with his wife, (is, are) planning to take a holiday. 5. ____________
6. A series of changes in office routines (is, are) expected soon. 6. ____________
7. News of the price decreases (has, have) reached the customers. 7. ____________
8. Six tons of coal (was, were) paid for on the last bill. 8. ____________
9. The number of marriages in the firm (is, are) increasing. 9. ____________
10. A number of filing clerks and secretaries (has, have) applied. 10. ____________

EXERCISE 6 — Agreement of Subject and Predicate

B. **Choose the correct predicate. Indicate whether the predicate is singular or plural—writing S if it is singular; P if it is plural.**

	PREDICATE	NUMBER
1. "Writing Better Letters" (is, are) a good book for secretaries.	1. ________	____
2. "Ideas on Office Improvement" (was, were) put aside for the new typist.	2. ________	____
3. The committee (has, have) decided to issue their report next week.	3. ________	____
4. The jury (was, were) asked by the judge to render its decision.	4. ________	____
5. The faculty of the school (seem, seems) to be against new proposals.	5. ________	____
6. Pearson, French, Hein and Jackson (is, are) a leading publishing house.	6. ________	____
7. The Providence Producing Company (appear, appears) on the top of the list.	7. ________	____
8. The members of the ANTA Playhouse Company (is, are) planning a road trip.	8. ________	____
9. A number of checks (was, were) returned marked "No funds."	9. ________	____
10. The number of books available for sale (is, are) low.	10. ________	____

EXERCISE 6 — Agreement of Subject and Predicate

C. **In the first space write the subject; in the second, write the predicate.**

	SUBJECT	PREDICATE
1. High among the winners (was, were) Jim Taylor.	1. ________	____
2. There (is, are) several ways of making stencil corrections.	2. ________	____
3. There (was, were) three comments in the suggestion box.	3. ________	____
4. None of the orders (have, has) been processed yet.	4. ________	____
5. None of the methods of transcription (is, are) beyond criticism.	5. ________	____
6. Some of the firm's investments (seem, seems) to have been affected by the market changes.	6. ________	____
7. Some of the carbons (have, has) been ruined by careless handling.	7. ________	____
8. Three-fifths of the crop (has, have) to be stored in silos.	8. ________	____
9. Forty per cent of the letters (have, has) to be corrected.	9. ________	____
10. Half of the order (appear, appears) to be on its way.	10. ________	____

EXERCISE 6 — Agreement of Subject and Predicate

D. **This problem deals with agreement of subject and predicate. In the space provided, write the correct predicate. Remember, first find the subject; then choose its predicate. If you have any trouble, review the Hints on Agreement of Subject and Predicate.**

1. Each order (has, have) been processed. 1. ____________
2. Each of the orders (has, have) been processed. 2. ____________
3. Anyone (know, knows) what the solution should be. 3. ____________
4. Walter Clark of Chicago, as well as his entire family, (intend, intends) to spend his summer here. 4. ____________
5. Either Mr. Burns or Mr. Jones (is, are) the logical candidate. 5. ____________
6. There (is, are) a table and a lamp still unshipped. 6. ____________
7. One million dollars (is, are) a lot of money 7. ____________
8. We feel that neither your office nor your plants (is, are) adequately equipped. 8. ____________
9. The committee (has, have) issued a final decree. 9. ____________
10. Each of the children, in addition to his parents, (is, are) entitled to a free pass. 10. ____________
11. A number of photos (were, was) taken. 11. ____________
12. Anybody with a sound mind (are, is) eligible to enter. 12. ____________
13. I feel that politics (has, have) entered a decade of turmoil. 13. ____________
14. The number of books available for sale (are, is) low. 14. ____________
15. Thirty-six percent of our total production (has, have) been sold. 15. ____________
16. None of the suppliers (has, have) called since our orders were sent. 16. ____________
17. Hundreds of teachers, together with their students, (hail, hails) our product. 17. ____________
18. Measles (is, are) a contagious disease. 18. ____________
19. This series of figures (is, are) much too confusing. 19. ____________
20. Here (is, are) the list of figures you requested. 20. ____________
21. Any number of consequences (is, are) possible. 21. ____________
22. Nearly one-third of our supply (has, have) been exhausted. 22. ____________
23. Mathematics as well as economics (is, are) required. 23. ____________
24. The members of the jury (is, are) in complete disagreement. 24. ____________
25. The jury and the judge, as well as the general public, (is, are) convinced of the defendant's innocence. 25. ____________

REVIEW EXERCISE — The Sentence

The letter below contains a number of intentional errors in sentence structure. Cross out all incorrect punctuation and incorrect words. Above each, write the proper form.

Dear Mr. Jones:

On looking over our records this week, we find that each of your offices has failed to renew its subscription to Modern Times. And we assure you we regret this very much. Each of our previous letters express our appreciation of having you as a subscriber. And explain to you our desire to have all your offices remain as regular subscribers.

Everyone on our staff are concerned over your failure to renew, was this failure due to something that somebody in my office have said or done? We would be very much pleased to hear any suggestions you may have, and assure you that we will take all steps possible to remedy any unfortunate situation.

You know "Modern Times" are the finest magazine in its field, whether drama, science, current events, or politics are your interest, "Modern Times" have articles of interest to you. "Modern Times" is read and enjoyed by men in all walks of life, it is read by doctors, it is read by lawyers, it is read by engineers, the list of readers are just endless.

We do hope that you will reconsider and forward your renewal so that we may again enter your name on our list of subscribers and friends. After all, are there anything more important than loyal friends?

Sincerely yours,

LESSON 2

NOUNS

1. the types of nouns **2. forming the plurals of nouns**

3. possessive nouns

Now that we have studied the sentence, let's turn to the words that make up the sentence. The names of most of these words are probably familiar to you – *nouns, pronouns, verbs, adjectives, adverbs, conjunctions,* and *prepositions.* You undoubtedly met most of these terms in your earlier schooling, but you may have forgotten their *exact* technical meaning. Don't let that worry you! Our purpose is to make you into an expert. We shall start from the very beginning and leave nothing to chance.

You may wonder, "Why must they plague me with technical terms like *nouns* and *verbs* and the like?" And that's a good question. We could have omitted all such terms and given them other, simpler names. We could have called nouns *name words* and called verbs *action words.* But would you really have gained by this? Probably not. More likely you would have become confused by the mixture in your mind of the new terms we would invent and those commonly used terms you would remember from grammar school.

So, we shall use the old familiar terms. If you don't remember them from your grammar-school days, that's no problem. We'll teach you all about them. If you happen to recall the meanings of these terms, all the better. We'll reinforce what you already know and teach you more.

Let's start with the words known as *nouns.*

1. the TYPES of nouns

Nouns are *name* words. We use nouns to *name* persons, places, things, or abstract qualities. Here are some examples:

Person	*Place*	*Thing*	*Abstract Quality*
man	**courtroom**	**chair**	**truth**
typist	**school**	**shorthand**	**initiative**
Smith	**lake**	**book**	**readiness**

You can divide all nouns into two classes: *common nouns* and *proper nouns.* A common noun names a *general* class of people, places, things, or abstract qualities. A proper noun names a *specific* person, place, or thing. Look at these paired examples:

Common Noun:	**boy**	**country**	**car**
Proper Noun:	**John**	**America**	**Buick**

The significance of the distinction between common nouns and proper nouns will become apparent when you study capitalization in a later lesson. As you will learn, proper nouns are always capitalized; common nouns are not.

2. forming the PLURAL of nouns

Nouns, as you know, may be either singular or plural.

Singular	*Plural*
book	**books**
child	**children**
alumnus	**alumni**

Do you know how to spell plural nouns correctly? How do you spell the plural of *attorney*? of *solo*? of *brother-in-law*? In business you will have to be able to spell these plural nouns properly at all times. Remember this basic rule: *WHEN IN DOUBT, LOOK IT UP!* Use your dictionary. Most dictionaries include a special note under each noun showing the proper spelling of the plural of that noun. Here is a typical dictionary entry. We have circled the notation that shows you how to spell the plural.

lynx (liŋks), *n.* [*pl.* LYNXES (-iz), LYNX; see PLURAL, II, D, 1], [ME.; L.; Gr. *lynx*], 1. any of a group of wildcats found throughout the northern hemisphere and characterized by a ruff on each side of the face, long legs, a short tail, long, tufted ears, and keen vision: the North American species are the

Extracted from WEBSTER'S NEW WORLD DICTIONARY, College Edition, Copyright 1958 by the World Publishing Co.

Of course, you should not be in doubt so often that you are *constantly* at your dictionary. You should commit to memory the plural forms of most frequently used nouns. To help you do this we have listed some rules to guide you.

These rules for forming plurals are not difficult. All they require is a little of your concentration.

RULE 1.

To form the plural of *most* nouns, simply add *s*.

cigarette	**cigarettes**
crowd	**crowds**
desk	**desks**
group	**groups**
European	**Europeans**
paper	**papers**
piece	**pieces**
receipt	**receipts**
town	**towns**
Mrs. Smith	**the Smiths**

RULE 2.

To form the plural of a noun that ends in the sound *s*, *sh*, *x*, or *ch*, add *es*.

box	**boxes**
bus	**buses**
bush	**bushes**
church	**churches**
gas	**gases**
glass	**glasses**
lash	**lashes**
lunch	**lunches**
tax	**taxes**
Mr. Rich	**the Riches**

RULE 3.

To form the plural of a noun that ends in *y* preceded by a *vowel (a, e, i, o, u)*, simply add *s*.

alley	**alleys**
alloy	**alloys**
attorney	**attorneys**
essay	**essays**
galley	**galleys**
play	**plays**
survey	**surveys**
trolley	**trolleys**
turkey	**turkeys**
valley	**valleys**

NOTE: Colloquies, soliloquies

RULE 4.

To form the plural of a noun that ends in *y* preceded by a *consonant* (any letter other than *a, e, i, o, u*), change the *y* to *i* and add *es*.

accessory	**accessories**
baby	**babies**
company	**companies**
country	**countries**
county	**counties**
laboratory	**laboratories**
lady	**ladies**
specialty	**specialties**
variety	**varieties**

When a *proper* noun ends in *consonant-y*, just add *s*.

the Henrys the Kellys the Murphys

RULE 5.

To form the plural of a noun that ends in *o* preceded by a *vowel*, merely add *s*.

cameo	**cameos**
embryo	**embryos**
patio	**patios**
portfolio	**portfolios**
radio	**radios**
ratio	**ratios**
studio	**studios**

RULE 6.

a. To form the plurals of many nouns that end in *o* preceded by a *consonant*, add *es*.

cargo	**cargoes**
echo	**echoes**
embargo	**embargoes**
hero	**heroes**
motto	**mottoes**
Negro	**Negroes**
potato	**potatoes**
tomato	**tomatoes**
veto	**vetoes**
volcano	**volcanoes**

b. To form the plurals of many *musical* terms and some other nouns that end in *o* preceded by a *consonant*, merely add *s*.

banjo	**banjos**
concerto	**concertos**
piano	**pianos**
solo	**solos**
soprano	**sopranos**
auto	**autos**
dynamo	**dynamos**
halo	**halos**
memento	**mementos**
tobacco	**tobaccos**
zero	**zeros**

RULE 7.

To form the plurals of many nouns that end in the sound of *f*, change the *f* to *v* and add *es*.

calf	**calves**
half	**halves**
knife	**knives**
leaf	**leaves**
life	**lives**
loaf	**loaves**
self	**selves**
shelf	**shelves**
thief	**thieves**
wife	**wives**

BUT NOTE:

bailiff	**bailiffs**
chef	**chefs**
chief	**chiefs**
dwarf	**dwarfs**
handkerchief	**handkerchiefs**
plaintiff	**plaintiffs**
proof	**proofs**
roof	**roofs**
safe	**safes**

RULE 8.

Certain old English nouns have irregular plural forms. You should find these words very familiar.

child	**children**
foot	**feet**
gentleman	**gentlemen**
goose	**geese**
louse	**lice**
man	**men**
mouse	**mice**
ox	**oxen**
woman	**women**

RULE 9.

Certain nouns have special plural forms. Below is a list of the most frequently used ones. Try to learn to recognize these words. If you are not certain of the precise meaning of any of these words, look it up in your dictionary.

Singular	*Plural*
alumna (female)	**alumnae**
alumnus (male)	**alumni**
analysis	**analyses**
antithesis	**antitheses**
axis	**axes**
basis	**bases**
crisis	**crises**
datum	**data**
hypothesis	**hypotheses**
oasis	**oases**
parenthesis	**parentheses**
phenomenon	**phenomena**
synopsis	**synopses**
synthesis	**syntheses**
thesis	**theses**

Some nouns have both foreign plural forms and also "Anglicized" plural forms. In the following list we have put the *preferred* spelling of the plural in the middle column.

Singular	*Preferred Plural*	*Acceptable Plural*
appendix	**appendixes**	**appendices**
criterion	**criteria**	**criterions**
formula	**formulas**	**formulae**
index	**indexes**	**indices**
medium	**mediums**	**media**
memorandum	**memorandums**	**memoranda**

RULE 10.

Many words are composed of two separate nouns that are linked together to form one word. Such words are called *compound* nouns. When a compound noun is written as one *solid* word, without hyphens, form the plural by making the *last* part plural.

blackboard	**blackboards**
bookcase	**bookcases**
classmate	**classmates**
courthouse	**courthouses**
cupful	**cupfuls**
grandchild	**grandchildren**
handful	**handfuls**
letterhead	**letterheads**
spoonful	**spoonfuls**
stepchild	**stepchildren**
stockholder	**stockholders**
workman	**workmen**

RULE 11.

When forming the plural of a compound noun that is written with one or more hyphens, make the *principal* or *most important* part plural. Sometimes it's difficult to decide just *which* part is the most important part. So study these examples:

brother-in-law	**brothers-in-law**
court-martial	**courts-martial** (or court-martials)
editor-in-chief	**editors-in-chief**
father-in-law	**fathers-in-law**
mother-in-law	**mothers-in-law**
sister-in-law	**sisters-in-law**

RULE 12.

Form the plurals of *numerals,* individual *letters,* and *characters* by adding *'s.*

9	**9's**	*	***'s**
56	**56's**	#	**#'s**
h	**h's**	**x**	**x's**

NOTE: These are the *only* instances in which you use an apostrophe to form a plural. Notice also that a number that is *written out* forms its plural in the usual manner, without an apostrophe.

nine	**nines**	**fifty-six**	**fifty-sixes**

You also form in the usual manner the plural of any *word* used simply as a word: **It must be done; we will stand for no <u>ifs</u>, <u>ands</u>, or <u>buts</u>.**

RULE 13.

What is the plural of *Mr.*? of *Mrs.*? of *Miss*? Often a business letter will be addressed to more than one person, and the plurals of these titles can become a problem. Here's how you solve that problem easily.

The plural of *Mr.* (Mister) is *Messrs.,* an abbreviation derived from the French word *Messieurs.* Accordingly, you may write: *Dear Messrs. Smith and Black.* Modern business usage, however, is tending away from this old-fashioned form, and many employers today prefer that you repeat the title of each person: *Dear Mr. Smith and Mr. Black.*

The plural of *Mrs.* is *Mmes.,* an abbreviation derived from the French word *Mesdames.* Accordingly, you may write: *Dear Mmes. Jones and Spencer.* Or you may follow the preferred modern usage and repeat the title: *Dear Mrs. Jones and Mrs. Spencer.*

The plural of *Miss* is *Misses.* Again, it is preferable to repeat the title rather than use the plural term: *Dear Miss Hale and Miss Holsey* rather than *Dear Misses Hale and Holsey.*

Why should you bother to learn these plural forms if they are no longer considered preferable? First, because *your* particular employer may prefer these time-honored forms. Second, because you should be able to recognize them when they appear on letters *received* by your firm. Third, because they are still used widely in *social* correspondence. Fourth, because if you are writing to a firm in which three brothers are partners, you would not write *Dear Mr. Kern, Mr. Kern, and Mr. Kern.* In this instance it is proper to write: *Dear Messrs. Kern.* Of course, it is sometimes less awkward to write *Gentlemen.*

RULE 14.

A few nouns are written the same in both the singular and the plural forms. When one of these nouns is the subject of a sentence, you must look to the meaning of the sentence to determine whether to use a singular or a plural predicate.

corps	**Japanese**
deer	**means** (method)
fish (quantity)	**series**
gross	**sheep**
head (of cattle)	**species**

Corps is pronounced *core* in the singular; it is pronounced *cores* in the plural.

Some nouns *look* plural but are really singular in meaning. Always use a singular predicate when one of the following words is the subject of a sentence: *news, measles, mumps, economics, physics, politics, ethics, molasses.* For example:

Politics <u>is</u> a vital field.

Some nouns are *always* plural, never singular. Always use a plural predicate when one of the following words is the subject of a sentence: *scissors, pants* (clothing), *trousers, proceeds* (money), *goods* (merchandise), *thanks, riches, headquarters, premises, auspices.* For example:

The proceeds <u>were</u> turned over to charity.

3. POSSESSIVE nouns

Another type of noun you will use frequently in business is the *possessive.* A possessive noun is one which shows ownership, authorship, or origin:

The *company's* factory (ownership)
Shakespeare's play (authorship)
The *lamp's* glow (origin)

The rules for the spelling of possessive nouns were quite complicated at one time. In those awful bygone days you had to be a genius to know whether to add *apostrophe s* (*'s*) or just *apostrophe* to the name *Charles* or *Roberts.* Today, fortunately, these complicated rules are no longer required. In fact, the modern rules for forming possessive nouns are extremely simple and will cause you no trouble.

RULE 1

Form the possessive of a noun that does not end in *s* by adding *'s.*

box	**box's**
children	**children's**
company	**company's**
hero	**hero's**
men	**men's**
John	**John's**

Note that it does not matter if the noun is singular or plural. If it does not end in *s*, add *'s*.

RULE 2

Form the possessive of a noun that ends in *s* by adding an *apostrophe* only. Again, note that the rule applies whether the noun is singular or plural.

boxes	**boxes'**
companies	**companies'**
grass	**grass'**
heroes	**heroes'**
Charles	**Charles'**
Mr. Roberts	**Mr. Roberts'**

Why do we use the apostrophe in a possessive noun? We use it for the same reason that we use the apostrophe in a contraction such as *can't* or in an abbreviation such as *gov't*—to indicate that something has been *omitted.*

The apostrophe in the possessive noun indicates that a phrase has been omitted from the sentence—generally, a phrase beginning with *of*. For example:

the company's factory = the factory of the company

Shakespeare's play = the play of Shakespeare

the lamp's glow = the glow of the lamp

Understanding this fact makes it easy for you to decide correctly on the use of the apostrophe in all possessive nouns. To determine whether or not a noun requires an apostrophe – and, if so, where to place it – simply test to see if an *of phrase* can be added in front of the noun in question.

If an *of phrase* can be added, then you place the apostrophe precisely at the end of the word as it would appear in the *of phrase*. For example:

1 **This (companies, companies', company's) policy ....**

TEST: The policy of this company ....

THEREFORE: This company's policy ....

(Apostrophe precisely at end of *company*. Add *apostrophe s* because the noun does not end in *s*.)

2 **These (companies, companies', company's) policies ....**

TEST: The policies of these companies . . .

THEREFORE: These companies' policies

(Apostrophe precisely at end of *companies*. No *s* added because the noun already ends in *s*.)

3 **.... in two (weeks, week's, weeks') time ....**

TEST: .... in the time of two weeks ....

THEREFORE .... in two weeks' time ....

Be particularly alert to the need for the apostrophe in this latter type of phrase which refers to a period of time. Other examples of this type:

a moment's hesitation
a few moments' hesitation

a minute's work
ten minutes' work

an hour's delay
four hours' delay

a day's passage
a few days' passage

a week's salary
three weeks' salary

a month's wait
six months' wait

a year's interest
twenty years' interest

Generally, avoid the use of the possessive with nouns that name *inanimate* objects. While such usage is permissible, it is usually considered awkward. The preferred usage is to employ our old friend, the *of phrase.*

AWKWARD: The building's architecture ....

PREFERRED: **The architecture of the building ....**

AWKWARD: The airplane's roar....
PREFERRED: **The roar of the airplane....**

Of course, there are some time-honored phrases that involve the possessive form of an inanimate object. There's no need to change these: *a stone's throw; a hair's breadth; an arm's length.*

HINTS ON FORMING POSSESSIVE NOUNS

HINT 1

A problem arises when you want to show joint ownership. How would you write this phrase in possessive form?

The operetta by Gilbert and Sullivan....

Answer: **Gilbert and Sullivan's operetta....**

To show joint possession, write only the *last* name in possessive form.

Smith and Miller's firm....

This means one firm owned jointly by Smith and Miller. Other examples:

Johnson and Johnson's bandages....

Rodgers and Hammerstein's play....

But, when you want to show separate possession of distinct items, write the name of *each* owner in possessive form.

Smith's and Miller's firms are strong competitors. This refers to two firms, one owned by Smith and the other by Miller.

New York's and Chicago's police forces are among the finest. This refers to the police force of each city separately.

HINT 2

To write the possessive form of an abbreviation, place the *apostrophe s* (*'s*) after the final period.

The U.S.A.'s tariff
The U.N.'s policy
John D. Rockefeller, Jr.'s, fortune
The Wainright Co.'s staff

HINT 3

To form the possessive of a *compound* noun, place the *apostrophe s* (*'s*) after the *last* word in the noun:

My brother-in-law's inheritance (One brother-in-law)

My brothers-in-law's inheritances (More than one brother-in-law)

HINT 4

Note where the apostrophe is placed in this type of expression:

Alexander the Great's conquests were vast.

Chrysler, the automobile manufacturer's, main plants are in Michigan.

These examples illustrate the use of the possessive in cases where an *explanatory phrase* follows the noun. In such case, you make the last word in the explanatory phrase possessive; you do not make the noun itself possessive.

HINT 5

Often an organization will choose to omit the apostrophe from a plural noun that appears in its official title even though that noun is in the possessive. Always follow the form that appears on the official letterhead or the official listing of the organization.

National Sales Executives Club
National Business Teachers Association
Columbia University Teachers College
Manufacturers Trust Company

EXERCISE 7 — Plural Nouns

A. Write the plural form of each of these nouns in the space provided.

1. book ______
2. invoice ______
3. office ______
4. mass ______
5. tax ______
6. match ______
7. facility ______
8. colony ______
9. body ______
10. journey ______
11. attorney ______
12. studio ______
13. hero ______
14. embargo ______
15. auto ______
16. wife ______
17. half ______
18. chief ______
19. plaintiff ______
20. proof ______
21. memorandum ______
22. workingman ______
23. bookkeeper ______
24. cupful ______
25. grandchild ______
26. handful ______
27. copyright ______
28. stepchild ______
29. father-in-law ______
30. commander-in-chief ______
31. Mr. Hatch ______
32. 26 ______
33. twenty-six ______
34. X ______
35. series ______
36. crisis ______
37. veto ______
38. bus ______
39. box ______
40. roof ______
41. laboratory ______
42. handkerchief ______
43. basis ______
44. shelf ______
45. thesis ______
46. watch ______
47. receipt ______
48. company ______
49. self ______
50. datum ______
51. radio ______
52. stimulus ______
53. valley ______
54. alumnus ______
55. criterion ______
56. Mrs. ______
57. zero ______
58. letterhead ______
59. census ______
60. deletion ______
61. analysis ______
62. court-martial ______
63. piano ______

(continued)

A. (continued)

64. medium ______________________
65. bureau ______________________
66. Miss ______________________
67. if ______________________
68. five ______________________
69. Mr. ______________________
70. scissors ______________________
71. agency ______________________
72. C.P.A. ______________________
73. Jones ______________________
74. spoonful ______________________
75. gas ______________________

EXERCISE 7 — Plural Nouns

B. **Below are listed 20 words. Some are singular; some are plural. Check the appropriate column and write the opposite form in the other column.**

	Singular	*Plural*
1. test	____________	____________
2. column	____________	____________
3. lighters	____________	____________
4. children	____________	____________
5. ladies	____________	____________
6. attorney	____________	____________
7. knife	____________	____________
8. shelves	____________	____________
9. phenomenon	____________	____________
10. alumnus	____________	____________
11. datum	____________	____________
12. alloys	____________	____________
13. volcanoes	____________	____________
14. cupful	____________	____________
15. brother-in-law	____________	____________
16. species	____________	____________
17. sheep	____________	____________
18. politics	____________	____________
19. zero	____________	____________
20. company	____________	____________

EXERCISE 8 — Plural Nouns

A. **This problem deals with recognizing improperly spelled plural nouns. In the following paragraph, 14 plural nouns are improperly spelled. Cross out each incorrectly spelled noun and write the correct form above it.**

Industrys of all sorts have flourished in the central vallies of the Acme Mountains. Each year, cargoes of tomatos and potatoes are shipped from the valleys in large quantities. The area is famous for its fine tobaccoes, which are bought by all the large cigar companys. In addition to these agricultural products the region has fine facilitys for steel foundrys and for the manufacture of radioes and pianoes. The Caseys', who are attornies and steel men, made fortunes in alloyes, datas for which came from their own formulaes.

EXERCISE 8 — Plural Nouns

B. **This problem deals with recognizing plural nouns. Choose the proper predicate in each of the following sentences. Remember, if the subject is singular, use a singular predicate. If the subject is plural, use a plural predicate.**

1. The data (has, have) been entered in the account book. 1. ____________
2. Our most successful media (is, are) radio and TV. 2. ____________
3. Our curriculum (include, includes) courses in many fields. 3. ____________
4. The bases for my contention (is, are) twofold. 4. ____________
5. (Were, was) the memoranda left on my desk? 5. ____________
6. The alumni (is, are) fully behind the dean. 6. ____________
7. The stimulus (has, have) been measured in electrical units. 7. ____________
8. The fathers-in-law (has, have) met for the first time. 8. ____________
9. The crisis in his illness (is, are) finally past. 9. ____________
10. The series of revisions (is, are) complete, at last. 10. ____________
11. Riches (is, are) something to be thankful for. 11. ____________
12. Proper ethics (was, were) the backbone of the new concern. 12. ____________
13. What (are, is) the major criterion in judging a letter? 13. ____________
14. The theses the philosopher expounded (was, were) stimulating. 14. ____________
15. How many international crises (has, have) there been lately? 15. ____________
16. The latest phenomena in the electronics industry (seems, seem) to be concerned with transistors. 16. ____________
17. Three handfuls of rice (was, were) thrown at the couple. 17. ____________
18. What new formulae (were, was) presented by him? 18. ____________
19. Parentheses (present, presents) occasional punctuation problems. 19. ____________
20. An editor realizes that plot synopses (is, are) important. 20. ____________

EXERCISE 9 — Possessive Nouns

A. **This problem deals with writing the possessive of nouns. Below is a list of 20 possessive phrases. Rewrite them using the correct possessive form.**

1. the clothes of the ladies — 1. ____________________
2. the ties of the men — 2. ____________________
3. the books of the boy — 3. ____________________
4. the wool of the sheep — 4. ____________________
5. the report of the boss — 5. ____________________
6. the meeting of the directors — 6. ____________________
7. the statement of the Vice-Presidents — 7. ____________________
8. the poetry of Burns — 8. ____________________
9. the finances of the firm — 9. ____________________
10. the letters of the secretaries — 10. ____________________
11. the store of John — 11. ____________________
12. the association of the teachers — 12. ____________________
13. the children of my brother-in-law — 13. ____________________
14. the policy of R. H. Macy — 14. ____________________
15. the home of Dickens — 15. ____________________
16. the editorials of the *New York Times* — 16. ____________________
17. the engine of the old bus — 17. ____________________
18. the daughter of my boss — 18. ____________________
19. the notes of the typists — 19. ____________________
20. the motor of the tape recorder — 20. ____________________

EXERCISE 9 — Possessive Nouns

B. **This problem deals with possessive nouns. Each of the following sentences contains one or more possessive nouns from which the apostrophe has been omitted. In the space provided, rewrite these possessive nouns properly.**

1. The chairmans report included details on the proposed workmens cafeteria. 1. __________
2. The camp directors view was that drastic changes had to be made in Johns outlook. 2. __________
3. At the sales meeting it was agreed that new desks should be installed in the salesmens office. 3. __________
4. Yesterdays techniques cannot succeed in todays market. 4. __________
5. You have one weeks time to accept or reject this companys offer. 5. __________
6. The managers, at last Wednesdays meeting, agreed to rebuild the executives recreation hall. 6. __________
7. The new sales managers plan was discussesd at the boards last meeting. 7. __________
8. Roberts trouble is that he takes nobodys advice. 8. __________
9. We agree with Mr. Johnsons plan for improving our office forces morale. 9. __________
10. We asked Charles opinion, but he refused to discuss Smiths plan. 10. __________
11. Miller and Jones is one of the citys finest firms. 11. __________
12. Miller and Jones policies are in complete agreement with the District Attorneys suggested code of conduct. 12. __________
13. Browns and Whites stores compete in the ladies garments line. 13. __________
14. Green and Blacks store handles a complete line of mens items. 14. __________
15. A committee to support the U. S. s policy in Europe sent a flood of telegrams to Senator Bass office. 15. __________
16. The A.A.A.s vehicle policy is under the I.C.C.s direction. 16. __________
17. My sister-in-laws child left college after two years work. 17. __________
18. Frederick the Wises policies are comparable to the fiscal policies of the Farmers National Alliance. 18. __________
19. The sales managers convention dealt with the new organizations policies. 19. __________
20. The Tribunes point of view is that a secretarys contributions sometimes exceed those of the employer. 20. __________

EXERCISE 10 — Nouns—Plural and Possessive

This problem tests what you have learned about the spelling of possessive nouns and plural nouns. Fill in the form of the noun called for in each column – singular possessive, plural, and plural possessive.

Singular	*Singular Possessive*	*Plural*	*Plural Possessive*
1. book			
2. child			
3. tax			
4. Smith & Smith			
5. wife			
6. ratio			
7. body			
8. criterion			
9. attorney			
10. workingman			
11. radio			
12. memorandum			
13. brother-in-law			
14. hero			
15. stockholder			
16. roof			
17. journey			
18. letterhead			
19. committee			
20. county			
21. boss			
22. medium			
23. lady			
24. ox			
25. attorney general			

REVIEW EXERCISE — Nouns

The following passage contains a number of errors in the use of possessive and plural nouns. Whenever you locate such an error, cross out the incorrect form and write the correct form above it.

Dear Reader:

In the worlds most famous museum, the Louvre in Paris, hangs a painting by Americas celebrated artist, James McNeill Whistler. This paintings formal title is "An Arrangement in Gray and Black," but it is better known by the simple name, "Whistlers Mother." Many studies have been made in an effort to explain the basises of this portraits almost universal appeal.

But what criterions can the art critic use in judging a painting? The critic is not like a scientist; he cannot set up a controlled experiment wherein a number of stimulus are shot into a subject and datums collected on the subjects reaction. No, the art critic must rely on his inner emotions and sensitivity when he analyzes a painting. His analyses of a painting is a very personal thing.

If you looked at "Whistlers Mother," what would you see? Would you recognize the source of this portraits greatness? Would you, like most of us, be left wondering what makes this painting a masterpiece?

(continued)

REVIEW EXERCISE (continued)

Dr. Felix A. Roberts has come forward to help you. Dr. Roberts new book, Art for the Layman, has just been published. For a limited period only, this fine book is being made available to you at a very special discount price.

In this books Table of Contents are listed such interesting topics as: Criterions of Evaluation; Mediums for Communicating Art to the Masses; The Artists Studio; The Analysis of Expression through Color.

After you have read this fine volume, you will find new meaning in such great works as "Whistlers Mother." New horizons of appreciation will be opened to you.

Send for your copy today. Don't delay. Make out your check, payable to the Art Lovers Book Club, and mail it at once.

Very truly yours,

LESSON 3

PRONOUNS

1. the forms of pronouns
2. possessive pronouns
3. the relative pronouns
4. pronouns and their antecedents
5. clarity in using pronouns

The pronoun is the efficient man's tool. It is a shortcut by which you can save time and space. How? The job of the pronoun is to stand in place of a noun. Since many nouns are long words and most pronouns are short, you can shorten statements by skillfully using pronouns. Compare the length of the following sentences:

WITHOUT PRONOUNS

The Coca Cola Bottling Company announced that the Coca Cola Bottling Company intends to double the sale of the Coca Cola Bottling Company's product.

WITH PRONOUNS

The Coca Cola Bottling Company announced that it intends to double the sale of its product.

1. the FORMS of pronouns

Pronouns take different forms, depending upon how they are used in a sentence. You have used these different forms automatically for most of your life, so they should cause no difficulty now.

	Singular	*Plural*
First Person (The person speaking)	**I**	**WE**
Second Person (The person spoken to)	**YOU**	**YOU**
Third Person (The person or thing spoken about)	**HE, SHE, IT**	**THEY**

These forms – called *personal pronouns* – are familiar to you, aren't they? Then let's move on to our major concern – the proper *use* of pronouns.

2. POSSESSIVE pronouns

You learned in the previous lesson that the possessive form of a noun is generally formed by adding an apostrophe-s (*'s*). For example:

firm	**firm's**
author	**author's**
John	**John's**
America	**America's**

Now look at the possessive form of these pronouns:

Person	*Singular*	*Plural*
First:	**my, mine**	**our, ours**
Second:	**your, yours**	**your, yours**
Third:	**its, his, her, hers**	**their, theirs**

What is the first thing you noticed about these possessive pronouns? That's right! You noticed that *none* is written with an apostrophe. If you learn nothing else about possessive pronouns, learn this one simple rule: The possessive pronouns *yours, hers, its, ours,* and *theirs* are written *without apostrophes.*

As an added warning, remember: The word *its* is a pronoun. The word *it's* is *NOT* a pronoun. *It's* is a contraction for the words *it is.*

For example:

It's illegal to sell liquor on Sunday.

(*It is* illegal to sell liquor on Sunday.)

The book lay on its side.

(The book lay on the book's side.)

It's going to be a cold winter.

The firm is proud of its history.

The officers say that it's not going to be sold.

How can your company increase its sales?

3. RELATIVE pronouns: Who, Whom, Which, That

The pronouns *who, whom, which,* and *that* are used to *relate* one thought to another. For this reason they are called *relative* pronouns.

Look at these examples. Do you see how the relative pronoun in each sentence *relates* one thought to another?

Here is the man who will be our next president.

The book, which had fallen, was soon found.

Shorthand is the subject that I like best.

When should you use *who, whom, which,* or *that?* The answer is simple:

1. Use *who* or *whom* to refer to a person (In a later lesson you'll learn how to select between *who* and *whom.*)
2. Use *which* to refer to an animal or a thing
3. Use *that* to refer to a person, an animal, or a thing

At one time there were complicated rules controlling the choice of *which* or *that.* Fortunately, today they may be used interchangeably to refer to animals or things.

4. pronouns and their ANTECEDENTS

England expects every man to do (her) (their) (his) duty.

How do you know which pronoun to use? Let's work this problem through together. You remember that the function of the pronoun is to replace a noun. We call the noun that is replaced by the pronoun the *antecedent* of that pronoun. (*Cede* means *to go* and *ante* means *before*. An *antecedent* goes before the pronoun.)

David says he is tired. (*David* is the antecedent of *he.*)

Mary knows she cannot succeed. (*Mary* is the antecedent of *she.*)

We have heard from our salesmen. They write that they cannot fill the quota. (*Salesmen* is the antecedent of *they.*)

Since a pronoun must stand in place of its antecedent, it should be as identical to the antecedent as possible. If the antecedent is singular, the pronoun must be singular. If the antecedent is plural, the pronoun must be plural. This is called agreement in *number*. If the antecedent is masculine, the pronoun must be masculine. This is called agreement in *gender*.

Now, let us return to our problem sentence:

England expects every man to do (her) (their) (his) duty.

First, what is the antecedent? Right! The antecedent is *man*. The antecedent *man* is clearly masculine, so we can eliminate *her* from our choice. Our problem is reduced to:

England expects every man to do (their) (his) duty.

The final step is to determine whether the antecedent is singular or plural. The antecedent *man* is singular. Therefore, we should use the singular pronoun *his*.

Our sentence should read:

England expects every man to do his duty.

Once you learn to recognize antecedents, you will never have trouble choosing the proper pronouns. The problem of agreement of a pronoun with its antecedent is very much like a problem you have already studied and mastered – the agreement of a subject and its predicate. Right now, go back to the section in Lesson 1 on agreement of subject and predicate and review all the Hints given there. Only when you have fully familiarized yourself with that topic should you proceed with the Hints given below on agreement of pronouns with their antecedents.

HINTS on AGREEMENT of PRONOUNS with their ANTECEDENTS

HINT 1.

Try this sentence. It should be easy.

Jack and Jill are on (his, their) way.

Obviously, *their* is correct. The antecedent of *their* is *Jack and Jill.* Always use a plural pronoun to represent two or more antecedents connected by *and.*

Mr. Johnson and Miss Smith are on their way here.

The Acme Company and the Ajax Company are merging their assets.

Now look at this sentence.

The Secretary and Treasurer rendered (his, their) report.

If the positions of Secretary and Treasurer are held by two different men, *their* is obviously correct. If the two positions are held by one one man, *his* is correct. If, however, two men hold the two posts, the sentence would be better written as follows: **The Secretary and the Treasurer rendered their report.** The inclusion of the second *the* clearly tells the reader that two men are involved.

HINT 2.

When two antecedents are connected by *or* or *nor,* have the pronoun agree in number with the *nearer* antecedent.

1 **Neither Johnson nor Smith knows his business.** (*Smith* is the nearer antecedent. *Smith* is singular. Therefore, use *his.*)

2 **Either Miss Smith or Miss Black will get her wish.** (*Miss Black* is the nearer antecedent. *Miss Black* is singular. Therefore, use *her.*)

3 **Neither the boys nor the girls are ready for their lessons.** (*Girls* is the nearer antecedent. *Girls* is plural. Therefore, use *their.*)

4 **Neither Mr. Smith nor his sons have done their best.** (*Sons* is the closer antecedent. *Sons* is plural. Therefore, use *their.*)

Note: In a sentence like this, where one antecedent is singular and the other is plural, always place the plural antecedent *last.*

HINT 3.

The following words or groups of words are always singular: *anybody, anyone, each, every, everybody, everyone, many a, nobody, no one, somebody, someone.* When used as an antecedent, therefore, each of these expressions calls for a *singular* pronoun. Naturally, if one of these expressions is the *subject* of a sentence, it calls for a singular *predicate* too.

Nobody is eager to risk his life.

Many a soldier has displayed his courage under fire.

Everyone does his work efficiently.

We have selected each of the men on the basis of his merit.

Note that *of the men* in the last sentence does not alter the requirement that a singular pronoun be used. *Each* is the antecedent. You may disregard the *of* phrase that follows it.

Each of our competitors has reduced his sales.

Each of the factories is operating at its fullest capacity.

HINT 4.

Which pronoun do you use in the following sentence?

Everyone in the class did (his) (her) homework.

Is *everyone* masculine or feminine? It could be either. In such case, where the sex of the antecedent is unknown, use a *masculine* pronoun.

For example:

Not a person left his seat before the last curtain.

One of the students left his books.

Of course, if the context of the sentence clearly indicates that the pronoun refers to a *feminine* antecedent, use a *feminine* pronoun.

Each student at Vassar College must attend her classes regularly.

Since Vassar is a girls' school, we know that *each student* calls for a feminine pronoun.

None of the airline stewardesses failed her flight examination.

Neither of the waitresses does her job well.

Now let's try this sentence.

Each man and woman in the audience enthusiastically showed (his, her) approval.

Here you specifically refer to a masculine *and* a feminine antecedent, *man and woman.* In this instance, to avoid confusion, you must use *both* the masculine *and* the feminine pronoun.

Each man and woman in the audience enthusiastically showed his or her approval.

Since this is clearly an awkward sentence, you would be wise to rephrase the sentence into a less awkward construction.

Enthusiastic approval was shown by every man and woman in the audience.

Awkward: The host or hostess should always personally greet his or her guests.

Better: Guests should be personally greeted by the host or hostess.

HINT 5.

When locating the antecedent, disregard a phrase beginning with *as well as, in addition to, and not.*

1 **John, as well as his brothers, is on his way.** (The antecedent is *John.* Disregard *brothers.*)

2 **The boys, in addition to John, are on their way.** (The antecedent is *boys.* Disregard *John.*)

3 **John, and not his brothers, is on his way.** (The antecedent is *John.* Disregard *brothers.*)

HINT 6.

Words like *committee, jury, class, crowd,* and *army* may be either singular or plural depending upon their meaning in the sentence. Each of these words refers to a group of people. When you are referring to that group as a single unit, use a singular pronoun.

The committee is holding its meeting.

The class is in its room.

When you refer to the individuals that make up the group, however, use a plural pronoun.

The committee were called at their homes one at a time.

The jury brought in their split verdict.

HINT 7.

You have already learned to recognize the relative pronouns – *who, which,* and *that.* The relative pronoun is often followed by a predicate verb that must agree in number with the antecedent of the relative pronoun. But recognizing the *real* antecedent may sometimes require all your reasoning skill. If you think through the problem carefully, however, you will come up with the correct answer. For example, try this sentence:

She is one of those girls who (is, are) conscientious in following directions.

In this sentence what word does *who* relate to, *one* or *girls?* Look at the sentence carefully and you will see that a statement is being made about a broad characteristic of *those girls. Who,* therefore, relates to the plural word *girls* and requires the plural verb *are.*

She is one of those girls who are conscientious.

Let's examine another example:

She is the one girl of all the applicants who (is, are) able to do the job.

Who shows the ability to do the job in this sentence – *all the applicants* or the *one girl?* Clearly *who* relates to *one girl;* it is therefore a singular subject and takes the singular predicate *is.*

5. CLARITY in using pronouns

When using pronouns in your writing, be sure that the meaning of each pronoun is clearly understood. Look at this sentence:

The manager told Brown that the meaning of his report was unclear.

Whose report is unclear—the manager's? or Brown's? From this sentence you cannot tell because the *reference* of the pronoun is ambiguous. Here's how this sentence could be improved.

The manager told Brown that the meaning of Brown's report was unclear.

This sentence, though better, is awkward; so let's rephrase it:

The meaning of Brown's report was unclear, the manager told him.

EXERCISE 11 — Possessive Pronouns

A. **This problem deals mainly with the possessive forms of pronouns. In the space provided, write the proper word. Remember, you do not write possessive pronouns with apostrophes.**

1. The book fell on (its) (it's)side. 1. ________
2. (Its) (It's) going to be a cold winter. 2. ________
3. The package on top is (ours) (our's). 3. ________
4. They claimed the package was (theirs) (there's) (their's). 4. ________
5. These men are certain (their) (they're) correct. 5. ________
6. Mr. Jones is a man (who) (that) can get his own way. 6. ________
7. Victory is (our's) (ours). 7. ________
8. The pact must stand or fall on (its) (it's) merits. 8. ________
9. (Yours) (Your's) truly, 9. ________
10. Here is the man (that) (which) I told you about. 10. ________
11. This car of (ours) (our's) is similar to (yours) (your's) (yours'). 11. ________
12. This work of (hers) (her's) is extremely clear in (its) (it's) analysis of (there) (their) accounting department. 12. ________
13. (Its, It's) not clear whether the package is (yours, your's) or (theirs, their's, theres, there's). 13. ________
14. Tell me (whose, who's) letter is more accurate, mine or (hers, her's). 14. ________
15. The company hurt (its, it's) reputation, (its it's) sad to say. 15. ________

EXERCISE 11 — Possessive Nouns and Pronouns

B. **This problem deals with the proper use of possessive nouns and pronouns. Wherever a possessive noun or pronoun is incorrectly spelled, cross it out and write the correct form above it.**

Dear Mr. Byrnes:

Thank you for your order of a years supply of Danity Perfumes which your buyer, Mr. Stoll, gave us yesterday.

Your's is an unusually large order and this, combined with Mr. Stolls extreme courtesy, is appreciated. Our's is a small firm, and an order the size of yours is very encouraging.

(continued)

B. **(continued)**

We know that our line of perfumes will meet the perfume needs of a number of your departments.

You will find Danity Perfume's are an especially good item for your Womens Toiletry Department. In addition, it's success has been proven in the Debs Department of many stores.

If we can be of any further service, please call upon us.

Very truly yours',

EXERCISE 11 — Personal Pronouns

C. **This problem deals with the various forms that pronouns take. Fill in the missing pronouns in the following table.**

	SINGULAR	PLURAL	SINGULAR POSSESSIVE	PLURAL POSSESSIVE
FIRST PERSON	I	________	my ________	________ ________
SECOND PERSON	________	________	your ________	________ ________
THIRD PERSON	________ ________ ________	they	________ ________ ________	their ________

EXERCISE 12 — Pronouns—Antecedents and Number

In this problem you are to identify pronouns and their antecedents. In the column marked Pronoun write the pronoun. In the column marked Antecedent write the antecedent. In the column marked Number write S if the antecedent is singular; write P if the antecedent is plural.

		PRONOUN	ANTECEDENT	NUMBER
1. The present equipment deserves all the praise given it.	1.	________	________	_____
2. Mr. Jones is certain of his grounds.	2.	________	________	_____
3. The Acme Laundry knows it can count on continued community support.	3.	________	________	_____
4. The boy's rackets were hung on their sides.	4.	________	________	_____
5. Mr. Jones can protect the firm if he acts quickly.	5.	________	________	_____
6. Our firm is proud of its record.	6.	________	________	_____
7. Somebody forgot his glasses.	7.	________	________	_____
8. Each of the players has his part.	8.	________	________	_____
9. Mr. Jones and Mr. Smith are on their way to the meeting.	9.	________	________	_____
10. Mr. Jones, as well as Mr. Smith, is on his way to the meeting.	10.	________	________	_____
11. Each man must do his very best.	11.	________	________	_____
12. The committee has been in its meeting room for hours.	12.	________	________	_____
13. Neither the desk nor the table is worth its price.	13.	________	________	_____
14. Mr. Roberts, in addition to the entire staff, will offer his resignation.	14.	________	________	_____
15. Neither Mrs. Jones nor the boys have saved their money.	15.	________	________	_____

EXERCISE 13 Agreement of Pronoun and Antecedent

This problem deals mainly with the agreement of a pronoun with its antecedent. In the spaces provided, write the proper pronouns.

1. Smith and Jones has grown till (it, they) is the largest firm in (its, it's, their) field. 1. ____________
2. If somebody does an outstanding job, (he, they) will be rewarded for (his, their) efforts. 2. ____________
3. The memoranda (is, are) in (its, their) proper place. 3. ____________
4. Every girl in that class knows (his, her, their) lessons. 4. ____________
5. The crisis (is, are) over but has left (its, their) mark. 5. ____________
6. Now is the time for all good men to come to the aid of (his, their) country. 6. ____________
7. Each good man should come to the aid of (his, their) country. 7. ____________
8. No one in this world is certain of (his, their) future; yet each must plan as best (he, they) can. 8. ____________
9. If a man does a valiant deed, (he, they) shall be honored wherever (he, they) goes. 9. ____________
10. Somebody tried to force (his, their) way through the crowd. 10. ____________
11. If Miss Smith or Miss Jones orders at once, (she, they) will receive the merchandise by return post. 11. ____________
12. Either Mr. Dunlap or Mr. Firestone left (his, their) lighter. 12. ____________
13. Every man, woman, and child owed (his, their) life to the Coast Guard. 13. ____________
14. James Randall is one man who realizes (his, their) own value. 14. ____________
15. James is one of those men who realize (his, their) own value. 15. ____________
16. Acme Lumber, in addition to Zenith Lumber, is launching (its, their) annual campaign. 16. ____________
17. The President, but not his Cabinet, is on (his, their) way. 17. ____________
18. All the members (has, have) received (his, their) invitations. 18. ____________
19. Each of the books (has, have) been autographed on (its, their) cover. 19. ____________
20. This is one of those problems that (is, are) not easily solved on (its, their) bare facts. 20. ____________
21. Neither Mary nor Madeline (was, were) able to do (his, her, their) special report on time. 21. ____________
22. None of the manufacturers (is, are) willing to make (his, their) contribution yet. 22. ____________
23. Mr. James, accompanied by his sons, (was, were) able to make (his, their) entrance at the appropriate moment. 23. ____________
24. He is one of those men who (is, are) always complaining about (his, their) tasks. 24. ____________
25. He is different from any of those executives who (remain, remains) calm when (he, they) (is, are) harassed. 25. ____________

REVIEW EXERCISE — Pronouns

The letter below includes many intentional errors. Cross out each incorrect word and write the correct word above it. Pay particular attention to the use of possessive pronouns and to the agreement of a pronoun with its antecedent.

Dear Miss Johnson:

We were extremely pleased to be invited by P.C.L. to attend it's annual convention. I know that each of the members of our staff felt it their personal duty and pleasure to attend. Mr. Smith, as well as Mr. Johnson, send their special thanks to you for the invitation.

I was especially thrilled by the talks given by Professor Poole and Dean Brown. Their's is an unusual combination of talents. I noticed that during there talks every member of the audience were glued to their seats. Its a rarity in this day and age to meet men who have such complete command of his English and his subject matter.

I also wish to congratulate you on the fine job done by your banquet committee. Every table decoration, every knife, every fork were in their proper places. The banquet speakers, especially Miss Green, did her work exceptionally well. By the way, Miss Green is the woman which I told you about at lunch last week. I'm very much pleased that talent such as her's was recognized by your committee. She is one of those women who is reliable and can be trusted to do her work to it's fullest extent. Neither Mr. Smith nor Mr. Johnson were disappointed in their expectations.

In closing, let me say that I believe wholeheartedly in the work of this organization of your's. Since ours' is a small firm, we are especially proud to be members. You will probably be pleased to know that neither Mr. Smith nor any of his associates has had a word of criticism of your organization.

Sincerely,

LESSON 4

VERBS

Verbs are the words in a sentence that pack the wallop. They give a sentence punch. They supply action.

The purpose of business communication is to promote decisive action. Well-chosen verbs in a business letter are the dynamos that generate the desired action. No matter what your position in business may be —executive, secretary, or clerk — verbs are the tools that will get things done for you. They are tools that you must use with facility and ease if you are to be a success in the business world.

Are you skilled in the use of these verb-tools? Can you, at this moment, state the precise difference between the proper use of the verbs *lie* and *lay* or *sit* and *set*? The correct use of such verbs is governed by a few relatively simple rules. You can master these rules with a little application. You *must* master them if you are to be a success in the business office.

1. the TYPES of verbs: action and linking

You probably remember from grammar school that a verb is a word that expresses *action.* Do you remember, however, that a verb may also be a word that merely *links* one part of the sentence to another but does not express action? Compare the two types of verbs below.

Action verbs: **run, hit, fly, explode, lie, sleep, sit.**

Linking verbs: **is, are, will be, seem, appear, taste, sound, look.**

Can you tell the difference between these types of verbs? You probably noticed that the action verbs depict an occurrence that you can easily picture in your imagination. On the other hand, the linking verbs refer to occurrences that are much more difficult to picture. Compare these two sentences:

(1) The automobile swerved off the road.

(2) It seems a good idea.

In your imagination you can probably picture the car *swerving,* but can you picture something *seeming?* Note that the linking verb *seems* can be replaced by the word *is.* This is true of all linking verbs. They do little more than stand in place of the word *is.*

It seems a good idea.
It is a good idea.

Another name for *linking verbs* is *state-of-being verbs.* In this course we shall call them simply *linking verbs.*

Many verbs may be either action verbs or linking verbs depending upon how they are used in a sentence. Compare the use of the verb *taste* in the following sentences:

(1) The gourmet tasted the soup with obvious delight.

(2) Candy tastes sweet.

In the first sentence *taste* is an action verb. It depicts the action of the gourmet in sampling the soup. You can almost picture him as he brings the spoon to his lips. In the second sentence, however, *taste* is a linking verb. It merely links the quality of sweetness to the subject *candy.* The word *is* could replace the word *tastes.*

Candy tastes sweet.
Candy is sweet.

Learn to recognize the distinction between action verbs and linking verbs, for you will have to apply it in later lessons. For the moment, remember these two points:

1. All forms of the verb *to be* are linking verbs. (Below is a list of all forms of the verb *to be.* You need not memorize this list; however, you should become familiar with these forms.)

is	**is being**	**shall be**	**has been**	**shall have been**
am	**am being**	**will be**	**have been**	**will have been**
are	**are being**	**should be**	**had been**	**should have been**
was	**was being**	**would be**		**would have been**
were	**were being**			

2. Verbs such as *become, seem, appear, prove, grow, remain, feel, taste, sound, look,* and *smell* are linking verbs when they can be replaced by the word *is.*

Candy tastes (is) sweet.
Stone appears (is) solid.
Velvet feels (is) soft.
Buttermilk smells (is) sour.

2. the SIMPLE tenses

Verbs change their form depending upon the time of the event they depict. We call the different forms a verb may take by the name *tenses*.

You undoubtedly know the three simple tenses: *the present tense, the past tense,* and *the future tense.* Certainly, in your daily conversation you have employed these tenses properly – perhaps without even realizing you were doing so. You would never say **I will go to the bank yesterday.** You realize, of course, that when you refer to an action that occurred *yesterday,* you must use the *past* tense of the verb *to go.* You would properly say **I went to the bank yesterday.**

Using the simple tenses is easy enough. You have used them correctly since you were an infant. Just as a review, here is an outline of the proper use of the three simple tenses:

1. The past tense refers to a *definite* past event or action.

I went to the movies yesterday.

I sold the books last year.

2. The future tense applies to events that will take place at a future time. You form the future tense by placing *will* or *shall* before the verb.

While many authorities permit the use of *will* or *shall* interchangeably, there are certain rules governing their proper use that you should learn just to be absolutely correct. These rules can be simply stated as follows:

a) To express ordinary future, use *shall* with the first person pronouns *I* and *we;* use *will* for all other pronouns *(you, he, she, it, they).* For example: **I shall see you tomorrow. They will be at the theatre in an hour.**

b) Reverse this rule to show great determination or emotion–using *will* with *I* and *we;* and using *shall* for all other pronouns. For example: **I will see you tomorrow, no matter what you say! They shall be at the theatre in an hour, even if I have to carry them.**

A simple way to remember these uses of *will* and *shall* is by memorizing this little sentence:

The king roared: "I will that you and he shall do it."

The king's will must be done–so in this sentence you tie together *I will, you shall,* and *he shall* to show determination. By memorizing this sentence, you'll always be able to remember how to use *will* or *shall* correctly.

Should and *would* are treated exactly like *shall* and *will.* Use *should* in those instances where *shall* is correct. Use *would* in those instances where *will* is correct.

I would like to see you immediately. (Determination)

I should like you to visit me when you can. (Ordinary future)

3. The present tense is used to denote three types of actions:

a) It describes action going on at the present time.

I am satisfied. **He is here.**

b) It describes action that is continued or habitual.

I see him every day. **We sell hardware.**

c) It is used to denote a general truth.

Cats are animals. **Candy is sweet.**

That's all there is to the present tense.

3. the PROGRESSIVE form

The progressive form is used to refer to an *unfinished* action.

1 I am working on the books right now.
This means that you are at work on the books at present and have not finished them yet. Your work is unfinished.

2 I was studying when John came in.
This means that your studying was interrupted by John. You were not through studying. Your studying was unfinished.

In Sentences 1 and 2 each verb is in the progressive form because the action it denotes is still progressing—is *unfinished.* Did you notice that these verbs end in *ing*? The *ing* ending is the sign of the progressive form. In addition, did you notice that each progressive verb is preceded by a form of the verb *to be*? This too is essential to the progressive form.

1. am working
2. was studying

The name we give to a verb to which *ing* is added is the *present participle. Working* is the present participle of the verb *work*; *studying* is the present participle of the verb *study.* The *ing*-verb is called a participle because it is *part* of the progressive form.

Learn these three things about the progressive form:

1. Use the progressive to show action that is, was, or will be unfinished;
2. Form the progressive verb by adding *ing* to the simple verb; and
3. Place a form of the verb *to be* before the progressive verb.

Occasionally you will have to decide whether to use a simple tense or the progressive form. Here's an easy way to solve this problem. Merely ask yourself one question: *Is or was the action finished?* If finished, use the simple tense. If unfinished, use the progressive.

1 I (walked, was walking) down the street yesterday when the wind blew my hat off.
Ask: Was the action finished?
Answer: *No.* It was interrupted by the hat incident.
Therefore: Use the progressive form.

I was walking down the street when the wind blew my hat off. (Past Progressive)

2 He (writes) (is writing) out the report at this very moment.
Ask: Is the action finished?
Answer: *No.* He is still working on the report.
Therefore: Use the progressive form.

He is writing out the report at this very moment. (Present Progressive)

3 We (swam) (were swimming) at the lake every day last summer.
Ask: Was the action finished?
Answer: *Yes.* It was completed by the end of last summer.
Therefore: Use the simple tense.

We swam at the lake every day last summer. (Simple Past)

4 They (worked) (were working) feverishly until dawn.
Ask: Was the action finished?
Answer: *Yes.* This is tricky. Dawn did not interrupt their work. It merely marked the moment when they stopped work.
Therefore: Use the simple tense.

They worked feverishly until dawn. (Simple Past)

5 I (listened) (was listening) to the radio when the accident occurred.
Ask: Was the action completed?
Answer: *No.* It was interrupted by the accident.

Therefore: Use the progressive form.

I was listening to the radio when the accident occurred. (Past Progressive)

6 I shall be swimming in the pool by the time you arrive. (Future Progressive)

By now you should know exactly why *shall be swimming* is correct, and not *shall swim.* Why?

4. the PERFECT tenses

Let's turn to the final tenses you are going to study – the *perfect* tenses.

They are called the perfect tenses because they always denote action that is *perfect*ed – that is, completed. In the progressive forms that you have just learned, an action is uncompleted when another action occurs. In the perfect tenses the reverse is true – an action is always completed *before* another action occurs.

The form of the verb that is used in all perfect tenses is called the *perfect participle* because this verb form is *part* of all perfect tenses. For example, *brought* is the perfect participle of the verb *bring*:

Present Perfect **has (or have) brought**
Past Perfect **had brought**
Future Perfect **shall (or will) have brought**

Remember, the perfect participle is simply the name given to that form of a verb that is used in all three perfect tenses. Now let's explore the three perfect tenses in detail.

A. THE PAST PERFECT:

I had shipped the order by the time the message arrived.

This means that I had completed the shipment of the order before another event occurred. The other event was the arrival of the message. *Had shipped* is called the *past perfect tense.* It is past perfect because it denotes an action that was completed before another event, *also in the past,* occurred. Remember this: Use the *past* perfect tense to show action that was completed before another event in the *past* occurred.

The sign of the past perfect is the word *had* before the verb.

He had left by the time I arrived.

They had hidden the prizes before the company sat down for dinner.

It had stopped raining by noon.

He had finished college before the war was over.

Occasionally you will be faced with a choice of using either the simple past tense or the past perfect tense. Both refer to events completed in the past, but they are easily distinguished. Remember, the *past* perfect always refers to an action completed *before another event in the past.*

1 We (printed) (had printed) the edition before the censorship order arrived.

Ask: Did one event occur before another occurred?

Answer: *Yes.* The books were printed *before the order arrived.*

Therefore: Use the past perfect.

We had printed the edition before the censorship order arrived.

2 We (suspected) (had suspected) his statements even before we received the police report.

Ask: Did one event occur before another occurred?

Answer: *Yes.* We *had suspected* before we received the report.

Therefore: Use the past perfect.

We had suspected his statements even before we received the police report.

3 **Spring (arrived) (had arrived) early last year.**

Ask: Did one event occur before another occurred?

Answer: *No.* There is only one event – the arrival of spring.

Therefore: Use the simple past.

Spring arrived early last year.

4 **Did he know that you (heard) (had heard) from the home office?**

Ask: Did one event occur before another occurred?

Answer: *Yes. You had heard* before *he did know.* Even though this sentence is in the form of a question, treat it as though it makes an affirmative statement. Remember, you learned to do this in determining the subject and predicate of a sentence back in Lesson 1. Treat this sentence as though it reads: *You had heard from the home office before he did know that.*

Therefore: Use the past perfect tense.

Did he know that you had heard from the home office?

B. THE FUTURE PERFECT:

By this time tomorrow I shall have finished my exams.

This means that my exams will be completed by a definite moment in the future. As you probably guessed, *shall have finished* is in the *future perfect* tense.

Remember this: Use the future perfect tense to show action that will be completed by a definite time in the future. The sign of the future perfect is the words *shall have* or *will have* before the verb.

By the time the message arrives, John will have left.

By June 30 our firm will have completed its expansion plans.

I shall have finished my report by noon tomorrow.

Since the future perfect is not used too frequently in business material, we won't bother you with any of the complications that it may cause. You should, however, be able to cope with it when it does come up. So, right now, reread this little section on the future perfect.

C. THE PRESENT PERFECT:

John has filed only one report so far.

This means that John filed a report and will probably file more. The *so far* tells us there will probably be more reports. *Has filed* is called the *present perfect* tense. It is present perfect because it refers to an action that was completed in the past but is part of a series of actions that continues into the present. The sign of the present perfect is the word *has* or *have* before the verb. Let's look at some more examples to make this clearer.

1 **He has shopped in our store many times.**
Has shopped indicates that you expect him to shop some more at your store. If you don't expect him back – let's suppose he had just moved to Pago-Pago – you would say **He shopped in our store many times.** By using the simple past tense *shopped,* you show that the action is completed once-and-for-all. It is not part of a continuing series.

2 **John and Jane's bickering has gone on for years.**
Has gone indicates that it is still going on. If the bickering had finally stopped – let's say that Jane divorced John and moved to Alaska – then you would say **John and Jane's bickering went on for years.**

3 **The Smiths have traveled to this park year after year.**

Do the Smiths intend to come back again? Certainly. *Have traveled* indicates they expect to continue to do so. If they didn't expect to return any more you would say **The Smiths traveled to this park year after year.**

Does the present perfect seem clearer to you now? Good. Let's see how you do with a few problems that we'll work through together.

1 Mr. Jones (came) (has come) to see us on numerous occasions.
Which is right, *came* or *has come*? The answer depends on what we mean. If Mr. Jones still comes to see us, then use *has come*. **Mr. Jones has come to see us on numerous occasions.** But if Mr. Jones doesn't like us any more and doesn't visit us any more, use *came*. **Mr. Jones came to see us on many occasions.**

2 The boys (spoiled) (have spoiled) their little sister.
If she is still being spoiled: **The boys have spoiled their little sister.** If she is no longer being spoiled: **The boys spoiled their little sister.**

3 Our offices (were) (have been) on the same corner for years. If they still are on that corner, use *have been*. **Our offices have been on the same corner for years.** If they have been moved elsewhere: **Our offices were on the same corner for years.**

Note: A common error many people make is to substitute the present tense for the present perfect tense. Note these examples – and avoid making the error.

Incorrect: **I am in this office for three months.**
Correct: **I have been in this office for three months.**
Incorrect: **I am living in this house since September.**
Correct: **I have been living in this house since September.**

5. SUMMARY of tenses

You have now studied all the tenses that you need know. Let's review the ground you have covered. In studying one tense at a time, you can easily lose track of the overall picture. Does the following outline help you get a better view of all the tenses?

TENSE	REFERS TO:	EXAMPLE
Simple Past	A completed past action	arrived
Past Perfect	A completed past action that came before another completed past action.	had arrived
Simple Future	A future action	will / shall } arrive
Future Perfect	A future action that will be completed by a definite time in the future.	will / shall } have arrived
Simple Present	An action going on in the present	arrive
Present Perfect	A completed action that is part of a continuing series of such actions.	has / have } arrived
Progressive	An action that is or was uncompleted.	is / was } arriving

6. verb FORMS

Look at how the verb *swim* changes depending upon its tense. In the present tense you use *swim*: **I swim every day that I can.** In the past tense you use *swam*: **I swam every day last summer.** In the perfect tense you use *have swum*: **I have swum every day this summer.**

These three forms – *swim, swam, have swum* – enable you to write all simple and perfect tenses of the verb *swim.* You have already learned how to do this.

1. *Swim* is the present tense. To form the future tense, place *shall* or *will* before *swim*: **He will swim again next summer. They shall swim this afternoon.**
2. *Swam* is the past tense. This is the *only* tense where *swam* is correct: **I swam yesterday.**
3. *Swum* is used in all the perfect tenses. As you have learned, it is called the *perfect participle* because *swum* is part of the three perfect tenses as follows:

   a) *Has swum* or *have swum* is the present perfect: **He has swum for hours.**

   b) *Had swum* is the past perfect: **He had swum for hours before he came out.**

   c) *Will have swum* or *shall have swum* is the future perfect: **In an hour I shall have swum my race.**

So, by knowing only three forms of the verb *swim,* you can form all simple and perfect tenses. This is true of all verbs. By knowing only *three* words you can write any simple or perfect tense.

Take another example – the verb *drink.*

1. **Drink**	Present Tense	I **drink** milk.
	Future Tense	I **will drink** milk.
2. **Drank**	Past Tense	I **drank** all the milk.
3. **Drunk**	Present Perfect	I **have drunk** milk for years.
	Past Perfect	I **had drunk** only milk till I was eighteen.
	Future Perfect	I **shall have drunk** a full quart by the time I finish this glass.

Here is another example – the verb *see.*

1. **See**	Present Tense	I **see** him.
	Future Tense	I **shall** see him.
2. **Saw**	Past Tense	I **saw** him.
3. **Seen**	Present Perfect	I **have seen** him....
	Past Perfect	I **had seen** him....
	Future Perfect	I **shall have seen....**

Here is a final example – the verb *go.*

1. **Go**	Present Tense	I **go.**
	Future Tense	I **will** go.
2. **Went**	Past Tense	I **went.**
3. **Gone**	Present Perfect	I **have gone....**
	Past Perfect	I **had gone....**
	Future Perfect	I **will have gone....**

To review, the above examples show that you can form any simple or perfect tense by knowing only three forms:

1. The present tense;
2. The past tense;
3. The perfect participle.

Now let us turn to choosing the proper forms of some other verbs.

7. REGULAR and IRREGULAR verbs

Most verbs are what we call *regular* verbs. By this we mean that they form the past tense by merely adding *d* or *ed* to the present tense, and they form the present perfect tense by placing the word *has* or *have* before the past tense. For example, the following are some regular verbs:

Present	Past	Present Perfect
receive	**received**	**has or have received**
like	**liked**	**has or have liked**
allow	**allowed**	**has or have allowed**
follow	**followed**	**has or have followed**

There are many so-called irregular verbs, however, which do not form their past and perfect tenses in this regular manner. You have already studied four irregular verbs – *swim, drink, see, go.* Some books on English list a hundred or more irregular verbs and tell you, "Memorize these!" Such books are actually making the task more difficult than it need be. While irregular verbs do not follow the pattern of regular verbs, we can still find other patterns within them. For example, there is obvious similarity among:

drink	**drank**	**has drunk**
sink	**sank**	**has sunk**
shrink	**shrank**	**has shrunk**

To enable you to master irregular verbs in record time, we have divided them into families. When studying these families, read them *aloud.*

SAY:

sing	**sang**	**has sung**
ring	**rang**	**has rung**
spring	**sprang**	**has sprung**

By reading these word-groups aloud, your mind will *hear* the pattern within each family. You will learn *by ear* – the simplest, most indelible way. Remember, the key to saving yourself hours of work is to *say* the words in each family aloud and let your mind *hear the pattern.*

To help you learn to *hear* the perfect tenses correctly, we have used the *present perfect* tense in which *has* is placed before the perfect participle. Remember that *have* would also be correct in the present perfect tense; *had* in the past perfect; and *shall have* or *will have* in the future perfect.

I. Present	Past	Perfect
bring	**brought**	**has brought**
buy	**bought**	**has bought**
fight	**fought**	**has fought**
seek	**sought**	**has sought**
teach	**taught**	**has taught**

II. Present	Past	Perfect
begin	**began**	**has begun**
swim	**swam**	**has swum**
ring	**rang**	**has rung**
sing	**sang**	**has sung**
spring	**sprang**	**has sprung**
sink	**sank**	**has sunk**
shrink	**shrank**	**has shrunk**
drink	**drank**	**has drunk**
run	**ran**	**has run**

III. Present	Past	Perfect
blow	**blew**	**has blown**
grow	**grew**	**has grown**
know	**knew**	**has known**
throw	**threw**	**has thrown**
fly	**flew**	**has flown**
draw	**drew**	**has drawn**
withdraw	**withdrew**	**has withdrawn**
wear	**wore**	**has worn**
swear	**swore**	**has sworn**
tear	**tore**	**has torn**
show	**showed**	**has shown**

IV. Present	Past	Perfect
bend	**bent**	**has bent**
lend	**lent**	**has lent**
spend	**spent**	**has spent**
deal	**dealt**	**has dealt**
feel	**felt**	**has felt**
keep	**kept**	**has kept**
sleep	**slept**	**has slept**
sweep	**swept**	**has swept**
weep	**wept**	**has wept**
mean	**meant**	**has meant**
leave	**left**	**has left**
lose	**lost**	**has lost**

V. Present	Past	Perfect
break	**broke**	**has broken**
choose	**chose**	**has chosen**
freeze	**froze**	**has frozen**
speak	**spoke**	**has spoken**
steal	**stole**	**has stolen**
forget	**forgot**	**has forgotten**

VI. Present	Past	Perfect
strive	**strove**	**has striven**
arise	**arose**	**has arisen**
take	**took**	**has taken**
mistake	**mistook**	**has mistaken**
shake	**shook**	**has shaken**
write	**wrote**	**has written**
typewrite	**typewrote**	**has typewritten**
underwrite	**underwrote**	**has underwritten**
eat	**ate**	**has eaten**
fall	**fell**	**has fallen**
forbid	**forbade**	**has forbidden**
give	**gave**	**has given**
hide	**hid**	**has hidden**

VII. The verbs in this group are irregular because they don't change at all. As you can see, they are the same in the present, past, and perfect tenses.

Present	Past	Perfect
bid	**bid**	**has bid**
burst	**burst**	**has burst**
cost	**cost**	**has cost**
cut	**cut**	**has cut**
forecast	**forecast**	**has forecast**
hurt	**hurt**	**has hurt**
let	**let**	**has let**
put	**put**	**has put**
quit	**quit**	**has quit**
spread	**spread**	**has spread**
thrust	**thrust**	**has thrust**

VIII. There is very little rhyme, and even less reason, in this group. Say the words aloud till they sound familiar.

Present	Past	Perfect
come	**came**	**has come**
become	**became**	**has become**
bleed	**bled**	**has bled**
lead	**led**	**has led**
flee	**fled**	**has fled**
get	**got**	**has got**
meet	**met**	**has met**
bind	**bound**	**has bound**
stand	**stood**	**has stood**
win	**won**	**has won**
hold	**held**	**has held**
stick	**stuck**	**has stuck**
strike	**struck**	**has struck**
string	**strung**	**has strung**
have	**had**	**has had**
say	**said**	**has said**
make	**made**	**has made**
do	**did**	**has done**
go	**went**	**has gone**

8. INFINITIVES

You've probably come across the word *infinitive* before. Like so many other terms that seem complicated, this one is really quite easy. An *infinitive* is simply a verb with the word *to* before it: *to love, to have loved; to see, to have been seen; to be, to have been.*

Take the infinitive *to see*. You may use any of the following forms:

To see Paris is exciting.

To have seen Paris is to have fulfilled a dream.

To be seen in Paris is chic.

To have been seen in Paris is something to talk about.

Let us remember then that infinitives may be used in different forms to express different ideas.

The pronoun used after an infinitive is exactly the same as the pronoun used after any other verb. For example: **The manager plans to visit him and me.** (*Him* and *me* are objects of the infinitive *to visit.*) **The boss says he wants to see me in the office.** (*Me* is object of the infinitive *to see.*) You've probably heard the expression *to split an infinitive.* Maybe you have heard it without knowing what it means. It simply means that a word has been placed between *to* and the verb, thereby splitting the infinitive. This is generally not considered perfect English.

Wrong: **I wish to frequently visit you.** To avoid such an awkward expression, you need merely keep the infinitive *to visit* unsplit: **I wish to visit you frequently.**

Wrong: **I have to sadly leave you.**

Right: **Sadly, I have to leave you.**

9. PARTICIPLES, dangling and otherwise

When you add *ing* to the verb, you have what is called a *present* participle. Sometimes the present participle is used as the progressive form of the verb that we described earlier in this lesson. For example: **I was working when you came in.** *Working* is the present participle, and *was working* is the progressive form.

Sometimes the present participle is used in a phrase that describes the subject of a sentence. Here is an example of such a *participial phrase*: **Working steadily, John finished his job by noon.** Do you see how the participial phrase *working steadily* describes the subject *John?* Your problem is to be certain that the subject being described is very clearly identified. Otherwise some most peculiar sentences will result, like these:

Walking down the street, the building came in sight.

Now buildings can't walk! Of course a man was doing the walking, and a man should be expressed as the subject of the sentence, like this:

Walking down the street, the man saw the building.

Examine this example: **Climbing the trees and swinging in the branches, the old lady noticed the monkeys.** Our old lady is not that agile! The climbing and swinging were done by the monkeys. The sentence should read: **Climbing the trees and swinging in the branches, the monkeys were noticed by the old lady.**

So remember that when a participial phrase begins a sentence, the person doing the *"ing-ing"* must be stated clearly *immediately after* the phrase. Otherwise you have the error known as a *dangling participle.*

Other examples: Wrong: **Lighting a match, the fire was started.** Right: **Lighting a match, he started a fire.**

Don't dangle any participles yourself. It might prove embarrassing!

10. verbs and OBJECTS of verbs

You know that a sentence must contain a noun or pronoun as its subject and a verb as its predicate; but you can combine a noun and a verb and still not have a meaningful sentence. *The secretary mailed ....* Though this expression contains a subject-noun *secretary* and a predicate-verb *mailed,* it is incomplete by itself. It lacks an explanation of *what* was mailed.

What is needed is an *object* of the verb *mailed* — a word that will tell us what was mailed. For example: *The secretary mailed the invoice. Invoice* is the object of the verb *mailed* because it tells us what was mailed.

To find the object of a verb, you merely ask yourself *Whom?* or *What?* after the verb. *The secretary mailed .... What?* The invoice. *Invoice* is the object of the verb *mailed. The President gave .... What?* A speech. *Speech* is the object of the verb *gave. John loves ... Whom?* Mary. *Mary* is the object of John's affections.

Of course, many verbs do not require objects to complete the meaning of a sentence. For example: *The President speaks.* Here the verb *speaks* is complete without an object. Or: *The plaster shook. The group met.* A verb that needs an object to make sense is called a *transitive* verb since the action *trans*fers to the object. *Frank put the letter on the table. Put* is transitive; *letter* is its object. A verb that does not take an object is called an *intransitive* verb. Its action is complete in itself. *Frank sleeps on the couch every afternoon. Sleeps* is intransitive. It does not take an object.

11. lie and lay—sit and set—rise and raise

You should learn the difference between verbs that require objects and verbs that do not. Once you have done so, you can easily master the proper use of such confusing verbs as *lie* and *lay, sit* and *set, rise* and *raise.*

A. LIE AND LAY

Probably no two words in the English language are more frequently confused than *lie* and *lay.* Yet *lie* and *lay* have entirely different meanings:

To lie means *to recline.*

To lay means *to place.*

An easy way to remember their different meanings is this little trick: There is an *i* in both *lie* and *recline.* There is an *a* in both *lay* and *place.*

As with all irregular verbs, the best way to learn the different tenses of *lie* and *lay* is to say them aloud: *SAY:*

Present	Past	Perfect
lie	**lay**	**has lain**
lay	**laid**	**has laid**

Another trick: Note that there is an *n* in both *recline* and *lain.*

Here are some sentences using *lie.*

Present Tense: **I lie on the grass.**

Past Tense: **I lay on the grass yesterday.**

Perfect Tense: **I have lain on the grass every afternoon this week.**

Here are some sentences using *lay.*

Present Tense: **I lay the book on the table.**

Past Tense: **I laid the book on the table yesterday.**

Perfect Tense: **I have laid the book on the table as you requested.**

There is another trick that makes distinguishing between *lie* and *lay* easy. *To lie* never needs an object to complete its meaning. It is always intransitive. *To lay* always needs an object to complete its meaning — it is always transitive. Observe these examples.

1. **I lay the book on the table.**
   Lay what? *The book.*
2. **I lie on the grass.**
   Lie what? No answer. *Lie* does not take an object.

3. **I laid the carpeting yesterday.**
Laid what? *The carpeting.*

4. **I lay in bed all day yesterday.**
Lay what? No answer. *Lay,* the past tense of *lie,* does not take an object.

5. **They have laid their cards on the table.**
Have laid what? *Their cards.*

6. **He has lain in a hospital bed for over a month.**
Has lain what? No answer. *Lain* does not take an object.

Let's try some problems using this method.

7. **The workmen have (laid, lain) the linoleum in the kitchen.**
Have (laid, lain) what? *The linoleum.* Therefore, *laid* is correct since *laid* always takes an object.
The workmen have laid the linoleum in the kitchen.

8. **The books have (laid, lain) on the shelves for years.**
Have (laid, lain) what? No answer. Therefore, use *lain* since *lain* never takes an object.
The books have lain on the shelves for years.

If you understand the difference between *lie* and *lay,* you will easily master the distinction between *sit* and *set* and between *rise* and *raise.* If you have any doubts about *lie* and *lay,* however, go back and restudy this lesson before you proceed further.

B. SIT AND SET

To sit means *to be seated.*
To set means *to place.*

Again, say the different tense forms aloud. *SAY:*

Present	Past	Perfect
sit	**sat**	**has sat**
set	**set**	**has set**

EXAMPLES:

The director sits at the head of the table.
The director sat at the head yesterday.
The director has sat at the head at every meeting.
He sets the book on the desk.
He set the book on the desk yesterday.
He has set the book on the desk.

Again, *sit* never takes an object to complete its meaning. It is intransitive. *Set* is transitive and always needs an object to complete its meaning. It requires a word to tell us what was set.

Grandpa used to (sit, set) in his chair by the hour.
(Sit, set) what? No answer. Therefore, use *sit* since *sit* never takes an object.
Grandpa used to sit in his chair by the hour.

C. RISE AND RAISE

To rise means *to get up.*
To raise means *to lift.*

Remember, say the different tense forms aloud. *SAY:*

Present	Past	Perfect
rise	**rose**	**has risen**
raise	**raised**	**has raised**

EXAMPLES:

I rise early every morning.
I rose early yesterday.
I have risen early every morning this week.

We raise the flag each morning.
We raised the flag at dawn this morning.
We have raised the flag every morning this summer.

Once more, *rise* never takes an object to complete its meaning. It is intransitive. *Raise* is transitive and always needs an object to complete its meaning. It requires a word to tell us what was raised.

1. **After he fell, he (rose, raised) himself from the floor.**
   (Rose, raised) what? *Himself.* Therefore, use *raised* since *raised* always takes an object.
   He raised himself.
2. **The balloon (rose, raised) from the ground.**
   (Rose, raised) what? No answer. Therefore, use *rose* since *rose* never takes an object.
   The balloon rose from the ground.

Now, here's a trick to tie all you have learned together. You have learned that all forms of the verbs *lie, sit,* and *rise* do not require objects to complete their meaning – that is, they are all intransitive. Just remember that *intransitive* begins with an *i,* and *lie, sit,* and *rise* also have *i's.* Whenever there is no answer to the question *what* after the verb, you know that the verb is intransitive and that it must be a form of the verbs, *lie, sit,* or *rise.*

12. GERUNDS and PARALLEL CONSTRUCTION

Sometimes a word ending in *ing* looks like a verb, but is really a noun. For example: *Swimming is fun.* For the word *swimming,* you could substitute *baseball* or any other noun, couldn't you? Such a noun coming from the *ing* form of a verb is called a *gerund.*

Logic and common sense would indicate the error in the following sentence: WRONG: **I like swimming, boating, and to hike.** In this sentence you are using as the objects of the verb *like* two gerunds (*swimming* and *boating*) and one infinitive (*to hike*). Of course, you should use the *same* form throughout. Either use all gerunds (**I like swimming, boating, and hiking**) or use all infinitives (**I like to swim, to boat, and to hike**). In other words, don't mix the types of verbs or gerunds used in a series, but rather keep them the same – what we call parallel structure.

Let's look at another example: WRONG: **I like to read, to paint, and playing the piano.** How would you correct this? It's easy! Either **I like to read, to paint, and to play the piano**; or **I like reading, painting, and playing the piano.**

13. IF I WERE...

There is one peculiarity of the verb *to be* that you should master. It is proper for you to say "*I were*" and "*he were*" in two instances:

a) to express a situation that you know to be contrary to fact:

If I were king, I would free all men from servitude.

If I were you, I would not talk so much.

If Mr. Jones were here, your demands would be quickly met.

Remember, you use this form only if the situation is *known* to be false. Note this sentence, for example:

If he was at the party, I didn't see him. You don't know for sure that he was not there, so you use the regular past tense, *if he was.* But if you know that he is not at the party, then you might say: **If he were at this party, it would be really lively.**

b) To express a wish:

I wish I were king.

I wish he were here now.

We wish we were able to answer your question more fully.

Would that I were king.

EXERCISE 14 Recognizing Action and Linking Verbs

A. **This problem deals with recognizing the difference between action and linking verbs. Below is a list of verbs. In the space next to each verb mark A if it is an action verb; mark L if it is a linking verb; mark E if it could be either.**

1. explode ________________
2. spend ________________
3. had been ________________
4. sleep ________________
5. lie ________________
6. were ________________
7. seem ________________
8. walk ________________
9. would have been ____________
10. looks ________________
11. was ________________
12. recline ________________
13. rested ________________
14. mail ________________
15. becoming ________________
16. thinks ________________
17. tastes ________________
18. attack ________________
19. receives ________________
20. feels ________________
21. taste ________________
22. smell ________________
23. touch ________________
24. appear ________________
25. desire ________________

EXERCISE 14 — Recognizing Action and Linking Verbs

B. **This problem deals with distinguishing between action and linking verbs. Below is a list of sentences. Find the verb (predicate) of each sentence and write it in the space provided. In the other space provided, write A if the verb is an action verb; write L if the verb is a linking verb.**

		Predicate Verb	*Action or Linking*
1.	This booklet will show our entire line of clothing.	1. ______________	______
2.	We feel certain of your success.	2. ______________	______
3.	Did you feel the texture of the cloth?	3. ______________	______
4.	The meal tasted wonderful.	4. ______________	______
5.	I tasted the soup.	5. ______________	______
6.	This business becomes tedious after a few weeks.	6. ______________	______
7.	The situation looks promising.	7. ______________	______
8.	He will be there.	8. ______________	______
9.	He looked me straight in the eye.	9. ______________	______
10.	Lie down before dinner.	10. ______________	______
11.	Mr. Smith looked for his papers.	11. ______________	______
12.	The exam looked very easy to everyone.	12. ______________	______
13.	The dinner smells delicious.	13. ______________	______
14.	I can smell the food from here.	14. ______________	______
15.	Don't those pies taste delectable?	15. ______________	______
16.	Did you taste them?	16. ______________	______
17.	I can feel the cold in my bones.	17. ______________	______
18.	I don't feel well.	18. ______________	______
19.	He feels bad about losing his job.	19. ______________	______
20.	His infected thumb feels the pain intensely.	20. ______________	______

EXERCISE 15 — The Simple Tenses

A. **This exercise deals with the use of the simple tenses. Here are five sentences. You are to change the verb to the indicated tense. Fill in the blanks.**

1. a. Present: **I work.**
   b. Past: They ________
   c. Simple future: We ________
   d. Emphatic future: You ________

2. a. Present: **He sells.**
   b. Past: You ________
   c. Simple future: I ________
   d. Emphatic future: They ________

3. a. Present: **They hear.**
   b. Past: We ________
   c. Simple future: You ________
   d. Emphatic future: I ________

4. a. Present: **You say.**
   b. Past: He ________
   c. Simple future: They ________
   d. Emphatic future: She ________

5. a. Present: **She is.**
   b. Past: He ________
   c. Simple future: They ________
   d. Emphatic future: It ________

EXERCISE 15 — The Progressive Form

B. **This problem deals with the proper use of the progressive form. In the space provided, write the proper verb for each of the following sentences. Remember, ask yourself: Is or was the action completed?**

1. They (work) when the bell rang. 1. ________
2. Mrs. Smith (see) Mr. Jones in his office at this very minute. 2. ________
3. Last year we (sell) hundreds of desks. 3. ________
4. While we (talk) the manager arrived. 4. ________
5. Miss Johnson (type) the letter right now. 5. ________
6. We (send) all our customers the new price list last month. 6. ________
7. Weren't you (visit) the home office when the explosion occurred? 7. ________
8. We (know) you can do a perfect job. 8. ________
9. They (leave) when the order was delivered. 9. ________
10. Yesterday we (file) the invoices that were received last week. 10. ________

EXERCISE 16 — The Perfect Tenses

A. **This problem deals with the proper use of the past perfect. In the space provided, write the proper verb for each of the following sentences. Remember, ask yourself: Did one event occur before another event, also in the past, occurred?**

1. The mail (arrive) before we opened the office. 1. ____________
2. Our department (ship) the order before we received your wire. 2. ____________
3. We (see) him walking in the street yesterday. 3. ____________
4. Your officers (be) very courteous to us during the entire party yesterday. 4. ____________
5. The inspector found that the crowd (be) dispersed before he arrived. 5. ____________
6. We saw the puff of smoke right after we (hear) the explosion. 6. ____________
7. As the bell rang, I (finish) my assignment. 7. ____________
8. By the time the bell rang, I (finish) my assignment. 8. ____________
9. My boss (dictate) five letters by noon. 9. ____________
10. Napoleon (conquer) Italy before his thirtieth birthday. 10. ____________

EXERCISE 16 — The Perfect Tenses

B. **This problem deals with the proper use of the present perfect. In the space provided, write the proper verb for each of the following sentences. Remember, ask yourself: Is this action part of a series of actions that continues up to the present?**

1. Ever since I entered the room, the clerk (do) nothing. 1. ____________
2. The baby (cry) since its mother left the room. 2. ____________
3. We (be) here for the past hour. 3. ____________
4. We (go) to the office many times last week. 4. ____________
5. The present governor (be) in office for seven years. 5. ____________
6. Since you left this office, there (be) very little activity. 6. ____________
7. I (be) in this office since 9 A.M. 7. ____________
8. The clerk (stay) on the job since 1942. 8. ____________
9. The printer (proofread) this paper before he left last night. 9. ____________
10. I (work) on this job since graduating. 10. ____________

EXERCISE 17 — Regular Verbs

A. **This problem deals with the way regular verbs change depending upon tense. Fill in the missing verbs in this table.**

	Present Tense	*Past Tense*	*Present Perfect Tense*
1.	work		has
2.		signed	has
3.	order		have
4.		replied	has
5.	return		has
6.			have complained
7.		expected	has
8.	interfere		have
9.		convened	has
10.	adjourn		have

EXERCISE 17 — Regular Verbs

B. **This problem involves working with regular verbs. In the space provided, fill in the proper form of the verb for each of the following sentences.**

1. Our firm (distribute) advertising leaflets for twelve years so far. 1. ____
2. By this time next week we (eliminate) this bottleneck. 2. ____
3. We hereby (acknowledge) receipt of your order. 3. ____
4. The Board (submit) the dispute to arbitration last week. 4. ____
5. We (expect) your reply by next Monday. 5. ____
6. Miss Johnson (leave) with her escort when she was called to the phone. 6. ____
7. We (describe) the project in our next letter. 7. ____
8. We (accumulate) too large an inventory last year. 8. ____
9. By this time last year we (accumulate) too large an inventory. 9. ____
10. The members of the committee (bicker) among themselves at last night's meeting. 10. ____
11. Yesterday we (invite) the Mayor to attend our banquet. 11. ____
12. So far, twelve people (answer) our questionnaire. 12. ____
13. The clerk (work) here since 1960. 13. ____
14. Last night she (type) in the office until midnight. 14. ____
15. Was he (allow) to see your accounts? 15. ____

EXERCISE 18 Irregular Verbs I

This problem deals with irregular verbs. On each line is printed the present tense of an irregular verb. Write the past tense and the present perfect tense of each of these verbs. Have you studied the irregular verbs carefully and recited them aloud?

Present	*Past*	*Present Perfect*
1. I am	I ______	I ______
2. You blow	You ______	You ______
3. It breaks	It ______	It ______
4. It bursts	It ______	It ______
5. They cost	They ______	They ______
6. You deal	You ______	You ______
7. We drive	We ______	We ______
8. I forbid	I ______	I ______
9. We fly	We ______	We ______
10. They go	They ______	They ______
11. I hide	I ______	I ______
12. She knows	She ______	She ______
13. I lead	I ______	I ______
14. You mistake	You ______	You ______
15. We pay	We ______	We ______
16. He reads	He ______	He ______
17. You seek	You ______	You ______
18. I shrink	I ______	I ______
19. We sing	We ______	We ______
20. You speak	You ______	You ______
21. I spend	I ______	I ______
22. They stand	They ______	They ______
23. We take	We ______	We ______
24. She teaches	She ______	She ______
25. We tear	We ______	We ______
26. You throw	You ______	You ______
27. I typewrite	I ______	I ______
28. He wears	He ______	He ______
29. I withdraw	I ______	I ______
30. You write	You ______	You ______

EXERCISE 19 — Irregular Verbs II

This problem deals with the correct forms of irregular verbs. In the space provided, write the correct form of the indicated verb in each of the following sentences. Have you recited the irregular-verb families so often that you know these verbs by ear?

1. I (awake) at the crack of dawn yesterday. 1. ____________
2. By the time he arrived, she had (become) very tired. 2. ____________
3. The general had (awake) by the time I called. 3. ____________
4. I (bid) $50 for the vase at yesterday's auction. 4. ____________
5. They were (bind) to each other by a common interest. 5. ____________
6. The tire had (blow) out. 6. ____________
7. Her heart had been (break) by the cad. 7. ____________
8. We will (build) a factory on the river. 8. ____________
9. Yesterday the pipe (burst) with a roar. 9. ____________
10. He was (choose) to accompany you. 10. ____________
11. He has (come) a long way. 11. ____________
12. By noon it had already (cost) me my entire salary. 12. ____________
13. It was (cut) across the top. 13. ____________
14. They were (deal) with in short order. 14. ____________
15. He has (do) no wrong. 15. ____________
16. This convention has (draw) a huge crowd. 16. ____________
17. He had (drink) too much water. 17. ____________
18. We discovered that prices had (fall). 18. ____________
19. Father (forbid) their leaving the house. 19. ____________
20. Planes have (fly) millions of miles. 20. ____________
21. The weather department has (forecast) clearing skies. 21. ____________
22. By morning the water had (freeze). 22. ____________
23. He has (get) too big for his breeches. 23. ____________
24. The prize was (give) to the bookkeeper. 24. ____________
25. All the members had (go) before the bell sounded. 25. ____________
26. Our nation has (grow) to enormous power. 26. ____________
27. He has not (hear) of your product. 27. ____________
28. The invoice was (hide) under a pile of paper. 28. ____________
29. He had (hurt) himself. 29. ____________
30. Have you (keep) up with the news? 30. ____________
31. Had I (know) of the detour, I would have chosen a different road. 31. ____________
32. He has (lose) his opportunity. 32. ____________
33. He has (lend) a fortune to the firm. 33. ____________
34. He (mean) what he said. 34. ____________

(continued)

EXERCISE 19 (continued)

35. He had (meet) most of them before. 35. ____________
36. I had (mistake) you for him. 36. ____________
37. Your account was (overdraw). 37. ____________
38. He has (prepay) the postage. 38. ____________
39. Have you (read) the contract? 39. ____________
40. We had (put) the matter before the board. 40. ____________
41. Had he (quit) the race by the end of the first mile? 41. ____________
42. The race had been (run) before noon. 42. ____________
43. He had (see) many examples, but could follow none. 43. ____________
44. They have (seek) the answer in vain. 44. ____________
45. The building had (shake) under the force of the earthquake. 45. ____________
46. Had he (show) you how to operate it? 46. ____________
47. The profits (shrink) last week to half their former level. 47. ____________
48. She has (sing) the song before royalty. 48. ____________
49. The ship had (sink) to the bottom. 49. ____________
50. I (sleep) until noon yesterday. 50. ____________
51. Had he (speak) to you about it? 51. ____________
52. We (spend) many hours discussing the problem last night. 52. ____________
53. The coil had (spring) from its covering. 53. ____________
54. Our company has (stand) for the finest quality for 100 years. 54. ____________
55. The two pieces had (stick) together. 55. ____________
56. Catastrophe had (strike) the city. 56. ____________
57. All year long he had (strive) for the top. 57. ____________
58. He was (swear) to secrecy. 58. ____________
59. The river had (sweep) all in its path. 59. ____________
60. I (swim) at the lake last week. 60. ____________
61. They have (take) more than their fair share. 61. ____________
62. Had I (teach) the course, I would have (teach) it differently. 62. ____________
63. Has he (tear) up those papers? 63. ____________
64. I had (think) he was much taller. 64. ____________
65. The President has (throw) out the first ball. 65. ____________
66. Cyrano (thrust) home with his sword. 66. ____________
67. His aunt (undertake) his obligations last week. 67. ____________
68. The company had (underwrite) all his debts. 68. ____________
69. Yesterday I (typewrite) the entire copy. 69. ____________
70. He has (wear) a hole through his sleeve. 70. ____________
71. They have (weep) for days. 71. ____________
72. Has he (win) his bet? 72. ____________
73. The Acme Co. has (withdraw) its bid. 73. ____________
74. Has she (write) to you in the past few weeks? 74. ____________
75. They (write) a letter to you last week. 75. ____________

EXERCISE 20 — Infinitives, Dangling Participles, Parallel Structure

A. **This problem deals with the proper use of infinitives, participles, and parallel structure in sentences. If the sentence is correct as it is, mark C in the space provided. If it is incorrect, use the space above the sentence to indicate the changes that have to be made.**

1. I intend to strongly complain about the errors in my bill. 1. ____
2. I was supposed to have gone to the party last night. 2. ____
3. He wants to see Frank and me and to carefully explain what to do. 3. ____
4. Typing at top speed, the letter was finished on time by the typist. 4. ____
5. We want to carefully proofread the manuscript. 5. ____
6. Reading the paper at lunch, the news upset him. 6. ____
7. Knowing the answer, he raised his hand. 7. ____
8. You must be sure to fully reply to this letter. 8. ____
9. Reading broadens a person, writing sharpens him, and to converse stimulates him. 9. ____
10. On a vacation we should plan to rest, to dream, and puttering in the garden. 10. ____

EXERCISE 20 — Was and Were

B. **This problem deals with the proper use of was and were. In the space provided, fill in the proper word.**

1. If I (was, were) you, I would change my mind. 1. ________
2. I wish I (was, were) President. 2. ________
3. He (was, were) not here yesterday. 3. ________
4. If he (was, were) to disappear into thin air, I could not be more pleased. 4. ________
5. I don't know if he (was, were) at the meeting. 5. ________
6. (Was, Were) I you, I would do the same. 6. ________
7. If I (was, were) the manager of this firm, I would do things differently. 7. ________
8. Since the report turned out to be false, I (was, were) relieved. 8. ________
9. Here is how I would act if I (was, were) in your shoes. 9. ________
10. I certainly wish it (was, were) cooler. 10. ________

EXERCISE 21	Verbs—and their Objects

A. This problem deals with the objects of verbs. Each of the following sentences contains a verb and its object. In the space provided, rewrite the verb and the object of that verb. Remember, to find the object, just ask yourself: Whom? or What? after the verb.

		Verb	*Object of Verb*
1.	John loves Mary.	1. ______	______
2.	Smith sent me to the factory.	2. ______	______
3.	Our firm makes the finest clothing.	3. ______	______
4.	We appreciate your letter of September 20.	4. ______	______
5.	We hear the important events of the day on the radio.	5. ______	______
6.	We will send our representatives next week.	6. ______	______
7.	Will you mail your remittance by return post?	7. ______	______
8.	We are enclosing a copy of the contract form.	8. ______	______
9.	We discussed the entire matter with him.	9. ______	______
10.	They advised him against the contract.	10. ______	______

EXERCISE 21	Verbs—Lie and Lay

B. This problem deals with the proper use of lie and lay. In the space provided, fill in the correct word. Remember: to lay means to place; to lie means to recline.

1. The book (lay, laid) on the shelf for months. 1. ______
2. (Lay, Lie) down before dinner. 2. ______
3. The President (lay, laid) down our basic foreign policy. 3. ______
4. It has (laid, lain) on a shelf for years. 4. ______
5. He will (lie, lay) the carpet tomorrow. 5. ______
6. Will you (lay, lie) down for a few moments' rest? 6. ______
7. He (lay, laid) the foundations for a solid business. 7. ______
8. They had (laid, lain) the goods on top of the table. 8. ______
9. The goods have (laid, lain) on the table for weeks. 9. ______
10. He had (laid, lain) his cards on the table and was ready to suffer the consequences. 10. ______

EXERCISE 21 — Verbs—Sit-Set and Rise-Raise

C. **This problem deals with the proper use of sit or set and rise or raise. In the space provided, fill in the correct word.**

1. (Sit, Set) down in that chair. 1. ________
2. They have (sat, set) in their rocking chairs for years. 2. ________
3. Can you (raise, rise) to the situation? 3. ________
4. (Set, Sit) the table down carefully. 4. ________
5. Will you (raise, rise) your hand if you agree. 5. ________
6. We must try to (raise, rise) above such petty bickering. 6. ________
7. Can you (sit, set) by doing nothing? 7. ________
8. He would have (raised, rose) prices had he foreseen the inflation. 8. ________
9. Prices (raise, rose) due to the inflation. 9. ________
10. (Sit, Set) the piano in the corner. 10. ________

EXERCISE 21 — Verbs—Transitive and Intransitive

D. **This problem deals with the proper use of lie or lay; sit or set; and raise or rise. In the space provided, fill in the proper word.**

1. Have you been (sitting, setting) here all afternoon? 1. ________
2. Prices had not (raised, risen) so fast as expected. 2. ________
3. The journal has (laid, lain) on the shelf for years. 3. ________
4. They were so tired they just (sat, set) right down on the ground. 4. ________
5. The plane will (rise, raise) beyond the clouds in a few moments. 5. ________
6. (Rise, Raise) the curtains and we will see better. 6. ________
7. The accountant (lay, laid) the checkbook on the table. 7. ________
8. Will you (lie, lay) down for a nap? 8. ________
9. A number of rockets have (rose, risen) beyond the stratosphere. 9. ________
10. He has (set, sat) in the same spot for hours. 10. ________
11. The blame was (laid, lain) at his doorstep. 11. ________
12. Will you (rise, raise) a fuss if they don't agree? 12. ________
13. (Sit, Set) down at the table before the guests arrive. 13. ________
14. Regulations have been (laid, lain) down by the Board. 14. ________
15. Have they (sat, set) long enough to be rested? 15. ________

REVIEW EXERCISE — Verbs

This problem deals with the proper use of verbs. In the following letter many verbs are in italics. If the italicized verb is correct, place a C above it. If the verb is incorrect, cross it out and write the correct form above it. Pay particular attention to the use of proper tenses and to irregular verbs.

Dear Mr. Robinson:

I *was* very disappointed that you *do* not send your representative to *watch* the test of our new Starfire car model last week. We are positive that he would *be* astounded by the way the Starfire *performed,* as *was* the hundreds of others who *was* there. Did he *forgot* the date of this demonstration test?

If he had *attended,* he would *be seeing* a new concept in automotive design and engineering. The Starfire *was* an all-new car. It *had* a new engine, new streamlining, new controls.

Until the new line of Starfires *were unveiled* last week, the automobile industry *has* been lagging behind other industries in the use of plastics. The Starfire *has* changed this.

At last week's demonstration tests, the Starfire *accelerated* to 90 miles per hour in under 25 seconds.

I needn't tell you how *astonished* the representatives of other firms *were* when they *seen* this spectacular performance. I'm sure that many of them *had* already told you about it themselves.

Until you have *seen* the Starfire and *drove* in it, you will be missing the thrill of your life. If I *was* you, I would make arrangements to *attendance* the next demonstration, which will be *holded* next Thursday at four o'clock at the Grand Plaza Arena. We *know* that by six o'clock next Thursday you *are* convinced that your going to the demonstration *were* one of the wisest moves of your life.

Moreover, Mr. Robinson, I am pleased to *inform* you that your firm *have* been chosen to enjoy a particular distinction at next week's demonstration. I am *forbid* to disclose anything further, but I can *forecast* with certainty that you will be *freezed* with surprise.

(continued)

REVIEW EXERCISE (continued)

You have *know* our firm for many years, Mr. Robinson. You have *seed* us become the leader in our field. You know that during the past three years we have *spended* many millions of dollars to *built* the Starfire and that we will *spend* many millions more to improve it. We have *stroved* to *shaken* off the shackles of conservative thinking that have *hold* the automotive industry back for years. We have *undertook* a difficult task these past three years. While others were *setting* in their easy chairs, or *laying* around relaxing, our research men were *stroving* for perfection.

The Starfire has been *brung* into being by this devotion to a concept. It has *sprang* into being out of the minds and energy of America's top automotive engineers. In the same way that the jet plane *shrunk* the highways of the air, so shall the Starfire *shrink* the highways on land.

We feel that with the Starfire we have *laid* the groundwork for all new automobiles. We have *setted* new standards in the field of transportation. *Won't* you find out for yourself all about the all-new Starfire?

Sincerely,

LESSON 5

ADJECTIVES

1. comparison of adjectives
2. adjectives after linking verbs
3. using adjectives
4. articles
5. repeating the article

An old Chinese proverb says: "A picture is worth a thousand words." In writing sentences, you paint pictures with adjectives. An adjective is a word that describes a noun or pronoun. Adjectives give color to an otherwise drab subject.

Compare these two classified advertisements. Which woman will win the job?

1. **WOMAN,** college education, looking for job as secretary in theatrical field.

2. **ATTRACTIVE,** energetic young woman, with college education and experience, desires challenging position as secretary to overburdened executive in theatrical field.

By using adjectives in a colorful, forceful manner, Woman No. 2 has created a positive image of herself in the prospective employer's mind. Remember this example when you apply for your job upon completion of your education. You can paint a positive, colorful portrait of yourself by the skillful use of adjectives.

1. COMPARISON of adjectives

The *simple* form of an adjective describes a *single* item or a single *group* of items.

fine book, pretty girls, fast cars, long letters

Adjectives, however, have an added power. They give you the ability to compare one item with others. If you are comparing *two* things, you add *er* to most *simple* adjectives to form what we call the *comparative*.

This is a finer book than that one.

Jane is prettier than Mary.

Sports cars are faster than stock cars.

These letters are longer than those.

Remember, use the *comparative* form only when comparing *two* items.

When you compare *three* or *more* items, add *est* to the simple adjective. We call this form the *superlative.*

This is the finest book I ever read.

Jane is the prettiest of the three girls.

This is the fastest sports car in the world.

This is the longest letter we have received.

Is the difference between the comparative and the superlative clear in your mind? To repeat: You use the *comparative* form only when comparing *two* items. You use the *superlative* when comparing *three or more.*

Why is the following sentence incorrect?

Wrong: He is the taller of the three boys.

If the answer is not obvious to you, you should review this lesson.

Not all adjectives, however, form their comparatives and superlatives by adding *er* and *est.* It would be very awkward for a suitor to whisper in his damsel's ear: **"You are the beautifulest girl in the world."** Long adjectives such as *beautiful* would become tongue-twisters if we were to add *er* or *est.* So, instead of adding *er* or *est* to the end of such an adjective, we simply place the word *more* or *most* in front of it.

To form the *comparative* of long adjectives we say:

more beautiful	**more grateful**
more difficult	**more durable**

To form the *superlative* we say:

most beautiful	**most grateful**
most difficult	**most durable**

Note, however, that the rule about comparatives and superlatives still applies.

More beautiful compares only *two.*

Most beautiful compares *three or more.*

By now you are probably wondering: How do I know when to add *er* or *est* and when to prefix the adjective with *more* or *most*? The best we can offer you is a rule of thumb. To most adjectives of *one* syllable add *er* or *est.* To most adjectives of more than two syllables add *more* or *most.*

Study the list of adjectives below. Note particularly the spelling of the different forms of these adjectives.

Simple	Comparative	Superlative
short	**shorter**	**shortest**
long	**longer**	**longest**
sad	**sadder**	**saddest**
happy	**happier**	**happiest**
lovely	**lovelier**	**loveliest**
lazy	**lazier**	**laziest**
dry	**drier**	**driest**
attractive	**more attractive**	**most attractive**
difficult	**more difficult**	**most difficult**

A few adjectives form their comparatives and superlatives in a different manner. Don't let that worry you. Not only are there very few of these irregular adjectives, but also you are familiar with most of them already.

Simple	Comparative	Superlative
bad	**worse**	**worst**
good	**better**	**best**
little	**less**	**least**
many / **much**	**more**	**most**
late	**later**	**latest**
	latter	**last**
far	**farther**	**farthest**
	further	**furthest**

2. adjectives after LINKING VERBS

Do you remember the linking verbs you learned about in Lesson 4 – verbs that express a *state of being* rather than an action? Linking verbs include all forms of the verb *to be* (for example: *am, was, shall be, should have been*) and also verbs like *feel, seem,* and *appear* when they are used in such a manner that they could be replaced by the verb *is.* (For example: **Candy tastes sweet. Candy is sweet.**)

What is the adjective in this sentence: **We have a heavy schedule.** Right. It is *heavy.* What is the adjective in this sentence: **Our schedule is heavy.** If you again said *heavy,* you are right. Even though *heavy* is separated from the noun it modifies (*schedule*) by the linking verb *is, heavy* is still an adjective and still modifies *schedule.* Pick out the adjectives in these paired examples:

This is a long day.

This day is long.

He stated a forceful argument.

His argument is forceful.

Of course the adjective in the first pair is *long*; in the second pair, it is *forceful.* Remember that an adjective is still an adjective even if it is separated from its noun by a linking verb. You'll learn more about the significance of this in a later lesson.

3. USING adjectives

A. Comparison with a Group

What is wrong with this sentence?

Wrong: I am smarter than any person in my class.

I am in my class. I cannot be smarter than myself. I must therefore exclude myself from the rest of the group by the use of the word *other* or the word *else* as follows:

Right: I am smarter than any other person in my class.

Right: I am smarter than anyone else in my class.

Do you see the point? It is subtle, but logical.

B. This and That

These is the plural of *this. Those* is the plural of *that.*

This book is perfect.

These books are perfect.

That mountain is farther than it looks.

Those mountains are farther than they look.

You may have trouble with these words where the noun that is modified sounds plural but is really singular—nouns such as *kind, sort,* and *type.* Be sure to write *this kind* or *that kind*—NOT, *these kind* or *those kind.* Write *those kinds* or *these kinds* since *kinds* is plural.

C. Less and Fewer

Less should be used to refer to items measured in bulk.

Fewer should be used to refer to items counted separately.

Less coal was mined this year.

Fewer men applied for the job than we anticipated.

D. Them

The word *them* is a pronoun, not an adjective. NEVER use *them* to modify a noun or another pronoun.

Right: Those books are mine.

(NOT: Them books are mine.)

Right: That kind is no good.

(NOT: Them kind is no good.)

In Lesson 8 you will learn when to use *them.* For the present learn when *not* to use it.

E. One Another and Each Other

Do you know what's wrong with this sentence?

Wrong: The two men knew one another.

One another always refers to three or more persons or things. In our sentence there are only two men. So we must use *each other* which is the proper form when there are only two persons or things.

Right: The two men knew each other.

Right: The three men knew one another.

F. Placement of the Word ONLY

The three sentences below show how we can completely change our meaning by merely moving the word *only*.

Only Bob was accused of lying. This means that no one else was accused.

Bob was only accused of lying. This means that he was accused, but not convicted.

Bob was accused of lying only. He was not accused of anything else.

From these sentences learn this rule of good English. Always place the word *only* as close as possible to the word it modifies so that its meaning is absolutely clear.

Right: I paid only eight dollars.

Wrong: I only paid eight dollars.

Right: I filed my application only a day late.

Wrong: I only filed my application a day late.

G. First and Last

When using the word *first* or the word *last* to modify a number, always place it *directly before* the number.

The first eight pages have been typed.

NOT: The eight first pages.

The last six people arrived late.

NOT: The six last people arrived late.

H. Misrelated Expressions

Sometimes an entire phrase will be used to modify a noun. Here is an example of such an *adjective phrase:* **The desk with the steel legs is sturdy.** The adjective phrase *with the steel legs* describes the noun *desk*. You should always place an adjective phrase as close as possible to the word it modifies. Failure to do so can result in strange sentences like these:

Wrong: They delivered the piano to the woman with mahogany legs.

Right: They delivered the piano with mahogany legs to the woman.

Wrong: I bought a fan for my friend that was reconditioned.

Right: I bought a fan that was reconditioned for my friend.

You have already met the dangling participle that leads to a similar problem:

Wrong: Serving lunch, a banana peel tripped the waitress.

Right: Serving lunch, the waitress tripped on a banana peel.

I. Farther — Further; Farthest — Furthest

Sometimes these forms of the adjective *far* are used incorrectly. The words *farther* and *farthest* should be used when an actual physical distance is thought of. An easy way to remember is to think of the *a* in *space* and the *a* in *farther* and *farthest*.

Our car will travel farther on less gas.

Alaska is the farthest state from Florida.

Use *further* and *furthest* in all other situations.

Study this chapter further.

If we delve further, we will find the solution.

J. Later and Latter

Later is the comparative form of the adjective *late* and refers to time.

I shall be there later.

The speech was given later than I had expected.

Latter means the second of two; it is usually used as the opposite of *former,* which means the first of two.

The latter part of the book is the more interesting.

Jones and Smith were both successful – the former through luck; the latter through hard work.

K. Capitalizing Proper Adjectives

Proper adjectives are adjectives that are derived from proper nouns – the names of specific people, places, or things. Words like *American, Asiatic,* and *Victorian* are capitalized just like the proper nouns from which they come.

Some proper adjectives, however, are no longer thought of in connection with the original proper noun. Here are a few of such adjectives that are not capitalized: *morocco binding, oriental rug, jersey wool.*

An interesting area is the study of trademarks that have become so common in everyday use that they have passed into the public domain and have lost their status as trademarks – and thereby their capital letters. Here are just a few examples: *aspirin, escalator, cellophane, shredded wheat, thermos bottle.* There are hundreds of others.

L. Unique

This jewel is unique. Since *unique* means *one of a kind,* nothing can be *more unique* or *most unique. Unique* is already a superlative; it cannot be compared.

M. Compound Adjectives

You have already met the word *compound* which means the uniting of two or more elements. You have studied compound subjects, compound predicates, compound sentences, and compound nouns. Now meet the *compound adjective;* for example: *well bred, up to date, well known, high grade.* The question is: When are compound adjectives hyphenated and when aren't they? Do you write *up-to-date* or *up to date?* The answer is simplicity itself. Compound adjectives are generally hyphenated when they immediately *precede* the noun they describe; they are usually not hyphenated when they come *after* the noun. Look at these examples:

Our up-to-date styles can't be surpassed.

Our styles are known to be up to date.

We sell first-class products.

The products we sell are first class.

A high-grade executive is hard to find.

We are looking for an executive who is high grade.

Compound adjectives are often formed by joining a numeral with words of measure like *inch, foot, mile, pound, month, quart.* Your basic rule still pertains:

a three-foot ruler	**a ruler three feet long**
a five-mile walk	**a walk of five miles**
a four-year period	**a period of four years**

Note that in the hyphenated adjectives that precede the noun the unit of measure is always singular: **A five-pound cake.** NOT: **A five-pounds cake.**

There are a few compound adjectives that are *always* hyphenated regardless of their position in a sentence.

A hyphen is used in all compound adjectives formed with *self.*

He is a self-made man.

This truth is self-evident.

A hyphen should be used in numerical adjectives from twenty-one through ninety-nine.

We celebrated our twenty-fifth anniversary.

He was elected on the thirty-second count.

This attempt was his one hundred and twenty-ninth.

4. ARTICLES

There are three words that we call *articles* – **a, an, the.** You've used these words all your life, so you should have little trouble with them.

Whether to use *a* or *an* depends upon the sound of the next word. When the next word begins with a *consonant* sound, you use *a*. A consonant sound is the sound of any letter in the alphabet except *a, e, i, o, u.*

a boy	**a happy boy**
a man	**a young man**

Note that you say: *a* happy boy. On the other hand you say: *an* honest man. Why? Because in the word *honest*, the *h* is silent. Since the word *honest* does not begin with a consonant *sound*, use *an*.

an hour	**a house**
an honor	**a hotel**

You use **an** wherever a word begins with a *vowel* sound. The vowels are **a, e, i, o, u.**

an apple	**an incident**
an event	**an orange**

an umbrella

Note that while you should say *an umbrella*, you also say *a university*. Why? Because the *u* in *university* sounds like the *y* in *you*. Remember, it is the *sound* that counts, not the spelling.

a union	**an ulcer**
a usurer	**an undertaking**

5. REPEATING the article

Occasionally, you will be faced with a problem of whether to repeat the article when you are listing a series of things. For example:

The red and (the) white coats are on sale.

Should you use the extra *the*? This depends upon what you mean. If each coat is part white and part red, then omit the extra *the*: **The red and white coats are on sale.** For the sake of clarity, you might better use hyphens here to express your meaning: **The red-and-white coats are on sale.** If, however, there are two types of coats – one all white and the other all red – then add the extra *the*: **The red and the white coats are on sale.**

Do you see this subtle distinction?

The President and the Chairman arrived. (Two men.)

The President and Chairman arrived. (One man holding both positions.)

The steel and the plastic cabinets are in place. (Some cabinets are all steel; some, all plastic.)

The steel and plastic cabinets are in place. (Cabinets of part steel and part plastic.)

EXERCISE 22 Recognizing Adjectives

A. **This problem deals with recognizing adjectives. Underline the adjective in each of the following sentences with one line. Then, underline the word each adjective modifies with two lines.**

1. He picked up the heavy case.
2. She prepared a light supper.
3. The colored lights were dimmed.
4. It was a very efficient system.
5. We have complete records.
6. Our latest records show a deficit.
7. We sent an order for farm machinery.
8. He slowly walked to his first class.
9. These are first-class goods.
10. Here is our new catalogue.
11. Send me your final approval.
12. Where is my brown hat?
13. Forgive my late reply.
14. The table has a smooth finish.
15. We went horseback riding.
16. It's a very smooth-riding car.
17. This is an easy problem.
18. This problem is easy.
19. I am hungry.
20. He feels hungry.

EXERCISE 22 Degrees of Adjectives

B. **This problem deals with the choice of the comparative or the superlative adjective. In the space provided, write the proper form of the adjective in parentheses. Remember, use the comparative when comparing two; use the superlative when comparing three or more.**

1. Although Mr. Smith and Mr. Jones are bright, Mr. Roberts is the (bright). 1. ____________
2. Which of this pair has the (bright) colors? 2. ____________
3. Though our Raleigh plant is large, the Durham plant is (large). 3. ____________
4. New York is the (exciting) of the two cities. 4. ____________
5. New York is the (exciting) city in the world. 5. ____________
6. She is the (tall) girl in the whole office. 6. ____________
7. The left sleeve is (long) than the right. 7. ____________
8. Of all our forty-three offices, the (large) is in Los Angeles. 8. ____________
9. Test this one, then that one, and choose the (good). 9. ____________
10. Which of the twins is the (pretty)? 10. ____________

EXERCISE 22 Degrees of Adjectives

C. **This problem deals with the three forms an adjective may take—simple, comparative, and superlative. On each line of the following table is written one of the three adjective forms. Fill in the other two forms. Pay special attention to proper spelling. Nothing less than perfect spelling is acceptable.**

	Simple	*Comparative*	*Superlative*
1.	pretty		
2.		busier	
3.	familiar		
4.			most
5.		less	
6.			last
7.		hotter	
8.	good		
9.			farthest
10.		sadder	
11.	difficult		
12.		worse	
13.	unusual		
14.			loveliest
15.	friendly		
16.	important		
17.	afraid		
18.	wealthy		
19.		happier	
20.	dry		

EXERCISE 23 — Comparison with a Group

A. **This problem deals with the comparison of a member of a group with the rest of the group. Of the following ten sentences, two are correct and eight are incorrect. If the sentence is incorrect, indicate the necessary corrections.**

1. My son is smaller than any boy in his class.

2. John is bigger, smarter, and more handsome than any of his classmates.

3. Mr. Smith is shrewder than anyone in his department.

4. Who is fairer than any girl in her group?

5. Mr. Jones is more popular than anyone.

6. Henry is better behaved than any child in his school.

7. Of all the tenants, Mr. Smith is least objectionable.

8. He is taller than any pupil in his class.

9. More level-headed than any man in his company, John was promoted.

10. This is the best and most efficient of any other system used today.

EXERCISE 23 — This and That

B. **This problem deals with the proper use of this and that, these and those. In the space provided next to each sentence, write the proper word. Remember, this and that are singular; these and those are plural.**

1. (This) (These) forms of designs are very effective. 1. ____________
2. (That) (Those) make of cars sells very well. 2. ____________
3. Our firm makes (this) (these) style of trousers. 3. ____________
4. (That) (Those) kind of book is for adults. 4. ____________
5. Where do you buy (this) (these) type of shoes? 5. ____________
6. I don't associate with (that) (those) kind of people. 6. ____________
7. I don't associate with (that) (those) people. 7. ____________
8. (This) (These) type of table is very sturdy. 8. ____________
9. Do you like (that) (those) kind of pants? 9. ____________
10. Would you call (this) (these) forms the best for us? 10. ____________

EXERCISE 23 — Less and Fewer

C. **This problem deals with the proper use of less and fewer. In the space provided, write the correct word, either less or fewer. Remember, use less to refer to quantities measured in bulk; use fewer to refer to items counted separately.**

1. They delivered (less) (fewer) coal than we had ordered. 1. ____________
2. They delivered (less) (fewer) tons of coal than we had ordered. 2. ____________
3. There were (less) (fewer) than ten customers today. 3. ____________
4. We can do the same amount of work with (less) (fewer) secretaries. 4. ____________
5. Your firm has sent (less) (fewer) orders than anticipated. 5. ____________
6. There is (less) (fewer) unemployment than anticipated. 6. ____________
7. This air conditioner uses (less) (fewer) electricity than any other model. 7. ____________
8. This air conditioner uses (less) (fewer) kilowatts of electricity than any other model. 8. ____________
9. This typewriter weighs (less) (fewer) than twenty pounds. 9. ____________
10. (Less) (Fewer) than ten people showed up. 10. ____________

EXERCISE 24 — Each Other—One Another

A. **This problem deals with the proper use of each other and one another. In the space provided, write the correct expression. Remember, each other refers to two; one another refers to three or more.**

1. The two men spoke to (each other) (one another). 1. ____________
2. The committee members spoke to (each other) (one another) until it was time to convene. 2. ____________
3. We are acquainted with (each other) (one another), he and I. 3. ____________
4. The men in the mob prodded (each other) (one another) to greater violence. 4. ____________
5. The two airmen helped (each other) (one another) survive in the jungle. 5. ____________

EXERCISE 24 — Only

B. **This problem deals with placement of the word only. In each of the following sentences, only is improperly placed. Indicate the proper placement of the word only. Remember, only should be placed directly before the word it modifies.**

1. The President only signed the first bill.
2. He only saw three familiar faces.
3. I only met him twice.
4. We only filed our applications one day late.
5. This hat only cost three dollars.
6. He only leaves early on Fridays.

(continued)

EXERCISE B. (continued)

7. He was only convicted of a misdemeanor.

8. He only promotes the younger, alert employees.

9. We have only seen him once.

10. It only is eleven o'clock.

EXERCISE 24 — First and Last

C. **This problem deals with the proper placement of the words first and last. In only one of the following five sentences is the word first or last properly placed. Write C in front of that sentence. Indicate the necessary changes to correct the other sentences. Remember, place the word first or last directly in front of the number it modifies.**

1. We enjoyed the two last weeks.

2. I don't understand the eight first pages.

3. We haven't heard from him for the last three days.

4. We have read all but the eight last pages.

5. Only the six first people were admitted.

EXERCISE 25 — Placement of Modifiers

A. **This problem deals with the proper placement of modifiers. Each of the sentences below is incorrect because of a misplaced modifier. Rewrite these sentences correctly in the space provided. Remember, place the modifier as close as possible to the word it modifies.**

1. People cannot fail to notice vast changes in business methods who are in touch with business offices.

2. We saw the new building walking down East Shore Drive.

3. The soldier saddled his horse who was wearing a new uniform.

4. Take the book to the man with the beautiful leather binding.

5. The dog ran toward his master wagging his tail.

6. Take the table to the shop with its four legs to be mended.

7. He watched the parade pass by standing at the corner.

8. The men took the chair to the woman with all four legs painted black.

EXERCISE 25 — Farther and Later

B. **This problem deals with the proper use of the adjectives farther-further and later-latter. Remember that farther refers to physical space, and that later is used only when time is involved. In the space provided, fill in the proper word.**

1. He threw the ball (farther, further) than I. 1. ____________
2. He sat in the chair (farthest, furthest) from the chairman. 2. ____________
3. I will go to the (farthest, furthest) place in the world for you. 3. ____________
4. (Further, farther) than that, I cannot go in compromising with you. 4. ____________
5. The (later, latter) we meet tonight, the less time we will have. 5. ____________
6. The (later, latter) part of the sermon contained some powerful points. 6. ____________
7. The former speaker introduced the guest; the (later, latter) spoke at length. 7. ____________
8. The two men spoke. The former said: "It is (later, latter) than you think." 8. ____________

EXERCISE 25 — Capitalizing and Hyphenating

C. **This problem deals with capitalizing and hyphenating adjectives. Remember that most adjectives derived from proper nouns are capitalized. Compound adjectives have hyphens if they come before the nouns they modify. In the space provided, fill in the proper word.**

1. The (American, american) Indian created (well-made, well made) tools. 1. ____________
2. The (Victorian, victorian) age occurred in the '80's. 2. ____________
3. A (Persian, persian) rug may be very valuable. 3. ____________
4. He heard (Martial, martial) music on the radio. 4. ____________
5. He was a (well-intentioned, well intentioned) worker who made mistakes. 5. ____________
6. The fact that he cannot perform the work is (self-evident, self evident). 6. ____________
7. A (first-rate, first rate) mechanic is difficult to get. 7. ____________
8. The battalion put up a (last-ditch, last ditch) effort. 8. ____________
9. This pie is obviously (home made, home-made). 9. ____________
10. In this office we need workers who are (well-disciplined, well disciplined). 10. ____________

EXERCISE 26 — Using Articles

A. **This problem deals with choosing a or an. In the spaces provided, write either a or an, whichever is correct.**

1. _____ man wearing _____ unusual jacket left _____ package.

2. _____ humorist is _____ human being with _____ peculiar sense of humor.

3. _____ understanding of all operations in our plant is _____ necessity for _____ foreman.

4. _____ hour before dawn is _____ inhuman hour for _____ human being to be awakened.

5. _____ union leader should be _____ honest man, for to lead _____ union is _____ undertaking of great responsibility.

EXERCISE 26 — Repeating the Article

B. **This problem deals with repeating the article. Indicate any necessary corrections.**

1. The secretary and vice-president met at noon.

2. He was elected to be both the vice-president and the secretary.

3. The car has a blue and a white finish.

4. We have in stock two cabinets, a chromium and aluminum one.

5. She wore a red and a green sweater.

REVIEW EXERCISE | Adjectives

The letter below includes many intentional errors. Cross out all errors and indicate the necessary changes in the spaces above them.

Dear Mr. White:

Have you heard about our sale on phonograph records? This sale is excitinger and spectacularer than any sale in this city's history.

Only during the two first weeks we have sold no less than 10,000 records in each of our two stores. You might be interested to know that the South Street store has sold the greatest number of records even though the store is furthest from the heart of town. This is a extremely unusual development.

We would be very grateful if you would visit our store. You can't miss it, walking down Sixth Avenue toward Elm. Mr. Johnson, our manager, and his assistant, Mr. Roberts, are very anxious to see you. I'm sure you three will enjoy chatting with each other.

Perhaps you will explain to these men why they have least sales than the South Street store. We want you to give them a honest opinion. See if you can help them catch up and surpass the South Street store during the three last weeks of the sale.

Sincerely,

LESSON 6

ADVERBS

1.forming adverbs **2. choosing between adverbs and adjectives**

3. using adverbs

You already know what words we use to give color to nouns or pronouns. That's right, *adjectives!* Now let's discuss those words that we use to give color to verbs – words we call *adverbs.* Adverbs are jacks-of-all-trades. Not only do they modify verbs, they also can modify adjectives and they can even modify other adverbs.

The ship sailed swiftly. The adverb **swiftly** modifies the verb **sailed.**

Broadway is an extremely wide street. The adverb **extremely** modifies the adjective **wide.**

The old man walked very slowly. The adverb **very** modifies the adverb **slowly.**

An *adverb* is a word that tells you *how, when, where,* or *how much.*

The book was printed carefully. Printed *how?* **Carefully.**
The order was shipped promptly. Shipped *when?* **Promptly.**
The officials came here. Came *where?* **Here.**
They were very pleased. Pleased *how much?* **Very.**

1. FORMING adverbs

You form most adverbs from adjectives by merely adding *ly*:

Adjective	*Adverb*
swift	**swiftly**
careful	**carefully**
familiar	**familiarly**
sole	**solely**

In spelling, remember that the *ly* adverb ending is simply attached to the existing word in most cases. Adjectives that end with *e* or *al* fall into the same category – just attach the *ly*.

separate + ly = separately
scarce + ly = scarcely
authoritative + ly = authoritatively
accidental + ly = accidentally
cordial + ly = cordially
official + ly = officially

When the adjective ends in *y*, to form the adverb change the *y* to *i* and add *ly*.

Adjective	*Adverb*
busy	**busily**
happy	**happily**
satisfactory	**satisfactorily**
temporary	**temporarily**

When the adjective ends in *able* or in *ible*, to form the adverb drop the final *e* and add *y*.

Adjective	*Adverb*
noticeable	**noticeably**
considerable	**considerably**
forcible	**forcibly**
horrible	**horribly**

Note the change in spelling when we transform these adjectives into adverbs.

Adjective	*Adverb*
due	**duly**
true	**truly**
whole	**wholly**

2. CHOOSING between adverbs and adjectives

On the job you will have to choose between using an adjective or an adverb in many sentences. Will you know which to use? For example: **The situation looks (bad) (badly).** Which is correct? By the time you finish this lesson, you will know how to solve such problems easily.

You learned in the chapter on verbs that there are two types of verbs – *action* verbs and *linking* verbs. If you don't know the distinction between them right now – and know it well – do not read further in this lesson. The whole problem of when to use adverbs and when to use adjectives hinges on the distinction between action and linking verbs. STOP! Review Lesson 4 right now if this distinction is not crystal clear in your mind.

The rule is very simple:
Use an *adverb* to modify an *action* verb.
Use an *adjective* after a *linking* verb.

The fire burned fiercely. *Burned* is an *action* verb; therefore, we used the *adverb fiercely.*

The material was sent promptly. *Sent* is an *action* verb; therefore, we use the *adverb promptly.*

The tiger attacked fiercely. *Attacked* is an *action* verb; therefore, we use the *adverb fiercely.*

The fierce tiger attacked. Here *fierce* describes the noun *tiger;* it is an adjective. What about this sentence: **The tiger is fierce.** In the lesson on adjectives you learned that *fierce* is still an adjective even though it is separated from its noun by a linking verb. **The tiger is fierce** is the same as saying **the fierce tiger.**

The same is true in this sentence: **The tiger looks fierce.** You know that *looks* in this sentence is a *linking* verb. *Looks* could be replaced by *is*: **The tiger looks (is) fierce.** So again we use the adjective *fierce* because it follows a linking verb and really describes the subject-noun *tiger* and not the verb *looks.*

What about this sentence: **He looked (fierce, fiercely) for the missing wallet.** Is *looked,* as used here, an action or a linking verb? Could it be replaced by *was*? No. Therefore, *looked* is an action verb (meaning *searched*) and requires the adverb *fiercely*: **He looked fiercely for the missing wallet.**

Earlier in this lesson, we gave as an example the problem-sentence: **The situation looks (bad) (badly).** You should be able to solve this easily now. *Looks,* as used here, is a *linking* verb; therefore, we use the adjective *bad*: **The situation looks bad.**

Here is a similar sentence: **The boy feels (bad) (badly).** It is conceivable that either word may be used if you stretch your imagination. How? If the boy has burned his fingers and they have become insensitive, you could say *The boy feels badly (with his fingers).* The adverb *badly* is then used to describe the *action* verb *feels.* Hardly likely, but possible!

For our purposes, however, *feels* in this sentence is a linking verb that really means *is.* **The boy feels** (*is*) **bad** (*unhappy*). Remember, therefore, to say **I feel bad** if you want to describe your emotional or physical condition – NOT: **I feel badly.**

3. USING adverbs

A. Good and Well

Dinner tasted (good) (well). Good is an adjective. *Well* is usually an adverb. Since *tasted* is a *linking* verb, we use the adjective *good.* **Dinner tasted good.** Note again that *tasted* really means *was*: **Dinner was good** or **a good dinner.** Simple, isn't it?

He performed (good) (well). *Performed* is an *action* verb; therefore, we use the adverb *well.* **He performed well.** The only exception to this rule occurs when *well* is used as an adjective meaning *healthy.* In such a case, since *well* is an *adjective,* it can be used after a *linking* verb. **He is well** (*healthy*). **He feels well** (*healthy*). **He looks well** (*healthy*).

BUT remember: **The flower smells good. He works well.**

B. Most and Almost

(Most, Almost) all the orders were sent. A simple test to determine whether to use *most* or *almost* is to substitute the word *nearly.* If *nearly* fits, then you know that *almost* is proper. **Nearly all the orders were sent.** Therefore: **Almost all the orders were sent.**

In the following sentence it is obvious that *nearly* would not fit, so *most* is proper: **Who had the most errors?**

BUT: **It was almost too late to catch the train.** The same as: **It was nearly too late....**

C. Double Negatives

Time and again you have heard people say that two negatives make a positive. For our purposes, two negatives generally make poor English; so you must avoid double negatives. What is a double negative? Here is a common example:

Wrong: **They don't know nothing.**

This sentence contains two negative words, *don't* and *nothing.* Each of these negatives destroys the other. By eliminating either one of them we get a correct sentence:

Right: **They know nothing.**

Right: **They don't know anything.**

Remember: Avoid double negatives.

1 **Right: He didn't say anything.**

Right: He said nothing.

Wrong: He didn't say nothing.

2 **Right: It was nothing.**

Right: It wasn't anything.

Wrong: It wasn't nothing.

You may have a little more difficulty with words that don't look negative but really are—words such as *scarcely, hardly, never, neither, but*. They will cause you no trouble if you remember that these words are *negative* in themselves. Never add the word *not* to them.

1 **We can scarcely see you in this fog.** NOT: We *can't* scarcely see you ....

2 **We could hardly have decided otherwise.** NOT: We *couldn't* hardly ....

3 **It could never happen here.** NOT: It *couldn't* never happen here.

4 **It was neither of them.** NOT: It *wasn't* neither of them.

5 **I understand all but one of them.** NOT: I *don't* understand all but one .... If you really mean what is said in the latter sentence, you'd be clearer to say **I understand only one of them.** Do you see why this means the same thing?

D. Real and Very

I am (real) (very) pleased. *Real* is an adjective that means *genuine*. *Very* is an adverb that means *extremely*. When faced with a choice of *real* or *very*, substitute *genuine* or *extremely*. If *genuine* fits, *real* is correct. If *extremely* fits, *very* is *correct*.

Our problem-sentence reads properly if we insert *extremely*: **I am extremely pleased.** Therefore, use *very*: **I am very pleased.** (NOT: *I am real pleased.*)

One further point about the use of the adverb *very*. It is considered less-than-perfect English to have *very* modify a verb *directly*. *Very* is a peculiar adverb that should modify only another adverb or an adjective. So for our problem-sentence to be perfectly correct, it should read: **I am very much pleased.** Similarly: **I am very much interested** is better than **I am very interested; I am very well satisfied** is better than **I am very satisfied.**

Returning to the use of *real* or *very*, let's substitute *genuine* or *extremely* to check a few other sentences:

Right: It gives me real (genuine) pleasure to introduce the next speaker.

Right: We are very (extremely) well pleased with the outcome.

Right: It was a real (genuine) diamond.

Right: It was a very (extremely) wonderful movie.

E. Comparison of Adverbs

Adverbs may be compared, just like adjectives. One- or two-syllable words add *er* and *est*: *soon, sooner, soonest*; *early, earlier, earliest*. Adverbs that are longer are usually formed by using the words *more* and *most*: *happily, more happily, most happily*; *sincerely, more sincerely, most sincerely*. Remember to use the *comparative* form when comparing *two;* use the *superlative* only when comparing *three or more*. **I will arrive earlier than he. Of them all, I arrived earliest.** How about this sentence: **I arrived earlier than any of them.** Why do we use the comparative when *them* tells us that there are at least two others? You are right (we hope). We use *earlier* because it compares you with *any* of *them*, and you know from Lesson 1 that *any* is always singular – it means *any one*.

F. Unnecessary Adverbs

Sometimes the adverbial meaning of *how, when, where,* or *how much* is expressed in other words in the sentence. In that case do not use the adverb unnecessarily. In the following sentences, why is each word in parentheses redundant and therefore unnecessary?

Recopy this page *(over)*.

I shall repeat the question *(again)*.

He has returned *(back)* **from Europe.**

They must co-operate *(together)* **to be a perfect pair.**

Erase this *(out)*.

G. Compound Words Confused With Adverbs

Sometimes you may be confused between compound expressions, usually beginning with **all**, that resemble adverbs, and the adverbs themselves. If you examine these expressions, however, you will see that the meanings are quite different.

all together (meaning *many combined*)
altogether (meaning *completely*)
They worked all together until they were altogether satisfied with the results.

all ways (meaning *every manner*)
always (meaning *forever*)
Always remember that there are all ways of reaching happiness.

all ready (meaning *completely prepared*)
already (meaning *previously*)
The employees were all ready at five o'clock, though some had already punched out.

Note: **All right** is always written as two words, never as one word. There is no such word as *alright* just as there is no such word as *alwrong.*

Correct: **all right all wrong**

H. Sure and Surely

Don't use the *adjective* **sure,** which means *confident* or *certain,* when you want to say *certainly* or *undoubtedly.* In that case you must use the *adverb* **surely.**

He (sure, surely) did an unusually effective job! We must use **surely** since we mean *certainly.*

(Sure, Surely) I'll go with you. (**Surely,** meaning *certainly.*)

BUT: **He is quite sure of himself.** (Confident)

EXERCISE 27 — Recognizing Adverbs

A. **This problem deals with recognizing adverbs. Underline the adverb in each of the following sentences with one line. Then, underline the word it modifies with two lines.**

1. The plane traveled swiftly.
2. We are very much pleased to hear from you.
3. We walked quietly to the side.
4. Quickly he leaped into his car.
5. The matter is entirely finished.
6. No two men are completely alike.
7. This occurrence is most unfortunate.
8. We strongly urge you to accept this offer.
9. Recheck thoroughly all outgoing mail.
10. They came here much later than expected.
11. He was essentially interested in securing a patent.
12. We were unusually surprised by his work.
13. All our customers are comfortably dressed when they leave us.
14. Watch this maneuver intently.
15. Mr. Jones arrived at the meeting exactly at the appointed hour.

EXERCISE 27 — Changing Adjectives into Adverbs

B. **This problem deals with changing adjectives into adverbs. Below is a list of adjectives. In the space next to each adjective, write the equivalent adverb.**

1. careful ____________
2. sole ____________
3. busy ____________
4. primary ____________
5. noticeable ____________
6. principal ____________
7. whole ____________
8. true ____________
9. considerable ____________
10. substantial ____________
11. real ____________
12. extraordinary ____________
13. extreme ____________
14. bad ____________
15. good ____________

EXERCISE 28 Review of Action and Linking Verbs

This is a review problem involving action and linking verbs. Underline the verb in each of the following sentences. Then, in the space provided, mark A if it is used as an action verb; mark L if it is used as a linking verb. Have you reviewed Lesson 4 on the distinction between action and linking verbs?

1. He looked at me with a piercing stare. 1. ____________
2. The office seems quite comfortable. 2. ____________
3. This bread smells very fresh. 3. ____________
4. John lay down on his bed after dinner. 4. ____________
5. This proposition is a once-in-a-lifetime opportunity. 5. ____________
6. Mr. Jones looks taller than his brother. 6. ____________
7. This situation seems positively uncanny. 7. ____________
8. John rests. 8. ____________
9. By tomorrow I shall have been there and back. 9. ____________
10. He knows the answer to our problems. 10. ____________

EXERCISE 29 Choosing Between Adverbs and Adjectives

This problem deals with choosing between an adjective and an adverb. Below is a series of sentences. In the space provided write the proper form of the word in parentheses in each sentence. Remember, use an adverb to modify an action verb; use an adjective after a linking verb.

1. Candy tastes (sweet). 1. ____________
2. He tasted the mixture (careful). 2. ____________
3. Return the merchandise as (quick) as possible. 3. ____________
4. He is very (content). 4. ____________
5. The situation seems (bad). 5. ____________
6. I am (extreme) tired from my long journey. 6. ____________
7. The plant grew more and more (quick). 7. ____________

(continued)

EXERCISE 29 (continued)

8. The whole garden smells (sweet). 8. ____________
9. We (certain) hope you are comfortable. 9. ____________
10. We feel he has been (extraordinary) competent at his task. 10. ____________
11. Ordinarily the bell tolls (soft), but today it sounds (loud). 11. ____________
____
12. Our situation has grown (bad). 12. ____________
13. She looks (beautiful). 13. ____________
14. We can accomplish our goals (easy). 14. ____________
15. He has done (good, well) in his new post. 15. ____________
16. Our product is becoming more and more (desirable) in its line. 16. ____________
17. Mr. Jones became (angry) and threatened his employee (loud). 17. ____________
____
18. He feels (indignant) because he cannot attend. 18. ____________
19. The whole story sounds (strange). 19. ____________
20. You are paying an (extreme) large amount. 20. ____________
21. We will (glad) repay your losses. 21. ____________
22. This is a very (poor) constructed problem. 22. ____________
23. The river flowed (rapid). 23. ____________
24. Do business conditions look (bad) to you? 24. ____________
25. Rewrite the entire page (correct). 25. ____________
26. Please have a clerk file these papers (quick). 26. ____________
27. Mr. Roberts certainly is a (quick) thinker. 27. ____________
28. When faced with an emergency, Mr. Roberts thought (quick). 28. ____________
29. There is no doubt about Mr. Roberts' being (quick). 29. ____________
30. Mr. Smith tasted his soup (hungry). 30. ____________
31. To Mr. Smith, the soup tasted (delicious) and (inviting). 31. ____________
____
32. The table was set (inviting). 32. ____________
33. I feel (bad) about your leaving. 33. ____________

EXERCISE 30 — Good and Well

A. **This problem deals with the proper use of good and well. In the space provided, write the proper word – either good or well.**

1. You did the job very (good, well). 1. ______
2. You did a very (good, well) job. 2. ______
3. It sounds (good, well) to me. 3. ______
4. You look (good, well) in your new suit. 4. ______
5. He performs (good, well) on the piano. 5. ______
6. The job was done quite (good, well). 6. ______
7. The proposition sounds (good, well). 7. ______
8. We feel confident you shall do (good, well) in your new position. 8. ______
9. Though he was sick, he is now completely (good, well). 9. ______
10. He was extremely (good, well) in the part of Hamlet. 10. ______

EXERCISE 30 — Most and Almost

B. **This problem deals with the proper use of most and almost. In the space provided, write the proper word. Remember, use almost only where the word nearly could be used as well.**

1. These are (most, almost) all of the supplies that are left. 1. ______
2. We found that (most, almost) people did not answer. 2. ______
3. He is (most, almost) as good as his competitor. 3. ______
4. (Most, Almost) everything was finished by noon. 4. ______
5. (Most, Almost) of the time we work quite hard. 5. ______
6. It was (most, almost) too good to be true. 6. ______
7. We feel that (most, almost) of our staff is doing a top-notch job. 7. ______
8. It seems that (most, almost) all of the men answered our plea. 8. ______
9. He can sell (most, almost) as (good, well) as any of our other salesmen. 9. ______ ______
10. (Most, Almost) anyone who dresses (well, good) can look (well, good). 10. ______ ______ ______

EXERCISE 30 — Double Negatives

C. **This problem deals with double negatives. Rewrite the following letter, correcting all double-negative expressions.**

```
Dear Mr. Bronson:
        Mr. Marshall from your office hasn't scarcely
visited us more than a few times in the past few months.
We certainly hope that we haven't done nothing to offend
him.  After all, we haven't hardly started in our associa-
tion with your firm, and we certainly wouldn't want to do
nothing that would jeopardize our fine relationship.
                                    Sincerely,
```

____

____

____

____

____

____

____

____

EXERCISE 30 — Real and Really

D. **This problem deals with the proper use of real and really. In the space provided, write the proper word.**

1. These diamonds are (real, really). 1. ________
2. He was (real, really) pleased to meet them. 2. ________
3. It gives us (real, really) satisfaction. 3. ________
4. We are (real, really) sorry we cannot comply. 4. ________
5. After a day's work he was (real, really) tired. 5. ________
6. Were the (real, really) situation known, there might be a scandal. 6. ________
7. The teachers were (real, really) concerned about her grades. 7. ________
8. This matter is (real, really) important. 8. ________
9. We have (real, really) valid reasons for our stand. 9. ________
10. Are you (real, really) sure of your facts? 10. ________

EXERCISE 30 — Unnecessary Adverbs

E. **This problem deals with the use of unnecessary adverbs. If an adverb is used unnecessarily, write it in the space; if there is no unnecessary adverb, write the letter C for correct.**

1.	Please repaint this wall again.	1. ______
2.	Exit out this way.	2. ______
3.	Return those papers back to me.	3. ______
4.	Cooperate together with your associates.	4. ______
5.	Please repeat the letter again.	5. ______
6.	Let us reconvene again on Monday morning.	6. ______
7.	In re-examining the ledger, they discovered the error.	7. ______
8.	We want nations to coexist together in harmony.	8. ______
9.	The new fan has conquered over all competition.	9. ______
10.	Try to cooperate as fully as you can.	10. ______

EXERCISE 30 — Compound Expressions

F. **This problem deals with compound expressions that are confused with single adverbs. In the space provided, write the proper word or words.**

1.	He is (all together, altogether) wrong in his approach.	1. ______
2.	In (all ways, always) this edition seems superior.	2. ______
3.	Many students have (all ready, already) taken some college courses.	3. ______
4.	(All together, Altogether) I counted thirty-three people.	4. ______
5.	It's (all right, alright) to leave before the bell.	5. ______
6.	The new firm failed (all together, altogether).	6. ______
7.	He is in (all ways, always) a model employee.	7. ______
8.	I think the bank tellers are (all ready, already) to end their day's work.	8. ______
9.	Conditions are neither (all right, alright) nor (all wrong, alwrong.)	9. ______ ______
10.	(All right, Alright), you may go when you are (all ready, already.)	10. ______ ______

REVIEW EXERCISE — Adverbs

The following letter contains many improper words. Cross out each improper word and write the correct word above it.

Dear Mr. Spears:

It was a genuine pleasure to see you at the Acme Convention in Pittsburgh. I thought you looked real good, considering the seriousness of your recent illness. We sure hope you enjoyed your visit to Pittsburgh and that everything was alright there.

The Acme Company is growing very quick. Last year's sales are a tiny fraction of our anticipated sales this year. Our situation is growing more better every day. I am certain that we can easily accomplish the goals we set for ourselves in Pittsburgh.

One situation I feel badly about is the growth of competition in the South. If one looks close at sales figures in the South, he will see that the rate of increase does not look as well as we had first thought. I am real concerned with this problem.

On the other hand, our Western office has done extremely good. They are real quick rising to Number One position in the nation. I wish that our other offices followed our advice as complete and thoroughly as they do.

By the way, John Raymond feels indignantly because he was not chosen as a speaker in Pittsburgh. Even though his speaking is real poorly, he is an important person. While I am not positive that there will be time for him at the next convention, I am most surely that we can squeeze him in.

Please write and let us know if you are feeling weller.

Sincerely,

LESSON 7

PREPOSITIONS

1. using prepositions **2. the right preposition**

Words such as the following are prepositions: **of, at, in, on, between.** Since most prepositions are very familiar words, they should give you little trouble.

A preposition is a word that connects a noun or pronoun with the body of the sentence. The noun or pronoun that the preposition connects to the body of the sentence is called the *object* of that preposition.

of John – John is the *object* of the preposition **of.**

at the time – time is the *object* of the preposition **at.**

in the room – room is the *object* of the preposition **in.**

on the way – way is the *object* of the preposition **on.**

between you and me – you and **me** are the *objects* of the preposition **between.**

The phrase that is introduced by a preposition is called simply a *prepositional* phrase. **I arrived on time.** In this sentence **on time** is a prepositional phrase. **On** is the preposition; **time** is the object of the preposition.

I went to his office. What is the prepositional phrase? That's right – **to his office. To** is the preposition; **office** is its object.

I went to his newly decorated office. The prepositional phrase is **to his newly decorated office.** The preposition is **to;** its object is still **office** despite the introduction of the descriptive words **newly decorated.**

In Lesson 8 you will be called upon to work with the *objects* of prepositions. For the moment let's just study the prepositions themselves. Here is a list of the most common prepositions. You undoubtedly recognize them all, but did you know they are all prepositions? Don't memorize this list, but learn to recognize these words as prepositions:

about, above, across, after, against, along, among, around, at, before, behind, below, beneath, between, beyond, but, by, concerning, down, during, except, for, from, in, into, of, off, on, over, regarding, respecting, since, through, throughout, till, to, toward, under, underneath, until, up, upon, with, within, without

In addition, there are a number of familiar word groups that are used as though they were prepositions. Learn to recognize these word groups as prepositions.

as to, as for, as regards, apart from, by way of, contrary to, devoid of, from out, from beyond, instead of, in place of, in regard to, in reference to, on account of, to the extent of, with respect to

1. USING prepositions

A. From and Than

Always use the word *from* after the word *different* when you mean that something is different *from* something else. It is *never* different *than* something else. (It may help you to remember that the *f* of *different* must be followed by the *f* of *from.*)

Right: **This may differ from what you had thought.**

Right: **My theory is different from the one held by my boss.**

Right: **Sing the song differently from the way you sang it last night.**

When *differ* is used as a verb meaning *disagree,* it calls for the preposition *with.*

We differ with your conclusion.

B. Among and Between

There is a difference of opinion (among) (between) you and me.

Between is proper only when there are *two* people or things involved. *Among* is proper when there are *three or more.* Our sentence should read *between you and me* since there are only *two* people involved – *you* and *me.*

Right: **Between you and me, we have nothing to fear.**

Right: **We shall place your display among the many others.**

Right: **We shall place your display between the other two.**

C. In and Into

What is the difference between these two sentences?

1. **The director is in the room.**
2. **The director went into the room.**

In means *within. Into* means *from the outside to within.* In other words, *into* expresses an action of moving from one place (outside) to another place (inside). *In* expresses no action.

The carbon is in the drawer.

He put his hand into the drawer to get the carbon.

You will note that the words *in* or *into* in the same sentence may change the meaning completely.

He ran in the ring. (Was he afraid?)

He ran into the ring. (Was he eager?)

D. Off and Of

Do not use the word *of* after the word *off.*

Right: **The radio fell off the table.** NOT: The radio fell *off of* the table.

Right: **The letter dropped off the file.**

Right: **He is coming off the gangplank.**

Do not use *off of* when you mean *from.*

Right: **He borrowed the money from me.**

NOT: He borrowed money *off of* me.

Do not use *of* when you mean *have.* Remember, the word *of* never directly follows the word *might, must, could, should,* or *would.* It is true that when you speak quickly, the helping verb *have* sounds like the preposition *of*; that should not be mislead you, however.

Right: **I might have gone.** NOT: I *might of* gone.

Right: **I would have been there by now.**

Right: **I should have known this would happen.**

E. Unnecessary Prepositions

You should avoid unnecessary prepositions that merely clutter your sentence without adding thought content.

1 **Right:** **Where are you going?** NOT: Where are you going *to?*

2 **Right:** **Where is your home?** NOT: Where is your home *at?*

3 **Right:** **I cannot help expressing my gratitude.** NOT: I cannot help *from* expressing my gratitude.

4 **Right:** **I want you to see this.** NOT: I want *for* you to see this.

5 **Right:** **Until yesterday, I would have agreed.** NOT: *Up* until yesterday, I would have agreed.

6 **Right:** **In two weeks it will be over.** NOT: In two weeks it will be over *with.*

F. Incorrect Prepositions

1. Do not use *over* for *to, at, during,* or *for. Over* means *on top of* or *in excess of.*

Right: **Come to my house tonight.** NOT: *over my house.*

Right: **Let's have the meeting at my home.** NOT: *over my home.*

Right: **We held the meeting during the weekend.** NOT: *over the weekend.*

2. In the lesson on verbs, you studied the word *to* as part of the *infinitive*: *to walk, to study,* etc. Now let's consider *to* as a preposition: *to the office, to next week,* etc. Do not use *to* for *at. At* indicates location whereas *to* indicates motion.

Right: **I was at a meeting last night.** NOT: *to a meeting.*

Right: **was at her graduation.** NOT: *I was to her graduation.*
BUT: **I went to her graduation.**

3. Do not use the adverb *too* (meaning *also* or *excessively*) or the numeral *two* (meaning *2*) for the preposition *to.*

Right: **There are too many people to give out only two prizes.**

Right: **Too much has been said to the public about the two world powers.**

4. Do not use *around* (meaning *circular*) for *about* (meaning *approximately*).

Right: **I'll be at the bank about an hour from now.**

Wrong: **I'll be at the bank around an hour from now.**

G. Beside and Besides

To avoid confusing these two prepositions, remember that *beside* means *by the side of.*

He sat down beside her (*at her side*).

Besides with the *s* has a completely different meaning: *in addition to.*

The office will send a supervisor besides the typist and me.

No one will be there besides us two.

Wrong: He sat down besides her.

H. Omitting Necessary Prepositions

Do not omit prepositions that are necessary.

Right: **What type of work do you do?** NOT: What type work do you do?

Right: **Tell him what style of cabinet we want.** NOT: what style cabinet.

Do not omit the preposition *from* after the verb *graduate.*

Right: **I was graduated from high school two years ago.** NOT: I graduated high school.

2. the RIGHT preposition

Certain words call for one preposition and not another. You will be constantly using many such words in your work as a secretary. Below is a list of words and their proper prepositions. Study this list carefully. Repeat each expression over and over until it becomes familiar to you.

abide by (a decision)

absolve from (to free from)

abstain from (usual combination)

accede to (to express approval or give consent)

accompanied by (a person)
accompanied with (an object)

according to (done according to directions)

adapted to (adjusted to)

adhere to (to give support or to hold fast)

affiliate with (to associate oneself)

agree with (an opinion)
agree to (terms)
agree among (more than two people)
agree between (two people)

angry with (a person)
angry at (an occurence or object)

annoyed with (a person)
annoyed by (that which annoys)

appropriate to (suitable to)

argue with (a person)
argue for (something)

attend to (heed; listen; to direct one's care)

beneficial to (not "for")

blame for (not "on")

borrow from (not "of")

buy from (not "of")

capable of (having sufficient intelligence, resources, or strength)

careless about (appearance)
careless in (performance of actions)
careless of (others)

cause for (an action)
cause of (a result)

choose among (three or more)
choose between (two)

compare to (suggest a similarity)
compare with (specific similarities)

complementary to (not "with")

comply with (not "to")

coincide with (usual combination)

concur in (an opinion)
concur with (a person or thing)

confer with (compare views or take counsel)

confide in (to tell confidentially)
confide to (to entrust)

consist of (is made up of)
consist in (lies in)

contrast to (or "with" when **contrast** is a noun)
contrast with (when **contrast** is a verb)

convenient to (a location)
convenient for (a purpose)

conversant with (well-informed)

correspond with (writing letters)
correspond to (equivalent)

dates from (not "back to")

deal in (kind of business)
deal with (people)

depend upon (or "on"; to become conditioned)

differ from (a thing)
differ with (an opinion)

disappointed at (or "in" a thing)
disappointed with (a person)

disgusted with (a person)
disgusted at (a thing)
disgusted by (behavior)

dispense with (not "of")

dissent from (not "with" or "of')

emerge from (to arise from)

enter into (inquire into or become a part of)
enter upon (a career)

entertained by (amused, diverted)

equivalent to (equal)
equivalent with (synonymous)

familiar with (conversant)

in accordance with (not "to")

in compliance with (usual combination)

identical with (uniform with)
identical to (equal to)

impose upon (or "on" meaning to infringe or abuse)

independent of (not "from")

indifferent to (equal to)

inquire of (to ask a person)
inquire about (interrogate or question)
inquire after (one's health)

inseparable from (incapable of being disjoined)

insight into (power of seeing into)

interfere with (a person)
interfere in (something)

labor under (difficult conditions)
labor for (a person)

lend to (to add, furnish, or provide)

live in (a town)
live on (a street)
live at (a certain address)
live by (means of livelihood)

necessity for (urgent need)
necessity of (unavoidable obligation)

need for (urgent occasion for)
need of (lack or want)

object to (to oppose)

offended at (action)
offended with (a person)

participate in (to take part)

payment for (an article)
payment of (a fee or bill)

proceed with (to continue)
proceed from (to come forth)

profit by (not "from")

prohibit from (is usual form)

provide for (to supply what is needed)

take exception to (usual combination)

talk to (to speak to a person)

EXERCISE 31 — Recognizing Prepositions

This problem deals with recognizing prepositions. In each of the following sentences underline all prepositions with one line. Then circle the objects of those prepositions.

1. Did you hear of the trouble at the office?

2. Mr. Atwood was in his office when you called.

3. The reputation of Empire Fans has been built on high standards and fair dealings at all times.

4. Between you and me, I feel certain that one of the representatives will call at your office within a week.

5. In regard to any orders from your firm, we feel sure of our ability to fill them in time for your fall shipment.

6. With respect to your claim for damages, we are certain of a recovery to the extent of $3,000.

7. Contrary to our expectations, you will be refused a passport for the duration of the present emergency.

8. They have agreed among themselves to honor, without any question, all of the demands made by our client.

9. Against all odds, we have succeeded beyond expectation in our endeavor to enlist support for our cause.

10. Instead of being discouraged by his failure, he seemed to gain the strength of a lion in all his subsequent attempts.

11. Walking into the hall, the President of the United States and the members of his cabinet were greeted by the assembled guests.

12. In spite of his aversion to the tactics of high-pressure salesmen, Mr. Jones was so impressed by this young man that he agreed to buy his full line of goods.

EXERCISE 32 — Using Prepositions

A. This problem deals with the use of from after the word different. In the space provided, write the proper preposition.

1. My idea is different ________________ yours.
2. Our course may differ ________________ what you had expected.
3. Approach the topic differently ________________ the way you did last time.
4. The Board differed ________________ the advice of the Director.
5. His designs are no different ________________ the designs he showed last time.
6. What we differ ________________ is your desire for haste.
7. The course they chose was different ________________ that outlined in the manual.
8. Our attorneys differ ________________ this report's interpretation of the facts.
9. Have you nothing different ________________ what you showed me last week?
10. The new car models are very different ________________ the old ones.

EXERCISE 32 — Among or Between

B. In the space provided, write either among or between whichever is correct.

1. There is a difference of opinion ________________ the two men.
2. There is a difference of opinion ________________ the jury.
3. The Big Three often differ ________________ themselves.
4. Chicago is ________________ New York and Seattle.
5. ________________ the people present were the President, the Vice-President, and the Secretary of State.
6. The jewelry was found ________________ his belongings.
7. ________________ you and me, this plan will be a huge success.
8. ________________ the reasons for his success were his wisdom, honesty, and fairness.
9. Is there a great difference ________________ the Ford and the Chevrolet?
10. There is little difference ________________ these five jacket models.

EXERCISE 32 — In or Into

C. In the space provided, write either in or into, whichever is correct.

1. He walked ____________ the room from the hall.
2. Behind a closed door, he paced back and forth ____________ his office all day.
3. There are some fascinating articles ____________ today's newspaper.
4. It doesn't take much to get ____________ a fight with him.
5. What sort of work would you like to get ____________?
6. Promotion is rapid, once you have established a name ____________ this field.
7. He opened the door and rushed ____________ his office.
8. I would tear this contract ____________ a thousand little pieces if I could.
9. Do you think you can get ____________ the public relations field?
10. You can work your way ____________ the confidence of your superior only by intense effort.

EXERCISE 32 — Misusing of Prepositions

D. In the space provided, write the proper word or words.

1. Money was stolen (off of, from) the safe. 1. ____________
2. The child fell (off of, off) the chair. 2. ____________
3. I could (have, of) completed the job by noon. 3. ____________
4. They took the receipts (off of, from) me. 4. ____________
5. We all got (off of, off) the elevator at the same floor. 5. ____________
6. He borrowed money (off of, from) John. 6. ____________
7. They should (have, of) known he was lying. 7. ____________
8. The idol has toppled (off of, from) its pedestal. 8. ____________
9. The shirt was almost ripped (off of, off) the crooner's back. 9. ____________
10. With luck he might (have, of) pulled through. 10. ____________
11. I stepped (off of, from) the moving car. 11. ____________
12. They could (have, of) made many changes (among, between) the three of them. 12. ____________
13. He would (have, of) had very different opinions (from, than) mine. 13. ____________
14. When you went (in, into) this field, you should (have, of) been prepared for a life very different (from, than) college life. 14. ____________
15. Standing (between, among) his brothers, John and Bob, he would (have, of) looked very different (from, than) either of them. 15. ____________

EXERCISE 32 — Unnecessary Prepositions

E. **This problem deals with eliminating unnecessary prepositions. Twelve of the following sentences contain unnecessary prepositions. Three of the following sentences are correct. Cross out each incorrect preposition and list it in the box provided at the end of the sentence. If the sentence is correct, write C in the box.**

1. This is the place where I am going. 1. ____________
2. Do you know where Mr. Smith is at? 2. ____________
3. Did the packages fall off of the shelves? 3. ____________
4. Here is a copy of the plans you ordered. 4. ____________
5. We wanted for him to receive the prize. 5. ____________
6. Up until last week we had not received any report. 6. ____________
7. Together we can seek out a solution. 7. ____________
8. It's a relief that summer is over with. 8. ____________
9. By the end of the summer your shipment will be ready. 9. ____________
10. Open up all the windows. 10. ____________
11. I didn't remember of having received the bill. 11. ____________
12. If I'd of known the answer, I would have won the contest. 12. ____________
13. In another few minutes it will be done with. 13. ____________
14. Of our many customers, you have been one our most pleasant. 14. ____________
15. Get the books off of the desk. 15. ____________

EXERCISE 32 — Choosing Prepositions

F. **This problem deals with prepositions that are incorrectly used. Write the correct word in the space provided.**

1. I had a fine time (over, at) my friend's house. 1. ____________
2. Frank sat down (beside, besides) his friend. 2. ____________
3. What (type, type of) suit are you going to buy? 3. ____________
4. I'll be there (during, over) the holidays. 4. ____________
5. (Beside, Besides) my employer and me, who else is invited? 5. ____________
6. He ordered a new (style, style of) wall decoration for the office. 6. ____________
7. I was (to, at) the celebration last week. 7. ____________
8. What can we do (beside, besides) writing a letter of complaint? 8. ____________
9. I want to go along (to, too, two). 9. ____________
10. (Two, to, too) many times I hear the same complaints. 10. ____________
11. Did you (graduate, graduate from) high school? 11. ____________
12. He (too, to, two) feels that (too, to, two) hours are enough. 12. ____________

EXERCISE 33 — The Proper Preposition

This problem deals with recognizing the proper preposition for a given word. In the space provided, write the preposition that best completes the thought. This problem not only reviews material in the text but also introduces you to the correct use of other prepositions.

1. Abide ______ a referee's decision.
2. Accompanied ______ his boss.
3. Accompanied ______ a full payment.
4. Agree ______ the terms of the contract.
5. Agree ______ his views on politics.
6. Agree ______ this method of attack.
7. Angry ______ the superintendent.
8. Angry ______ the rainy weather.
9. Buy ______ a salesman.
10. Borrow ______ a friend.
11. Comply ______ your request.
12. Convenient ______ all trains.
13. Convenient ______ all business needs.
14. Correspond ______ his firm by mail.
15. Correspond ______ my understanding.
16. Differ ______ his outlook on life.
17. Agree ______ the three of us.
18. Disappointed ______ the outcome.
19. Take advantage ______ an offer.
20. Deal ______ a problem.
21. Deal ______ stocks and bonds.
22. In contrast ______ other methods.
23. To contrast ______ other methods.
24. Agree ______________ the two of us.
25. Provide ______ future needs.
26. Equivalent ______ a full gallon.
27. Emerge ______ the depths of despair.
28. Labor ______ pleasant conditions.
29. Labor ______ a kind employer.
30. Labor ______ a difficult task.
31. A necessity ______ promptness.
32. Inseparable ______ one another.
33. In accordance ______ the vast majority.
34. Familiar ______ the entire process.
35. An exception ______ the rule.
36. Dates______last June.
37. Lend ______ a friend.
38. Accompanied ______ a cash payment.
39. Agree ______ the terms.
40. Indifferent ______ others.

(continued)

EXERCISE 33 (continued)

41. Inquire ______ one's neighbor.
42. In contrast ______ his former work.
43. Accede ______ his wishes.
44. Angry ______ the drop in sales.
45. Conversant ______ all details.
46. Agree ______ a plan of attack.
47. Adapted ______ your needs.
48. Talk ______ his audience.
49. Adhere ______ my previous decision.
50. Distinguish ______ the two methods.
51. Comply ______ orders from headquarters.
52. Different ______ other methods.
53. Consist ______ wood and metal.
54. Enter ______ an agreement.
55. Impose ______ your neighbors.
56. Insight ______ complex matters.
57. Profit ______ former mistakes.
58. Coincide ______ the plans of others.
59. Approve ______ his behavior.
60. Dispense ______ all formality.
61. Correspond ______ air mail.
62. Capable ______ doing a fine job.
63. Depend ______ his parents.
64. Correspond ______ a friend overseas.
65. Accompanied ______ his mother.
66. Attend ______ business.
67. Conscious ______ the risks involved.
68. Appropriate ______ the occasion.
69. Participate ______ games.
70. Confide ______ his brother.
71. Correspond ______ his understanding.
72. Entertained ______ the comedian.
73. Identical ______ the original.
74. Confer ______ your doctor.
75. According ______ our contract.
76. In accordance ______ our contract.
77. Prohibited ______ doing an illegal act.
78. Concur ______ an opinion.
79. Abide ______ the court's ruling.
80. Depend ______ your wits.
81. Angry ______ his employee.
82. Proceed ______ the current plan.
83. Accompanied ______ invoices.
84. Absolve ______ all guilt.
85. Abstain ______ voting.
86. Convenient ______ buses and trolleys.
87. To object ______ certain conditions.
88. Different ______ his neighbor.
89. Agree ______ your opinion.
90. Participate ______ a contest.
91. Comply ______ your requests.
92. Correspond ______ our picture of events.
93. In contrast ______ other products.
94. Disagree ______ our opponents.
95. Differs ______ our old desk.
96. Disgusted ______ his boss.
97. In compliance ______ your order.
98. Differs ______ his boss.
99. Choose ______ the three.
100. Correspond ______ telegram.

REVIEW EXERCISE — Prepositions

In the following letter many prepositions are improperly used. Cross out each improper preposition and write the correct preposition above it.

Dear Mr. Smith:

I am afraid that I cannot agree upon your interpretation of our contract. Your interpretation is entirely different than mine. Unfortunately, my attorney, accompanied with his family, is at a vacation so that I have been unable to obtain his advice. I am trying to correspond to him by mail, but up until today have been unable to locate him.

This difference of opinion among you and me must be reconciled at once. You realize that I am not angry at you. I am angry at the conditions that brought about this situation.

I am quite willing to comply to all the provisions in Paragraph X, but I cannot agree to your interpretation of Paragraph XI. When I agreed to enter in this contract, I interpreted Paragraph XI very differently than your present interpretation.

Was it merely convenient to you to change your mind once I was bound to the contract? You cannot be indifferent to standard business practice, and my understanding to the contract is in complete accord to standard business usage. Paragraph XI is identical to Paragraph VII of the Standard Business Contract No. 109.

I am forwarding a copy of this letter, accompanied by a copy of Paragraph XI, up to the National Business Board.

I will abide with their decision if you will agree to abide with it too.

Respectfully,

LESSON 8

MORE ABOUT PRONOUNS

1. types of pronouns
2. using pronouns
3. who and whom
4. whoever and whomever
5. whose and who's
6. any one, anyone
7. like as a preposition
8. but, meaning except

"Me Tarzan. Me king of jungle." A movie script may sound like that, but your daily conversation had better not. Undoubtedly, you use the pronouns **I** and **me** properly most of the time, which is more than we can say for Tarzan. You automatically say:

> **I** want it. NOT: **Me** want it.
> Give it to **me.** NOT: Give it to **I.**

But in complicated sentences, your choice may become more difficult. Try this sentence, for example:

> **He thought it was (I) (me) who had ordered the circulars.**

Do you know whether **I** or **me** is correct? Do you know how to distinguish between the use of **he** and **him, she** and **her, we** and **us,** or **they** and **them**? Do you know when to use **who** and when to use **whom?** If you use these words properly at all times, you are a rare and fortunate person. In fact, you are probably a genius and we would advise you not to read further in this lesson. If, however, you are an ordinary mortal like the rest of us, you will occasionally have difficulty choosing the proper pronoun and this lesson is designed for you. We're going to show you how to make the choice of pronouns easy.

1. TYPES of pronouns

Look at these sentences. They show you when to use **me** rather than **I.**

❶ **Give it to me.** (**Me** is the *object* of the preposition **to.**)

❷ **He thanked me.** (**Me** is the *object* of the verb **thanked.**)

Learn this simple rule: Always use **me,** not **I,** when the pronoun is the *object* of a preposition or the *object* of a verb. In fact, **me** is called the objective case of the pronoun **I.** Similarly, **him** is the objective case of **he**; **her** is the objective case of **she**; **us** is the objective case of **we**; and **them** is the objective case of **they.**

Give it to him . . . . to her . . . . to us . . . . to them.

He thanked him . . . . thanked her . . . . thanked us . . . . thanked them.

Quickie Review: What should you know about *objective* pronouns? Only these two simple points:

1. The *objective* pronouns are: *me, him, her, us, them.*

2. You use *objective* pronouns as *objects* of verbs or *objects* of prepositions. That's all.

When do you use the pronoun *I, he, she, we,* and *they*? Do these examples answer your question?

❶ **I want to go.** (**I** is the *subject* of the sentence.)

❷ **It is I.** (**I** follows the *linking verb* **is.**)
That's all there is to it. Use *I, he, she, we,* or *they*:

1. as the *subject* of a sentence or of a clause;

2. after a *linking* verb.

I want to go. He . . . . She . . . . We . . . . They want to go.

It is I. It is he. It is she. It is we. It is they.

NEVER: *It's me.*
I, he, she, we, or *they* is called the *nominative* case of the pronoun because it *names* the subject of a sentence (or its equivalent after a linking verb).

Do you recognize the subject of a sentence when you see it? Do you remember what a clause is? If not, review Lesson 1 on the parts of a sentence. Do you recognize a linking verb when you see one? You should by now. You studied linking verbs in Lessons 4, 5, and 6. Review Lesson 4 right now if you are at all uncertain of linking verbs.

Quickie Review: What should you know about the *nominative* pronouns *I, he, she, we, they*? Remember these two points:

1. Use **I, he, she, we,** or **they** as the *subject* of a sentence or of a clause.

2. Use **I, he, she, we** or **they** after a *linking* verb.

Now look again at the problem sentence you had at the beginning of this lesson: **He thought it was (I) (me) who had ordered the circulars.** Isn't this sentence easy now? The pronoun (*I* or *me*) comes after the *linking* verb *was.* After a linking verb what do we use? That's right! *I.* Therefore: **He thought it was I who had ordered the circulars.** Simple, isn't it? (It it isn't, you had better reread this lesson.)

Let's take a few more difficult sentences. We'll show you a technique to make them easy. How would you complete this sentence:

1 The invoice was sent by John and (I) (me).
You would have no trouble if the sentence read:

2 The invoice was sent by (I) (me).
By just reading Sentence 2 aloud, you would hear that *me* is correct.

The invoice was sent by me.
Me is the object of the preposition *by*.
In Sentence 1, ignore the word *John* and use the same pronoun you would use if the pronoun were alone.

The invoice was sent by (John and) me.
Learn this simple rule: Use the same form of a pronoun when it is joined with another pronoun or a noun that you would use if the pronoun were alone.

Look at these examples:

1. *I* will move. (Subject of a sentence.)
   (Bob and) *I* will move.
2. *He* is an expert. *I* am an expert.
   He and *I* are experts.
3. Did you know it was *he*? (After linking verb.)
   Did you know it was (Bob and) *he*?
4. The order was sent to *me*. (Object of preposition.)
   The order was sent to (John and) *me*.
5. The report interests *me*. The report interests *him*. (Object of verb.)
   The report interests *him* and *me*.
6. Send *me* the folder. Send (Lou and John and) *me* the folder.
   Send *them* and *me* the folder.
7. Submit the report to either (*him or her*) (*he or she*).
   Submit the report to *him*. Submit the report to *her*.
   Submit the report to either *him or her*.

2. USING pronouns

A. Us and We

Here's a tricky sentence: **(We) (Us) secretaries have interesting work.**
To solve this problem-sentence, merely leave out the word **secretaries.**

(We) (Us) have interesting work.

Answer: **We** have interesting work.

Therefore: **We secretaries have interesting work.**

Here are some similar examples :

1. The prize was given to (*we*) (*us*) girls.
   Omit *girls*. The prize was given to *us*. (NOT: . . . to *we*.)
   Therefore: The prize was given to *us* girls.
2. The director asked (*us*) (*we*) boys to be present.
   The director asked *us* . . . . (NOT: asked *we*.)
   Therefore: The director asked *us* boys to be present.
3. (*We*) (*Us*) students should be cheerful and efficient.
   We should be . . . . (NOT: *Us* should be.)
   Therefore: *We* students should be cheerful and efficient.

B. Than and As

1 She is a better stenographer than (I, me.)

2 She was not so good as (he, him).

Here's a technique that will make it easy for you to choose the proper pronoun after *than* or *as*. Add a little word that completes the meaning of the sentence – a word such as *am, do,* or *was.*

For example:

1 **She is a better stenographer than (I, me).** This means:
She is a better stenographer than (I, me) *am.*
Answer: .... *I am.* NOT: *me* am.
Therefore: She is a better stenographer than *I.*

2 **She was not so good as (he, him).** This means:
She was not so good as (he, him) *was.*
Answer: .... *He was.* NOT: *him* was.
Therefore: She was not so good as *he.*

3 **She does a better job than (I, me).** This means:
She does a better job than *I (do).*

4 **He would rather eat with John than (me, I.)** This means:
He would rather eat with John than (*with*) *me.*

C. Between You and Me

Between you and (I, me), there's nothing to worry about.

If you remember from Chapter 6 that *between* is a *preposition,* you know that *me* must be correct because *me* is the *object* of the preposition *between.* Always say *between you and me*—never, *between you and I.*

Between you and me, I think this will work.

Between you and me, who do you think will win?

The profits were divided between Mrs. Smith and him.

3. Who and Whom

Whom is the *objective* case of the pronoun *who.* From this fact, you immediately know that you use *whom* as:

1. The *object* of a verb
2. The *object* of a preposition.

Who is in the *nominative* case, so you know that you use *who*:

1. As the *subject* of a sentence or a clause
2. After a *linking* verb.

Many people find the choice of *who* or *whom* difficult, but here's a technique that will make this choice easy for you. Whenever you choose between *who* and *whom,* merely substitute *he* or *him.* If *he* fits, *who* is correct. If *him* fits, *whom* is correct.

Remember: **He = Who .... Him = Whom.**
Note the *m* in both hi**m** and who**m**.
Let's try some examples:

1 **(Who, Whom) is it?**
Substitute *he* or *him.*
He is it. NOT: *Him* is it.
Therefore: **Who is it?**

2 **It is (who, whom)?**
Substitute: **It is he.** NOT: It is *him.*
Therefore: **It is who?**

3 **(Who, Whom) do you want?**
Substitute and place *he* or *him* at the end of the question for the sake of clarity: **Do you want him?** NOT: Do you want *he*?
Therefore: **Whom do you want?**

4 **You were referring to (who, whom)?**
Substitute: **You were referring to him.**
NOT: You were referring to *he.*
Therefore: **You were referring to whom?**

5 **(Who, Whom) threw the overalls into Mrs. Murphy's chowder?**

You should know the answer to this one. Test it by substituting *he* or *him*.

6 **He is a man (who, whom) is loved by all.**

This sentence can be broken into two parts that you know we call *clauses* because each part has a subject and a predicate:

a. **He is a man . . .**

b. **. . . (who, whom) is loved by all.**

In such a sentence test *who* or *whom* in its own clause. Whichever form is correct in its own clause is correct in the entire sentence.

Substitute: b. . . . **he is loved by all.** NOT: *him* is loved by all.

Therefore: **He is a man who is loved by all.**

7 **He is a man (who, whom) we all love.**

This sentence also divides into two clauses:

a. **He is a man . . .**

b. **. . . (who, whom) we all love.**

Again we test *who* or *whom* in its own clause.

Substitute: b. . . . **we all love him.** NOT: we all love *he*.

Therefore: **He is a man whom we all love.**

8 **There is an urgent need for men (who, whom) we can trust.**

Substitute: . . . **we can trust him.** NOT: *he*.

9 **He is a man (who, whom) I am positive can be trusted.** Do not let *I am positive* fool you. This sentence can be rearranged to read: **I am positive he is a man (who, whom) can be trusted.**

The rearranged sentence can be broken into:

a. **I am positive he is a man . . .**

b. **. . . (who, whom) can be trusted.**

Substitute: **He can be trusted.** NOT: *Him* can be trusted.

Therefore: **He is a man who I am positive can be trusted.**

10 **(Who, Whom) did you say was at the door?**

Rearrange this sentence to read: **Did you say (who, whom) was at the door?**

Substitute: **He was at the door.** NOT: *Him* was at the door.

Therefore: **Who did you say was at the door?**

11 **The man (who, whom) I think will be our next president will be here soon.**

Break this sentence down as follows:

a. **The man . . . will be here soon.**

b. **. . . (who, whom) I think will be our next president.**

Substitute in its own clause: **I think he will be our next president.**

NOT: I think *him* will be . . . .

Therefore: **The man who I think will be our next president will be here soon.**

12 **The man (who, whom) I believe we all love is standing next to me.**

a. **The man . . . is standing next to me.**

b. **. . . (who, whom) I believe we all love . . .**

Substitute in its own clause: **I believe we all love him.** NOT: we all love *he*.

Therefore: **The man whom I believe we all love is standing next to me.**

We pointed out earlier in this chapter that *whom* (like *him*) is in the objective case and should be used as the object of a verb or the object of a preposition. *Who* (like *he*) is in the nominative case and should be used as the subject of a sentence or after a linking verb. To double check your use of *who* and *whom* in the above sentences, re-examine them now to determine why your choice is correct. Why do we require the nominative case wherever we use *who?* Why the objective case wherever we use *whom*?

4. Whoever and Whomever

Whomever is in the objective case. *Whoever* is in the nominative. Once again we can use a variation of our *he-him* trick and make the choice easy. Disregard ALL words in the sentence that come BEFORE *whoever* or *whomever*; then substitute:

he = whoever

him = whomever.

Let's study a few examples to see how this works.

1 **(Whoever, Whomever) answers the phone should be pleasant.**

Substitute: **He answers the phone.** NOT: *Him* answers the phone.

Therefore: **Whoever answers the phone should be pleasant.**

2 **Give the prize to (whoever, whomever) you please.**

Disregard all words in the sentence before *whoever* or *whomever.*

Disregard: **Give the prize to.**

Substitute: **You please him.** NOT: You please *he.*

Therefore: **Give the prize to whomever you please.**

3 **Give the prize to (whoever, whomever) deserves it.**

Disregard: **Give the prize to.**

Substitute: **He deserves it.** NOT: *Him* deserves it.

Therefore: **Give the prize to whoever deserves it.**

4 **She always accepts help from (whoever, whomever) will give it.**

Disregard: **She always accepts help from.**

Substitute: **He will give it.** NOT: *Him* will give it.

Therefore: **She always accepts help from whoever will give it.**

5. Whose and Who's

These two words are sometimes confused. Remember, however, that the apostrophe in *who's* indicates the *contraction* of two words, *who + is.*

Who's going to the luncheon?

Who is going to the luncheon?

Whose, without the apostrophe, is the *possessive pronoun.* We learned that possessive pronouns do not have apostrophes (*yours, his, hers, its, ours, theirs*).

Whose book is lost?

I don't know whose pen I have.

6. Any One, Anyone

No one is *always* written as two words.

There is sometimes confusion about whether to write *anyone, someone,* or *everyone* as one word or two. A simple rule to follow is to write it as *two words* when it is followed by an *of* phrase and to write it as one word at other times.

Everyone was present.

Every one of the salesmen was present.

Can anyone enter the contest?

Let any one of the members enter.

7. LIKE as a preposition

Which is correct: **She swims like (I, me).** Since *like* is used here as a preposition, *me* is correct because it is the object of the preposition: **She swims like me.**

Why is it not correct to say: **She swims like I do.** It's wrong for the same reason that this famous cigarette slogan is grammatically incorrect: **Winston tastes good like a cigarette should.** *Like* is *never* a conjunction; it is a preposition. The slogan requires a conjunction to make it grammatically correct. *Winston tastes good* **as** *a cigarette should.* Our problem-sentence too requires a conjunction to make it grammatically correct. **She swims as I do.**

If you are not too clear on the proper use of conjunctions, don't worry; you'll learn all about them in the next lesson.

8. BUT meaning EXCEPT

Sometimes the word *but* is used as a preposition meaning *except:* **All but him are welcome.** You know that prepositions are followed by the objective case.

I want anybody but him for the position. NOT: I want anybody but *he*...

EXERCISE 34 — Action and Linking Verbs

A. **This is a review problem dealing with action and linking verbs. In each of the following sentences there is an italicized verb. In the space provided, mark A if it is an action verb; mark L if it is a linking verb.**

1. It *would have been* easier had we been better prepared. 1. ____________
2. Can we *expect* you before noon? 2. ____________
3. It *became* difficult for him to work. 3. ____________
4. He *tasted* the food with gusto. 4. ____________
5. Things *look* bad for the moment. 5. ____________
6. He *lay* down to rest. 6. ____________
7. It *sounded* like a good idea. 7. ____________
8. He *rose* at dawn. 8. ____________
9. This *is* the truth. 9. ____________
10. *Was* it he who met you? 10. ____________

EXERCISE 34 — Objects of Verbs and Prepositions

B. **This is a review problem that deals with the objects of verbs and the objects of prepositions. Underline each object of a verb or of a preposition in the following sentences. Write OV above the word if it is the object of a verb; write OP above the word if it is the object of a preposition.**

1. John still loves Mary.
2. All of the men were dissatisfied with the wage offer.
3. It seemed to him that all was lost.
4. Send the books to us by fast mail.
5. Thank you for your cooperation.
6. We should like to place a definite order for holiday goods.
7. This is no time for him to leave the firm.
8. This is how we know when to start the machine.
9. We shall have our fall order ready for delivery as soon as we get word from our buyer.
10. We explained to your salesman that we did not want the shoes before August because we have our annual sale during July.

EXERCISE 35 — Forms of Pronouns

A. **This problem deals with the different forms a pronoun can take. In the space provided, write the objective case and the possessive cases of each pronoun.**

Nominative Case	*Objective Case*	*Possessive Cases*	
1. I	________	________	________
2. you	________	________	________
3. he	________	________	________
4. she	________	________	________
5. it	________	________	________
6. we	________	________	________
7. they	________	________	________

EXERCISE 35 — Nominative Case Pronouns

B. **This problem deals with the use of the nominative case pronoun as the subject of a sentence. In the space provided, write the correct pronoun. These problems should be easy.**

1. (I, me) am extremely pleased with his progress. 1. ________
2. (He, Him) is an exceptionally gifted salesman. 2. ________
3. Last night (us, we) went to the theater after dinner. 3. ________
4. In the long run (her, she) will undoubtedly succeed. 4. ________
5. Contrary to our advice (them, they) all agreed to the resolution. 5. ________
6. During our last convention (we, us) presented the new idea. 6. ________
7. To preserve our position as leader in our field, (I, me) propose a new concept. 7. ________
8. In the beginning (she, her) was uncertain of her duties. 8. ________
9. Until now (he, him) has the best selling record. 9. ________
10. Despite their opposition (them, they) agreed to abide by our decision. 10. ________
11. (Us, We) are certain (us, we) can stop their gains. 11. ________
12. If it were my decision, (I, me) would tell them that either (them, they) work with us or (us, we) take drastic action. 12. ________

EXERCISE 35 — Pronouns After Linking Verbs

C. **This problem deals with the form of the pronoun after a linking verb. In the space provided, write the proper pronoun. Remember, use the nominative case after a linking verb.**

1. It is (I, me). 1. ________
2. It is (he, him). 2. ________
3. It is (her, she). 3. ________
4. It is (us, we). 4. ________
5. It is (them, they). 5. ________
6. It was (I, me). 6. ________
7. It was (he, him). 7. ________
8. It was (her, she). 8. ________
9. It was (us, we). 9. ________
10. It was (them, they). 10. ________
11. I thought it was (he, him). 11. ________
12. I thought it was (her, she). 12. ________
13. I thought it was (them, they) 13. ________
14. It was (he, him) who sent the order. 14. ________
15. If it was (he, him) who sent the order, (he, him) should be congratulated. 15. ________
16. The last person to leave was (her, she). 16. ________
17. The winners of the award were (them, they). 17. ________
18. If I were (he, him) and he were (I, me), this would be a different world. 18. ________
19. It must have been (her, she) who delivered the message. 19. ________
20. That is (them, they) walking toward us. 20. ________
21. That's (he, him) at the door now. 21. ________
22. Could it have been (us, we) who swayed his opinion? 22. ________
23. That might be (her, she) calling on the phone. 23. ________
24. It was not (I, me) who made the error. 24. ________
25. The man to get the promotion should have been (he, him). 25. ________

EXERCISE 35 — Pronouns as Objects of Verbs

D. **This problem deals with the use of the proper pronoun as the object of a verb. In the space provided, write the correct pronoun. Remember, use the objective case as object of a verb.**

1. They hired (I, me) for the job. 1. ________
2. They hired (he, him) for the job. 2. ________
3. The decision shocked (he, him.) 3. ________
4. The explosion knocked (her, she) out of her chair. 4. ________
5. In the end he lent (us, we) his support. 5. ________
6. Send (them, they) the letters at once. 6. ________
7. Permit (I, me) to voice my disapproval. 7. ________
8. You have told (us, we) a most fascinating story. 8. ________
9. They would not allow (he, him) to leave. 9. ________
10. The director told (us, we) that his decision had been reached. 10. ________

EXERCISE 35 — Pronouns as Objects of Prepositions

E. **This problem deals with the use of the proper pronoun as the object of a preposition. In the space provided, write the correct pronoun. Remember, use the objective case as object of a preposition.**

1. The message was sent to (I, me). 1. ________
2. The message was sent by (he, him). 2. ________
3. We had learned a great deal from (her, she). 3. ________
4. The committee sent its congratulations to (us, we). 4. ________
5. Mr. Smith walked right by (them, they) without even acknowledging their presence. 5. ________
6. He came directly to (I, me) for the information. 6. ________
7. They stared at (he, him) as he entered the room. 7. ________
8. The idea came to (them, they) at the same instant. 8. ________
9. The order was delivered directly to (us, we). 9. ________
10. John stood between (I, me) and the door. 10. ________

EXERCISE 36 — The Proper Pronoun—I

A. **This problem deals with the use of the proper pronoun. In the space provided, write the correct pronoun.**

1. The letter was sent directly to (he, him). 1. ____________
2. We knew that (she, her) would accept the offer. 2. ____________
3. It was (I, me) who ordered the books from (they, them). 3. ____________
4. Did you see (us, we) at the theater? 4. ____________
5. If I were (her, she), I would demand a raise. 5. ____________
6. Are you certain that (they, them) will not accept your invitation? 6. ____________
7. Was it (he, him) who spoke to the representative? 7. ____________
8. Deliver this message to (they, them) at once. 8. ____________
9. Permit (I, me) to differ with (he, him). 9. ____________
10. Stop (I, me) if you've heard this. 10. ____________

EXERCISE 36 — Joining Proper Pronouns

B. **This problem deals with the use of the proper pronoun when it is joined with another pronoun or a noun. Fill in the correct pronoun in the space provided. Remember, use the same pronoun you would use if it were alone.**

1. Bob and (he, him) will go. 1. ____________
2. The men congratulated Mr. Robinson and (I, me). 2. ____________
3. Mr. Smith will introduce you and (he, him) to the staff. 3. ____________
4. Our office is certain that you and (her, she) will get the job. 4. ____________
5. (He, Him) and (I, me) will leave on the early train. 5. ____________
6. They gave raises in salary to (he, him) and (I, me). 6. ____________
7. The winners of the prizes were (he, him) and (he, she). 7. ____________
8. Between you and (I, me), this is a dangerous proposition. 8. ____________
9. The salesmen in your territory are Mr. Johnson and (I, me). 9. ____________
10. The boys and (I, me) feel certain that the contract will be awarded to you and (they, them). 10. ____________

EXERCISE 37	The Proper Pronoun—II

This is an overall problem dealing with choosing the proper pronoun. In the space provided, write the correct pronoun.

1. Give it to (he, him). 1. ________
2. (He, Him) likes this method of accounting. 2. ________
3. This will shock (he, him). 3. ________
4. It was (he, him) who started the trouble. 4. ________
5. This message is for (she, her). 5. ________
6. Here is a story that will astound (they, them). 6. ________
7. Was it (I, me) you saw at the theater? 7. ________
8. Are you sure you sent (I, me) the bill? 8. ________
9. John and (he, him) are next on the list. 9. ________
10. Give the order to Charles and (he, him). 10. ________
11. (We, Us) salesmen must plan our campaign carefully. 11. ________
12. (He and I) (Him and me) will leave at dawn. 12. ________
13. Was it (he, him) you spoke to? 13. ________
14. The order directed (us, we) secretaries to come to work fifteen minutes earlier. 14. ________
15. He is not so clever as (I, me). 15. ________
16. This man is a better salesman than (I, me). 16. ________
17. He would rather work with John than (I, me). 17. ________
18. Between you and (I, me), this work is easy. 18. ________
19. Mr. Roberts is as good a manager as (he, him). 19. ________
20. It was (she, her) who cut the endowment fund. 20. ________
21. The trophy was presented to Smith and (I, me). 21. ________
22. He is pleased with (their, they're) success. 22. ________
23. Is Judith taller than (she, her)? 23. ________
24. They would rather choose Robert than (I, me). 24. ________
25. It is up to (us, we) girls to show her the proper procedure. 25. ________

EXERCISE 38 — Who and Whom

A. **This problem deals with the choice of who or whom, whoever or whomever. In the space provided, write the proper word. Remember, substitute: He = who or whoever; Him = whom or whomever.**

1. (Who, Whom) is at the door? 1. ______
2. (Who, Whom) do you want to meet? 2. ______
3. (Who, Whom) did you say called? 3. ______
4. Our choice is a man (who, whom) you all know. 4. ______
5. Our choice is a man (who, whom) is known by all. 5. ______
6. He likes (whoever, whomever) is kind to him. 6. ______
7. He is a man (who, whom) I think can be fully trusted in his position. 7. ______
8. (Who, Whom) were you speaking of? 8. ______
9. (Who, Whom) among you knows the answer? 9. ______
10. (Whomever, Whoever) gets there first wins the prize. 10. ______
11. He likes (whoever, whomever) he meets. 11. ______
12. She is a woman (who, whom) I feel confident we can rely on. 12. ______
13. Upon (who, whom) will you bestow the award? 13. ______
14. She is a person (who, whom) is most talented. 14. ______
15. She is a person (who, whom) we know to be talented. 15. ______
16. One man (who, whom) was chosen for accomplishment refused to take the job. 16. ______
17. Choose (whoever, whomever) you think best. 17. ______
18. It is the intelligent man (who, whom) succeeds. 18. ______
19. Have you determined (who, whom) you want for the job? 19. ______
20. Please tell me (who, whom) you think will win. 20. ______
21. The woman (who, whom) I expected did not show up. 21. ______
22. Show me the boy (who, whom) you suspect of having stolen the money. 22. ______
23. They want (whoever, whomever) comes to be on time. 23. ______
24. (Who, Whom) will check the results in the files? 24. ______
25. The story will be divulged to (whoever, whomever) you choose. 25. ______
26. Their agent said that Mr. Smith, (who, whom) is one of his friends, is the man for the job. 26. ______
27. They will select (whoever, whomever) they think best. 27. ______
28. I know a man (who, whom) I am sure can do a perfect job. 28. ______
29. Of all the people (who, whom) I know, he is the one (who, whom) can be counted on. 29. ______ ______
30. It was (he, him) to (who, whom) you spoke yesterday. 30. ______ ______

EXERCISE 38 — Proper Use of Pronouns

B. **This problem deals with the proper use of certain pronouns. Cross out any incorrect words in the following sentences and write the correct word above it. There may be more than one error in a sentence.**

1. Tell me whose coming today so that no one but he will be expected.
2. Everyone of the officials except he has been assigned a post.
3. Who's typewriter needs repairing, his or your's?
4. There's would be a most difficult task for any one.
5. There roles would be exciting for any one with courage.
6. Every one wishes they could sing like he.
7. Between you and I, no one is sure of his part.
8. The salesman whose coming looks like him.
9. Our's is a perfect relationship, and every one knows it.
10. Your's is not so accurate as our's.

REVIEW EXERCISE — More About Pronouns

A number of pronouns in the following letter are misused. Cross out each incorrectly written pronoun and write the proper pronoun above it.

Dear Mr. Backrack:

I would like to tell you more about Robert Gilbert, the man who I started to describe to you last week. Mr. Gilbert is a man who has been constantly employed in top executive positions. Ten years ago it was him and Bob

(continued)

REVIEW EXERCISE (continued)

Anthony whom raised the Eighth National Bank to its present position. It was him whom gave the Smith Company it's shot in the arm. It was him whom the Jones Corporation called upon when it needed help.

There are few such men left in the business world. If it were left to I, I would definitely choose Robert Gilbert for the Presidency of this firm. He is a man whom I believe can lead us out of our present difficulty. He is a man whom I believe we can accept as a leader and an inspiration. He is a man whom I believe will lead us to the top position in our field.

I am sure that whoever the Board chooses as President will do a fine job; however, I would choose Robert Gilbert. I cannot think of a man whom is better qualified, whom is more trustworthy, and whom will do a better job than him. If it were up to we salesmen, we would choose noone but he as a man whose reliable.

Respectfully,

LESSON 9

CONJUNCTIONS

1. conjunctions and sentence structure

2. using conjunctions **3. interjections**

A conjunction is the *glue* that we use to attach a word or thought to a related word or thought. **And, but, because, or, yet** – these are just a few of the hundreds of conjunctions in our language.

Conjunctions do more than just *connect* two or more ideas; they show the *relationship* between ideas. In your writing, use your conjunctions carefully so that they express the *precise* relationship you intend.

For example, in each of the following sentences which conjunction better shows the relationship between the ideas it connects:

1. **This book is heavy to carry, (and) (but) it is light reading.**
2. **This book is heavy, (and) (but) it is bulky too.**

Obviously, to convey the exact meaning intended in Sentence 1, **but** is proper. In Sentence 2 **and** is proper. There are hundreds of conjunctions in our language offering you a rich choice of words to show *precise* shades of relationship. Here are just a few that you use constantly: **accordingly, as soon as, besides, consequently, hence, inasmuch as, in order that, moreover, nothwithstanding, otherwise, therefore, though, thus, until, whereas**

1. Conjunctions and SENTENCE STRUCTURE

Let's review what we already know about how sentences are composed, and then let's add some new concepts involving the proper use of conjunctions.

You know that a simple sentence must contain two essential parts–a subject and a predicate–and that it must express a complete thought. In its simplest form you might have something like this: *Snow fell.* To add greater meaning to our simple sentence, you can add words and phrases that describe the subject or the predicate or both. For example: *Freezing snow fell on the highway.* This is still a simple sentence, but it provides added description. We have built up our simple thought by the addition of *modifiers* that describe our subject and predicate – an adjective, *freezing,* and a prepositional phrase, *on the highway.* We still have only a simple sentence consisting of a subject plus a predicate.

You have also learned that a simple sentence can have more than one subject or more than one predicate. For example: **Snow and sleet fell.** This is a simple sentence with a *compound* subject. Or we might have written: **Snow fell and froze.** This is a simple sentence with a *compound predicate.*

But now look at this example: **Snow fell and sleet froze.** Is this still a simple sentence? No. In effect, we have two complete sentences that are connected by the conjunction **and**: *Snow fell.* (AND) *Sleet froze.* The sentence **Snow fell and sleet froze** is called a *compound* sentence. A compound sentence is a sentence that is composed of two or more simple sentences that are joined together by a conjunction or a semicolon. We call each simple sentence that is part of a compound sentence by the name *independent clause.* In our example-sentence, **Snow fell** is an independent clause; **sleet froze** is an independent clause. They are *independent* because they can stand by themselves as complete sentences.

In a compound sentence, the conjunction that connects one clause with another is called a *coordinate conjunction.* **And, but, or, yet** – these are coordinate conjunctions. They are called *coordinate* because they connect two *coequal* parts. In a compound sentence they connect two coequal independent clauses.

Coordinate conjunctions can also be used as part of a compound subject – for example, **snow and sleet** – in which case they connect two coequal subjects; and coordinate conjunctions can be used as part of a compound predicate—for example, **fell and froze** – in which case they connect two coequal predicates. For the moment let us concentrate on the use of coordinate conjunctions in joining independent clauses to form compound sentences.

How many independent clauses can you weld together into one compound sentence? Theoretically, as many as you like. You have undoubtedly heard the tiresome talker who links all his thoughts together in one endless sentence that sounds something like this: **So snow fell and the wind blew, and I couldn't see enough to drive straight, so my car ran off the road, and I found myself in a ditch.** Of course, William Faulkner won the Nobel Prize for writing stories in which some sentences ran for pages without stopping. At the other extreme is another Nobel Prize winner, Ernest Hemingway, who wrote with a rat-a-tat style of short simple sentences: **Snow fell. The wind blew. I couldn't see to drive.**

How long should *your* sentences be? We would advise that you aim for a middle ground somewhere between the styles of these two great literary figures. In business correspondence your objective should be to say what you have to say as simply as possible. Thus you should tend toward the use of short simple sentences. By themselves, however, such sentences sound choppy and quickly become monotonous. Also, you will often find that simple sentences alone do not enable you to express certain *relationships* between ideas. So you will frequently want to use longer sentences composed of more than one clause. You have already learned about one such type of sentence – the compound sentence. Now, let's turn to another type of sentence – the *complex* sentence.

In Lesson 1 you learned about the *dependent* clause. This is a clause that contains a subject and predicate but does *not* express a complete thought by itself. For example, **since the snow fell** is a dependent clause. By itself, it leaves you up in the air without expressing a complete thought. It *depends* upon another thought to complete its meaning. Thus we might complete it like this: **We have received no shipments since the snow fell.** Now we have a complete sentence composed of an independent clause—**we have received no shipments**—and a dependent clause—**since the snow fell.** As you also learned in Lesson 1, this type of sentence composed of an independent clause plus a dependent clause is called a *complex* sentence. Observe in the following examples of complex sentences how two thoughts—an independent clause and a dependent clause—have been combined to show the relationship of one to the other.

We selected their product because it is best.

We will ship the order unless we hear from you by Thursday.

They will be on time if the weather is good.

In each of the above examples, observe the conjunction that introduces the dependent clause—**because, unless, if.** Each of these conjunctions is called a *subordinate conjunction* because when it is added to an independent clause, it makes that clause incomplete by itself and dependent upon another clause for completion. In other words, it *subordinates* that clause to an independent clause.

Let's look at a few examples to see how this works. If we start with the independent clause **Snow falls** and add to it a subordinate conjunction like **if, when, although,** or **in case,** we end with a dependent clause:

If snow falls....
When snow falls....
Although snow falls....
In case snow falls....

There are hundreds of subordinate conjunctions. Here are just a few of the commonly used ones:

after	**notwithstanding**	**though**
although	**on condition that**	**unless**
as	**otherwise**	**until**
as soon as	**provided**	**when**
because	**since**	**where**
except	**supposing**	**whereas**
if	**that**	**while**

For practice, try to compose complex sentences using ten of these subordinate conjunctions. Note that in a complex sentence, the so-called *natural sequence* is for the independent clause to come first. For example:

Natural sequence —

We shall pay the bill unless we hear from you.

Independent Clause *Dependent Clause*

You can reverse this sentence if you like.

Reverse sequence —

Unless we hear from you, we shall pay the bill.

Dependent Clause *Independent Clause*

The most important point to notice is that you use a comma to separate the clauses *only* when you follow the *reverse* sequence. Observe these paired examples:

This plant will close when the patents expire.
When the patents expire, this plant will close.

The luncheon will be held even if it rains.
Even if it rains, the luncheon will be held.

An easy way to remember the natural sequence is to think of a dependent clause as being like the tail on a dog. The dog can get along without the tail, but the tail can't get along without the dog. Naturally, the tail ordinarily follows the dog; so if you put the tail in front of the dog, you've got an unnatural sequence. The comma is put into a reverse-order sentence to warn the reader: "Watch out! Don't expect this sentence to be in natural sequence. This tail comes *before* the dog."

Let's take a moment now to review what you have learned about the different types of sentences. You have met three types of sentences: the *simple* sentence; the *compound* sentence; and the *complex* sentence. The simple sentence is composed of a subject and predicate that express a complete thought. The compound sentence is composed of two or more independent clauses connected by a coordinate conjunction such as **and, or, but,** or by a semicolon. The complex sentence is composed of an independent clause connected to a dependent clause that contains a subordinate conjunction such as **since, if, because.**

At this stage you may wonder why people ever came to evolve so many different types of sentences. The first reason is to add variety to our language. With the different types of sentences available to you, you are able to add interest and change of pace to what otherwise might be dull and monotonous. In addition, by using complex and compound sentences, you are able to combine thoughts so as to pass along to your reader necessary shades of meaning and relationship.

In all your writing, therefore, strive for these twin objectives: 1) maintaining interest by employing variety in your sentence structure; and 2) expressing the relationships among your thoughts by intelligent use of conjunctions in compound and complex sentences.

2. USING conjunctions

A. Pairs of Conjunctions

Certain conjunctions act together to connect ideas. They are called *correlative conjunctions* because they correlate one thought with another.

1. **Either . . . or: Either** you work harder **or** you leave.
2. **Neither . . . nor:** We want **neither** sympathy **nor** charity.
3. **Both . . . and:** The true leader is **both** self-confident **and** humble.
4. **Not only . . . but also:** We want you **not only** to visit our office **but also** to inspect our plant.
5. **Whether . . . or: Whether** you act now **or** wait is a matter of great concern.

The major points to remember about these paired conjunctions are these:

1. With **neither** always use **nor** (NOT **or**).

   We want neither sympathy nor charity.

Remember that **neither** and **nor** go together; the positive equivalents are **either** and **or.**

2. With **not only** always use **but also** (NOT **but** alone).

   We want you not only to visit our office but also to inspect our plant.

3. Paired conjunctions should stand as near as possible to the words they connect.

Right: My job has given me both pleasure and satisfaction.

WRONG: **My job has both given me pleasure and satisfaction.**

Do you see why this is wrong?

Right: The announcer has reported neither the time nor the place of the event.

WRONG: **The announcer has neither reported the time nor the place of the event.**

B. LIKE and AS

In the lesson on prepositions, you learned that **like** can be used as a preposition but never as a conjunction. You learned why this cigarette slogan is incorrect:

"Winston tastes good like a cigarette should." Properly, it should read: "Winston tastes good *as* a cigarette should." In other words, it requires a conjunction (*as*) rather than a preposition (*like*). Don't make the error of confusing **like** with **as**.

Right: He looks like me.

Right: It was done as you wanted.

Right: As I said, this is a great day.

NOT: **Like I said, this is a great day.**

C. TRY AND . . .

This sentence is wrong: **You must try and do it.**

You should say: **You must try to do it.**
Do you see why the logical relationship of thoughts dictates the use of *try to* rather than *try and*?

D. PROVIDED and PROVIDING

Provided is a conjunction. **Providing** is *not* a conjunction and should never be used to join two parts of a sentence.

Right: We will arrive on time provided we have a tailwind.

Right: Provided there is time, you can give your speech.

WRONG: **We will arrive on time, providing we have a tailwind.**

E. SO . . . SO . . . SO . . . SO

Have you ever heard a poor speaker drag on his remarks by connecting them with interminable **so's**? **So** is a conjunction that should be used cautiously; do not use it too frequently.

WRONG: **I asked my boss for a raise. So he refused me. So I thought of another approach. So the next day, etc.**

It is better to use words like **therefore, consequently,** and **accordingly** to join ideas so that you have interest and variety in your speech and writing. Moreover, these words enable you to express sharply and exactly the precise relationship of ideas that you intend.

Better: **I asked my boss for a raise, but he refused me. Rather than despair, I thought of another approach, which I promptly tried the next day, etc.**

F. AS . . . AS

When two *affirmative* statements are joined by paired conjunctions, use **as . . . as**; when *negative* statements are joined, use **so . . . as.**

Right: He is as tall as a tree.

Right: He is not so tall as I had thought.

G. WHERE for THAT

Don't use the conjunction **where** for **that.** Again, simple logic should show you why this is correct.

Right: I read in the magazine that the price had been lowered.

WRONG: **I read in the magazine where the price had been lowered.**

Note: Never say **the reason was because.** Say **the reason was that.** For example: **The reason was that I was tired.**

H. Conjunctions and Prepositions

You may sometimes wonder whether to use the objective case (**me, him**) or the nominative case (**I, he**) after words like **before, after, but**. These words may be used either as conjunctions (followed by the nominative case) or prepositions (followed by the objective case), depending upon how you want to use them.

Right: **I got to the office after him.** (Preposition)

Right: **I got to the office after he did.** (Conjunction)

Right: **She filed the letters before me.** (Preposition)

Right: **No one will go but him.** (Preposition meaning *except*)

Right: **She filed the letters before I did.** (Conjunction)

Right: **No one will go but he may come later.** (Conjunction)

3. INTERJECTIONS

Just one word about interjections. That's all they deserve. An interjection is a word or group of words that expresses strong feeling. Always follow an interjection with an *exclamation point.*

Good! Surprise! Well done! Oh! Magnificent!

EXERCISE 39 Independent Clauses

A. **Underline each independent clause. Be sure to underline all words in the clause.**

1. Since we went away, time has flown.
2. Forgetting his manners, he remained seated.
3. We won't forget this if we live to be a hundred.
4. They came; they saw; they conquered.
5. I feel satisfied.
6. Mail a check for the balance as soon as possible.
7. They tried to resist, but they could not.
8. Either they go or we do.
9. Although he is on in years, he is sprightly.
10. Won't you come in without further delay?

EXERCISE 39 Dependent Clauses

B. **Underline each dependent clause, if any. If there is no dependent clause in a sentence, leave it blank.**

1. Since we went away, time has flown.
2. Forgetting his manners, he remained seated.
3. We won't forget this if we live to be a hundred.
4. They came; they saw; they conquered.
5. Although I am tired, I feel satisfied.
6. Mail a check for the balance as soon as possible.
7. They tried to resist, but they could not.
8. We will go if we must.
9. Although he is on in years, he is sprightly.
10. We will come in if we are invited.

EXERCISE 39 — Types of Sentences

C. **In the space to the right of each sentence, indicate what type of sentence it is — simple, compound, or complex.**

1. Since we went away, time has flown. 1. ____________
2. Forgetting his manners, he remained seated. 2. ____________
3. We won't forget this if we live to be a hundred. 3. ____________
4. They came; they saw; they conquered. 4. ____________
5. I feel satisfied. 5. ____________
6. Mail a check for the balance as soon as possible. 6. ____________
7. They tried to resist, but they could not. 7. ____________
8. Either they go or we do. 8. ____________
9. Although he is on in years, he is sprightly. 9. ____________
10. Won't you come in without further delay? 10. ____________

EXERCISE 39 — Complex Sentences

D. **In the space to the right of each of these complex sentences, mark N if the sentence follows the natural sequence; mark U if the sequence is in unnatural order. Insert a comma in any sentence from which it is omitted.**

1. As soon as we arrived the festivities began. 1. ____________
2. Assuming that he was right he proceeded without further instructions. 2. ____________
3. We will order now although we are overstocked. 3. ____________
4. Until I hear from you I shall say no more. 4. ____________
5. We won't despair while there is still hope. 5. ____________
6. Although he is still a minor he is old enough to be responsible. 6. ____________
7. Because he was modest he refused adulation. 7. ____________
8. We will fight back until they retreat. 8. ____________
9. Don't underestimate the opposition if you hope to conquer them. 9. ____________
10. Before I leave let me congratulate you. 10. ____________

EXERCISE 40 — Correlative Conjunctions

A. **This problem deals with choosing the proper conjunction. In the space provided, write the correct word.**

1. Either you ship the goods (or, and) I will sue. 1. ____________
2. Neither the chair (or, nor) the desk is in perfect condition. 2. ____________
3. Both the fan (and, or) the motor were defective. 3. ____________
4. He not only refused to accept the goods (but, but also) refused to pay. 4. ____________
5. Neither the dictionary (or, nor) the glossary included the term. 5. ____________
6. He not only gave us dinner (but, but also) invited us to stay for the evening. 6. ____________
7. They are willing to offer you not only a discount (but, but also) a bonus gift. 7. ____________
8. They offered either a straight salary (and, or) a commission. 8. ____________
9. Our latest model is not only functional (but, but also) artistic. 9. ____________
10. Either the ledger (or, nor) the receipt (is, are) incorrect. 10. ____________

EXERCISE 40 — Proper Conjunctions

B. **This problem deals with choosing the proper conjunction. In the space provided, write the proper word.**

1. I acted (as, like) you advised. 1. ____________
2. Would you try (and, to) correct the error. 2. ____________
3. We will accept (provided, providing) you lower your price. 3. ____________
4. We would appreciate it if you would try (and, to) locate the lost files. 4. ____________
5. The computer was fully (as, so) large as a room. 5. ____________
6. We will go not only to Paris (but, but also) to London. 6. ____________
7. This contract is valid (provided, providing) the shipment arrives on schedule. 7. ____________
8. (Like, As) I said yesterday, this must stop. 8. ____________
9. Neither time (or, nor) effort is to be spared (provided, providing) they cooperate. 9. ____________
10. It looks very much (like, as) your automatic washer. 10. ____________

EXERCISE 40 — Correcting Conjunctions

C. **Wherever necessary, cross out incorrect words or insert correct words. Two sentences are correct.**

1. He is not as smart as I thought he was.
2. I read in a book that censorship is on the increase.
3. The reason I left was because I was tired.
4. The reason he was discharged was because he had been late too often.
5. Acme Products is not as large as General Electric.
6. The gain is not so great as I had anticipated.
7. I notice in the newspapers where employment figures are increasing.
8. I read where China and Russia are feuding.
9. I heard where Frank was promoted in his firm.
10. This looks excellent like I expected.

REVIEW EXERCISE — Conjunctions

In the following copy, cross out all errors and write your corrections in the space above each. Insert any omitted punctuation.

Like I said in my last letter, sales have not only fallen but we have lost some salesmen too. This is not as bad as you might think since we were going to try and hire some new salesmen anyway. You probably have read in the papers where the reason sales are down is because demand has fallen. Providing this downward trend in demand is reversed I feel confident our sales will soon be back to record levels.

LESSON 10

COMMON ERRORS

In this lesson, twenty-six common mistakes are discussed from A to Z. Note that some of the mistakes discussed here are also covered elsewhere in this book. We have repeated them for extra emphasis.

A. DOUBLE SUBJECT

Mr. Smith, our President, will attend the dinner.

This sentence is correct, but look at the following sentence:

WRONG: Mr. Smith, our President, *he* will attend the meeting.

Obviously, the word *he* is just excess baggage. It tells us absolutely nothing new about our subject. Since it adds nothing, throw it out.

Right: Mr. Smith, our President, will attend the dinner.

Right: Our firm, The Acme Company, is the finest in its field.

WRONG: Our firm, The Acme Company, *it* is the finest in its field.

Right: Mr. Roberts and Mr. Smith will arrive soon.

WRONG: Mr. Roberts and Mr. Smith *they* will arrive soon.

B. DOUBLE COMPARISON

This sentence is correct:

I am happier than a lark.

Happier than a lark, however, is not happy enough for some people. To show how ecstatic with joy they are (and how bad their English is) these people say:

WRONG: I am *more* happier than a lark.

More **happier** is an unhappy combination of words. **Happier** by itself is all right. **More happy** is permissible. But NOT *more happier*. As we pointed out in Lesson 5, such *double comparisons* are wrong.

Right: This is the best job I've ever had.

WRONG: This is the *bestest* job I've ever had. (If you speak this way, you won't have the job very long. There is no such word as *bestest*. You can't be better than **best.**)

Right: This is the best job I've ever had.

WRONG: This is the *most* best job I've ever had. (Once again, **best** is as good as you can get. Drop *most.*)

Note that *unique* is already a superlative, meaning *one of a kind*. Accordingly, avoid the phrase *most unique* which is a double comparison.

C. THIS HERE

Do you ever make these errors:

WRONG: This *here* book is interesting.

WRONG: That *there* desk is beautiful.

WRONG: These *here* books are heavy.

WRONG: Those *there* desks are light.

If you ever say these things, STOP doing so at once. It is a sure sign of a poor education to say *this here, that there, these here,* or *those there.* The word *here* or *there* is unnecessary in each of the sentences above.

SAY:

Right: **This book is interesting.**

Right: **That desk is beautiful.**

Right: **These books are heavy.**

Right: **Those desks are light.**

D. KIND OF

It is bad usage to say the following:

WRONG: He is a fine kind of *a* man.

The *a* before *man* is unnecessary.

Right: **He is a fine kind of man.**

Never use *a* after *kind of, sort of,* or *type of.*

Right: **This is the type of job I like to see.**
(NOT: type of *a* job ....)

Right: **What sort of problem have you encountered?**
(NOT: sort of *a* problem ....)

E. HAS GOT

Do not use *has got* to indicate possession.

Right: **He has a fine idea.**
(NOT: He has *got* a fine idea.)

Right: **What have you in your file?**
(NOT: What have you *got* in your file?)

Right: **They have a few things to say.**
(NOT: have *got* a few ....)

Right: **This boy has to go.**
(NOT: has *got* to go.)

• TURN TO Exercise 41

F. TEACH – LEARN

Do not confuse the words *teach* and *learn.*

To **teach** means to *give* knowledge *to* someone else.

To **learn** means to *receive* knowledge *from* someone or something.

The teacher teaches her class.

The class learns from the teacher.

G. LEND – BORROW

A frequent mistake is this:

WRONG: Can I *lend* your pencil?

What you mean to say is:

Right: **May I borrow your pencil?**

Lend means to *give* someone else your property temporarily.

Borrow means to *accept* someone else's property temporarily.

I borrowed John's typewriter last week and returned it to him yesterday.

John lent me his typewriter.

Another error is this: WRONG: *Loan* me your pencil. **Loan** is a noun. A **loan** is the *thing* that is lent. Remember, it is a *thing,* not an action. **Lend** is a verb. It is the *act* of giving a loan.

Right: **I need a loan of $500.**

Right: **I will lend it to you.**

Right: **The company asked for a thousand-dollar loan.**

Right: **The bank agreed to lend the thousand dollars to the company.**

H. STAYED – STOOD

There is a famous story of the fight promoter who, upon seeing his prize boy being decisively beaten, tore at his hair and moaned those classic words of despair: **I shoulda stood in bed.**

This language may be all right if you are a prize-fight promoter; but if you are planning to go into any other line of business, you had better learn the difference between **stayed** and **stood.**

Stayed is the past tense of **stay.**

Stayed means the same as **remained.**

I should've stayed in bed.

We stayed to watch the fight to the very end.

Stood is the past tense of **stand.**

The soldier stood at attention throughout the ceremony.

I don't know how he stood the strain.

Of course, there is no such word as *shoulda.* You should say **should have** or use the contraction **should've.**

So our unhappy fight promoter should have said: **I should've stayed in bed.** If he had, his sentence would have been grammatical, but his cry of despair would probably have been forgotten long ago.

I. CAN – MAY

Can means *is capable of. In other words,* **can** refers to physical *ability.*

May means *has permission to.* In other words, **may** refers to *consent.*

May I leave work an hour early? (Means: Will you give me *permission* to leave early?)

Can you spare me? (Means: are you *capable* of getting along without me?)

May we have the car tonight?

I understand the car is being repaired. Can we have it by tonight?

J. TWO – TOO – TO

Two is a number – **2.**

Send me two pairs of shoes.

They ordered two dozen shirts.

To is a *preposition.*

I am going to another department.

He rose to his feet.

To is also part of the *infinitive.*

I want to go at once.

To err is human.

Too is a word that *intensifies* the meaning of something. It means *more than* or *also.*

I want to go too.

There is too much work.

Our inventory is too large.

To help you choose between **to** and **too,** remember that the double **o** in **too** *intensifies* the word. So use **too** when you want to *intensify* your meaning.

• TURN TO Exercises 42 and 43

K. BEING THAT

There is no such conjunction as *being that.* It just does not exist, so erase it from your vocabulary.

Right: Since you don't want to go, I'll go alone.

WRONG: *Being that* you don't want to go, I'll go alone.

Right: Because he is ill, I'll stay late.

WRONG: *Being that . . . .*

L. AIN'T

The word *ain't* is not good English usage. To use it is to advertise your poor English.

SAY:

I am not going. (NOT: I *ain't* going.)

He isn't going. (NOT: He *ain't* going.)

I'm doing rather well, am I not?
(NOT: . . . *ain't* I?)

M. NOWHERES – SOMEWHERES – ANYWHERES

There are no such words. The correct words are:

nowhere, somewhere, and **anywhere.**

Remember: Omit the **s** at the end.

Right: **He could find it nowhere.**

Right: **Somewhere over the rainbow, skies are blue.**

Right: **Put the machine anywhere that's convenient.**

N. REGARDLESS

There is no such word as *irregardless.* **Regardless** is all that you need.

Regardless of the weather, we shall leave on time.

These stocks will maintain their value regardless of the market.

O. OVER YOUR HOUSE

A common error in some parts of the country is to say something like this:

WRONG: Let's play bridge *over* my house.

Can you just picture what this means? Can't you see the bridge table suspended in mid air about thirty feet above the chimney? We doubt if you would accept an invitation to play bridge in such a precarious position.

What your host should say is:

Right: **Let's play bridge at my house.**

So avoid the *over my house* habit.

Right: **Come on to my house.**

WRONG: Come on over my house.

Right: **Let's go to Jane's house.**

WRONG: Let's go over Jane's house.

• **TURN TO Exercise 44**

P. GERUNDS

In the chapter on verbs you learned that by adding **ing** to a verb you form the progressive tense.

I sing. I am singing.

I write. I am writing.

You also learned that it is possible to use the word **singing** or **writing** not as a *verb,* but as a type of *noun* called a *gerund.*

My singing has improved.

His writing is too uneven.

As used in each of the above sentences, **singing** and **writing** are *gerunds* and are the equivalent of nouns. Do you see why they are acting like nouns? That's right; because each of them *names* an activity. You remember that a *noun* is a word that *names.*

Here are a few other examples of *gerunds*:

What did you think of his acting?

Filing is a mechanical skill.

His thinking is very logical.

We felt his playing had improved.

Now that you have learned to recognize *gerunds,* try a sentence like this:

We thought that (him) (his) writing had improved.

Obviously **his** is correct.

We thought that his writing had improved.

Next, try this sentence:

What do you think of (him) (his) winning the bonus?

Do you know which is correct? Let's reason it out. **Winning** is a *gerund* (noun). You modify a noun with the *possessive* pronoun (**his**) rather than the objective pronoun (**him**). For example, you would say:

Look at his coat. (NOT: Look at *him* coat.)

So, since **winning** as used here is a *noun,* you should say:

What do you think of his winning the bonus?

Learn this rule: When modifying a *gerund,* use a *possessive* noun or pronoun.

We were pleased with John's receiving the award.

His losing the account was unforgivable.

The Board's deciding not to vote came as a shock to us all.

Of course, don't confuse *gerunds* with the *progressive verbs* you studied in Lesson 4.

We could see him running in the distance. (**Running** as used here is a *verb*.)

The jury, obeying the judge, arrived at a verdict.

The manager, going over the problem, found no solution.

But:

We watched his running with keen interest.

The jury's obeying the judge can lead to no other verdict.

The manager's studying of the problem brought no solution.

• TURN TO Exercise 45

Q. LET-LEAVE

Leave (left) means *to go away*. It should not be confused with **let** meaning *to allow or permit*.

Right: Let me work alone.

WRONG: *Leave* me work alone.

Right: You should have let him go.

WRONG: You should have *left* him go.

Note: **Leave me alone** and **Let me alone** are both correct, but each has a different meaning. **Leave me alone** suggests politely that you go away. **Let me alone** suggests more brusquely that you should stop irritating me.

R. LEAD (verb), LEAD (noun), LED (verb)

Don't incorrectly substitute the present tense of the verb **to lead** (rhymes with *need*) for the past tense **led** (rhymes with *red*).

Right: He led the company in sales last week.

WRONG: He *lead* the company in sales last week.

Just remember that **lead** as a verb is pronounced like *need*. Do not confuse **led,** the past tense, with the noun **lead** (also pronounced like *red*) meaning the metal used for plumbing.

Right: The general led the army yesterday.

Right: He has led a virtuous life.

Right: He may lead his class in marks.

Right: The lead was mined as an ore.

S. RESPECTFULLY – RESPECTABLY – RESPECTIVELY

Some writers make the error of substituting **Respectably** (in a decent fashion) for the proper letter closing—**Respectfully** (full of respect). **Respectively** is also quite unrelated; it means in *proper sequence* or *in order*.

Right: Please answer soon. Respectfully yours,

Right: He spoke respectfully (full of respect) **to the minister.**

Right: He was dressed respectably (in a decent fashion) **for the occasion.**

Right: I want Charles and James respectively to address the group. (In the named sequence or order.)

Right: Roosevelt, Truman, and Eisenhower respectively had their impacts on the American people.

T. LOSE-LOOSE

The verb **lose** is always pronounced *looz.* It means *to suffer loss.* This is quite different from **loose**, pronounced like *moose,* which means *free, not close together,* or as a verb, *to untie, to make free.* Just remember that **lose** means a *loss,* with one *o* in each word; **loose** means *free,* with a double vowel in each word.

Right: Did you lose your books?

Right: I shall lose my temper soon.

Right: The animals broke loose.

Right: Let's pull the loose ends together.

WRONG: You will *loose* your wallet if it sticks out of your pocket.

U. ANXIOUS for EAGER

Anxious is an adjective that is derived from the noun **anxiety,** meaning *worry.* An anxious person is therefore someone who is perplexed, concerned, or disturbed. **Eager** comes from **eagerness,** meaning *enthusiasm, interest, desire.* An eager person, therefore, is enthusiastic.

Right: I am eager to go on vacation.

Right: I am anxious about my father's health.

WRONG: I am *anxious* to see my girl friend tomorrow. (If you were worried, not eager, you would say: I am **anxious** about my girl friend's reaction to me tomorrow!)

• TURN TO Exercise 46

V. ANGRY and MAD

Years ago we were told that dogs go mad and froth at the mouth while people simply get angry. Do not use *mad* to imply anger or peevishness. *Mad* means insane.

Right: I am angry at his impertinence.

Right: A mad person may be confined to an asylum.

WRONG: She is *mad* at him because he snubbed her.

W. DISINTERESTED for UNINTERESTED

The prefix **dis** means *away from* or *apart.* A **disinterested** person is interested, but his interest is away from or apart from the issue. In other words, a *disinterested* person is *impartial, fair, interested but aloof.* A judge should always be disinterested, but never uninterested. The prefix **un** means *not. Uninterested* means *not interested.* Would we want an umpire to be uninterested or disinterested?

Right: I want a disinterested arbiter to make the decision.

Right: I am uninterested in impressing people.

WRONG: He yawned at his desk showing he was *disinterested* in the work.

X. MYSELF for ME

Pronouns ending in **self** are reflexive; that is, like a knee reflex, the action *comes back* to the doer.

Right: I hurt myself.

Right: The boy cut himself.

Do not use this **self** or reflexive form when a simple pronoun is required.

Right: Frank and I went to the movies.

WRONG: Frank and *myself* went there.

Y. AND or BUT as Sentence Openers

In the lesson on conjunctions you learned that **and** and **but** are coordinate conjunctions – words that join equal words, phrases, or clauses. Remember that you should *not* begin a sentence with **and** or **but.**

This is a common error and it generally reveals poor writing ability. If **and** and **but** are connecting words, they must have something to connect. Otherwise you have a sentence fragment.

Right: **saw Frank, but he didn't see me.**

WRONG: I saw Frank. *But* he didn't see me.

Great authors have privileges that good letter writers may not have. Some authors occasionally begin sentences with *and* or *but* to avoid a long compound sentence. Since in business you will not be aiming for a Pulitzer Prize, avoid **and** or **but** as an opening word.

Z. THAN and THEN

Do not use **then** meaning *at that time* or *later* (an adverb) when you want to use the conjunction **than** which indicates a comparison.

Right: **He is bigger than I.**

Right: **John is taller than Jack.**

Right: **If you ask, then I will answer.**

WRONG: He is older *then* I.

• **TURN TO Exercise 47 and Review**

EXERCISE 41 — Common Errors—A-E

A. **Each of the following sentences contains an unnecessary word or words. Cross out all unnecessary words and all improper punctuation.**

1. The Ajax Company, it will open its fall season campaign soon.
2. Our sales this year have been the most highest in our history.
3. This here gentleman is interested in your offer.
4. This sort of an investment should pay big dividends.
5. Mr. Smith has got a slight cold.
6. Bob, walking down the street, he fell.
7. This sample of lace is more finer than the last one you sent.
8. That there desk would fit perfectly.
9. What type of a man is he?
10. What has he got in mind?
11. Miss Jones, our representative, she will call on you soon.
12. Undoubtedly, this is the most best model we have ever put on the market.
13. Those there machines will be the answer to your needs.
14. This kind of a job will be fine.
15. He has not got a good reason for his absence.

EXERCISE 41 — A-E Review

B. **Cross out the improper words in the following sentences. Note that there may be more than one mistake in a sentence.**

1. Our experience shows that the Acme Company is the most best producer of farm machinery.
2. Mr. Jones he is the sort of a man you can trust.
3. This here office it is located on a residential type of a street.
4. These here salesmen, Mr. Robertson and Mr. Johnson, they have done an excellent job.
5. Did you forget to send that there message to Mr. Woodburn?
6. Mr. Roberts is a more finer man than any other man I know.
7. He is the type of a man that you are proud to know.
8. According to our latest reports, Jones and Company it is not the type of a firm that you would like to do business with.
9. These here invoices they should have been filed long ago.
10. What's this here I hear about your resigning?

EXERCISE 42 — Common Errors—F-J

In the space provided, write the correct word.

1. When students do not like a teacher, she will find it difficult to (teach, learn) them. 1. ____________
2. I had to (borrow, lend) money from my employer to get home. 2. ____________
3. I (stood, stayed) at the office until well after dark. 3. ____________
4. (Can, May) you reach the shelf if you stretch? 4. ____________
5. There are (to, too, two) many people in the office force. 5. ____________
6. A student who studies hard has no difficulty (learning, teaching) his lessons. 6. ____________
7. I am sure you will repay this (lend, loan) as soon as you have the money. 7. ____________
8. They (shoulda, should've) asked us before they (lent, borrowed) the money from the bank. 8. ____________
9. (Can, May) we be excused from the exercises? 9. ____________
10. Send the (to, too, two) packages (to, too, two) the Acme Agency. 10. ____________
11. Our bitter experience has (learned, taught) us to avoid risky deals. 11. ____________
12. The bank was very willing to (lend, loan) us the money despite the size of the (lend, loan) we were seeking. 12. ____________
13. The men (stayed, stood) at attention until the ceremony was over. 13. ____________
14. (Can, May) he attain the goals he set for himself? 14. ____________
15. (To, Too, Two) many cooks spoil the broth. 15. ____________

EXERCISE 43 — Review of Common Errors A-J

Proofread this paragraph, crossing out all errors and writing corrections in the space above each error.

Can I offer you some good advice? My opinion is that one should not lend money from a bank unless he is certain he will be able to repay the lend when it is due. I was learned my lesson by sad experiences when I was to young to know any better. Experience learned me that I should have stood away from borrowing.

EXERCISE 44 — Common Errors—K-O

A. Cross out any errors and write your corrections in the space above each error.

1. Being that it is a cold winter, our heaters will sell exceptionally well.
2. I ain't seen no one around here for weeks.
3. Our reports could be found nowheres.
4. Irregardless of your feelings in the matter, we must go on.
5. Would you study over my house?
6. We feel that he will do a good job being that he is so intelligent.
7. There ain't no reason for this delay.
8. Somewheres you will locate the man who can handle the job.
9. They will go ahead irregardless of all obstacles.
10. Let's have dinner over my house.
11. They will complete the job on time being that they are working so hard.
12. Ain't we going to leave before noon?
13. You will find it nowheres.
14. I would buy that necklace irregardless of its price.
15. They are having a meeting over the plant.

EXERCISE 44 — Review K-O

B. Cross out all errors, writing your corrections in the space above each error.

Being that the proper handling of incoming mail is a matter of great importance in any office, irregardless of it's size, it should be handled with the greatest care. The morning mail, which is usually the most heaviest, should not be opened just anywheres. Over our office our clerks use a large vacant table to make sure that the letters ain't mixed with other papers that might be laying around. The first thing they do is to separate the first-class matter from all other's – catalogues, circulars, packages, and even unsolicited letters to.

EXERCISE 45 — Gerunds

A. **Underline any gerunds in the following sentences. Don't confuse gerunds with progressive verbs.**

1. We went hunting last winter.
2. Realizing his mistake, he retreated.
3. I am thrilled by his winning of the race.
4. Filing is a routine skill.
5. It was a thrilling victory.
6. They will keep fighting until it is too late.
7. Our entering the contest was a wise move.
8. Have you heard of his forgetting his speech?
9. We are forging ahead into a lead.
10. Don't forget their signing of the agreement.

EXERCISE 45 — Possessives with Gerunds

B. **In the space provided, write the proper word.**

1. We heard about (him, his) winning the contest. 1. ____________
2. Despite the fog, they could see (him, his) swimming in the distance. 2. ____________
3. How good is Miss (Smith, Smith's) typing? 3. ____________
4. (Our, We) working together has brought substantial results. 4. ____________
5. They say that (me, my) writing shows definite possibilities. 5. ____________
6. What did you think of Senator (Jones, Jones') voting against the tariff? 6. ____________
7. There is no reason for (him, his) working late tonight. 7. ____________
8. (We, Our) checking of all receipts did not disclose the error. 8. ____________
9. The (bookkeeper, bookkeeper's), seeing the error, made all necessary corrections. 9. ____________
10. We tried to prevent (him, his) seeing the results until they were published. 10. ____________

EXERCISE 46 — Common Errors Q-U

A. In the space provided, write the correct word.

1. He won't (let, leave) me finish my work. 1. ____
2. John (lead, led) all the students in his class. 2. ____
3. He closed the letter, "(Respectfully, Respectably, Respectively) yours." 3. ____
4. The dentist worked on the (lose, loose) tooth. 4. ____
5. I am (anxious, eager) to get a fresh start in my job. 5. ____
6. He (let, left) the room angrily. 6. ____
7. He has (lead, led) an athletic existence for years. 7. ____
8. He gave a (respectful, respectable, respective) salute to the officer. 8. ____
9. Whatever you do, do not (lose, loose) your head in an emergency. 9. ____
10. He was (anxious, eager) about the hospital report. 10. ____
11. If you will (let, leave) him be, he will not be so irritable. 11. ____
12. The (lead, led) in the pencil is too soft. 12. ____
13. James Wilson was second in sales in his firm, a highly (respectful, respectable, respective) position. 13. ____
14. That rattle seems to come from a (lose, loose) bolt in the chassis. 14. ____
15. One should be (anxious, eager) about the effects of smoking. 15. ____

EXERCISE 46 — Review Q-U

B. Cross out all errors, writing your corrections in the space above each error.

Leave us point to a few factors that may save you from loosing a fine job opportunity the next time you apply. Let us assume that a classified ad has lead you to an interview. Of course, you are anxious to make a good appearance; so dress appropriately. After the receptionist has lead you into the interviewer's office, don't sit until asked to do so. Act respectably toward your interviewer, but don't be so timid that you loose the opportunity to explain all your qualifications. Let the interviewer lead the discussion, and don't be so anxious to reply that you interrupt. When he indicates that the interview is over, thank him respectively; then take your leave without losing another moment.

EXERCISE 47 — Common Errors V-Z

In the space provided, write the correct word.

1. Don't be (mad, angry) with me. 1. ____________
2. A good judge must be (disinterested, uninterested) in the case before him. 2. ____________
3. This secret is between Frank and (me, myself). 3. ____________
4. Are these sentences punctuated correctly? I know that every office worker must do his part. And I will do mine too. (Answer: *Yes* or *No*) 4. ____________
5. He studies harder (than, then) she. 5. ____________
6. The designer liked the new colors so much, he seemed to be (mad, angry) about them. 6. ____________
7. His failure shows he was (disinterested, uninterested) in the school work. 7. ____________
8. The ball hurt (me, myself) as it hit my face. 8. ____________
9. Are these sentences punctuated correctly? A sales manager has problems. But he must overcome them. (Answer: *Yes* or *No*) 9. ____________
10. Go to the office and (than, then) look for the document. 10. ____________
11. Never show that you are (mad, angry) if you are kept waiting for an appointment. 11. ____________
12. A clerk who is (disinterested, uninterested) in his firm will probably not succeed. 12. ____________
13. I cut (me, myself) as I opened the file. 13. ____________
14. Is this sentence punctuated correctly? The director tried to give the report to his colleague, but he refused it. (Answer: *Yes* or *No*) 14. ____________
15. She takes dictation faster (than, then) any other employee. 15. ____________
16. He appeared to be (mad, angry), so a psychiatric examination was requested. 16. ____________
17. The referee was selected because he was (disinterested, uninterested) in the two sides presented. 17. ____________
18. It isn't right for me to praise (me, myself) for my excellence. 18. ____________
19. Are these sentences punctuated correctly? Nothing succeeds like success. And all of us secretly want it. (Answer: *Yes* or *No*) 19. ____________
20. He cashed the check and (than, then) went home. 20. ____________
21. The good salesman never gets (mad, angry) with the customer. 21. ____________
22. (Disinterested, Uninterested) United Nations observers were sent to the scene. 22. ____________
23. The prank boomeranged and the boys hurt (them, themselves). 23. ____________
24. Are these sentences punctuated correctly? The transcript seemed correct. But the letter was not folded properly. (Answer: *Yes* or *No*) 24. ____________
25. A faster tennis player (than, then) Pancho Gonzales at his prime would be hard to find. 25. ____________

REVIEW EXERCISE — Common Errors from A-Z

The following paragraph contains many errors. Cross out all incorrect words and phrases, and write the correct forms above them.

Dear Mr. Abrams:

Regardless of your business, you will find at the Exposition all the equipment that your office should have got. Here is your opportunity to test, to compare, and for choosing the office machinery that will fit your particular office needs.

These kind of an exhibit is most unique among business shows. It is the result of the combined efforts of the exhibitors, local civic figures, the police department, and with the local business organizations.

Unless your office has got all the equipment it will ever need, you and your staff should attend this important meeting. We are certain that you visiting and seeing this exposition will be an important turning point in your business career. Plan to make your ticket reservations in the very near future.

Do not leave this opportunity pass, for if you loose this chance, you undoubtedly will be mad at yourself later on. We are anxious to see you at the Exposition, and we know you will not be disinterested in the equipment. We, therefore, respectively urge that you be more alert then some of your competitors. And make your reservation now.

Respectably yours,

ACME EQUIPMENT

LESSON 11

PUNCTUATION

1. the period
2. the question mark
3. the exclamation point
4. the comma
5. the colon
6. the semicolon
7. quotation marks
8. the apostrophe
9. the hyphen
10. parentheses
11. the dash
12. ellipses
13. capitalization

Can you read this:

marksofpunctuationtellthereaderwhentopause

Now, try it this way:

Marks of punctuation tell the reader when to pause.

Easier, isn't it? What a difference a few little spaces make. These spaces make a sentence easier to read because they break a long mumble-jumble of letters into easy-to-understand words. In the same manner, marks of punctuation make sentences easier to read because they break a mumble-jumble of thoughts into easy-to-understand ideas.

If you want your writing to say exactly what you mean, you must learn to punctuate correctly and carefully. Improper punctuation will not only confuse the reader but also may completely mislead him. For example, see how a comma completely changes the meaning of this sentence:

No price is too high.

No, price is too high.

In business you must be able to punctuate perfectly, so study this section thoroughly and carefully. Your mastery of the rules of punctuation will pave your way to a higher-paying position.

1. THE PERIOD (.)

The use of this mark of punctuation is very easy. You have probably used it properly throughout your life, so the five rules below should be a review for you.

RULE 1.

Place a period at the end of a sentence that makes a statement.

The shipment will be delivered by Friday.

Note 1: Review what you learned in Lesson 1 concerning the proper use of the period at the end of a *complete* sentence and the avoidance of sentence fragments and run-on sentences.

Note 2: When typing a sentence, *space twice* after the period before starting the next sentence.

```
Please pay the bill.  It is long
overdue.
```

RULE 2.

Place a period at the end of a sentence that states a command.

Bring it here.

Don't leave.

Order the goods immediately.

Note 1: When the command is phrased in the form of a question for the sake of politeness, use a period rather than a question mark.

Will you put it here, please.

Note 2: Use the period after a condensed expression that stands for a full statement or command.

Yes. Go. Next. Sit.

RULE 3.

Place a period after an abbreviation.

Mr. **Dr.** **N. Y. C.**

e.g. **J. Gordon Jones, Jr.**

Note 1: When a sentence ends with an abbreviation, use only *one period.*

Address the letter to Fulton Boyd, Esq.

The shipment goes to Morris Van Lines, Inc.

BUT: **The plant is open for inspection all day (9 a.m. to 5:30 p.m.).**

Note 2: **Miss** is *not* an abbreviation. **Mr., Mrs., Messrs.,** and **Mmes.** are abbreviations.

Dear Miss Smith: **Dear Mrs. Smith:**

Note 3: Abbreviations composed of a series of lower case letters should be typed with no space after each period. Space only after the final period; then use a single space unless you are starting a new sentence, in which case you use a double space.

```
The price quoted is f.o.b.
Detroit.
```

```
We received a c.o.d. shipment
from the Denver warehouse.
```

Note 4: Abbreviations composed of *capital* letters should be typed with a single space after each period. Pay particular attention to this spacing in typing the abbreviations in a person's name.

```
The C. P. A. examination is
scheduled for early June.
```

```
Our new Chairman is J. P.
Roberts.
```

Note 5: Certain abbreviations are written in solid capital letters, without either periods or spaces. Consult a dictionary when you are unsure of the correct abbreviation.

YMCA **VA** **NOMA** **FHA**

Note 6: At the end of this book appears a listing of the official United States Post Office abbreviations for the names of the fifty states. In business correspondence avoid abbreviating the names of states except in tabulations. Also avoid abbreviating the names of cities.

Note 7: Recognize the difference between a contraction and an abbreviation. A contraction that is written with an apostrophe does not require a period.

Gen'l Gov't Rec't Sec't Sup't

Note 8: The following numbers are considered contractions and do not require periods: **1st, 2nd (2d), 3rd (3d), 4th, 5th . . . 10th . . . 23rd . . . 100th . . . etc.**

RULE 4.

Use a period to separate cents from dollars in a money amount.

$2.58 $10.10 $4,372.27

Note 1: Do not put a period after a dollar amount if no cents are indicated.

$2 $10 $4,372

BUT: **$2.00 $10.00 $4,372.46**

Note 2: Use the period as a decimal point.

.0 .06 .006 3.1416

Note 3: Do not space after the period used in a dollar amount or in a decimal.

`$2.58 3.1416`

RULE 5.

A period may be used in tabulations. When a list is numbered or lettered, put a period after each number or letter. Do not put a period or other mark of punctuation after the items in the tabulation unless each item is a full sentence.

Basic to our way of life are these fundamental rights:

1. **Freedom of speech**
2. **Freedom of assembly**
3. **Freedom of religion**
4. **Freedom of the press**

Note 1: When a list is numbered or lettered, you may enclose the numbers or letters in parentheses. In this case, do not use a period.

Basic to our way of life are these fundamental rights:

(a) Freedom of speech
(b) Freedom of assembly
(c) Freedom of religion
(d) Freedom of the press

2. THE QUESTION MARK (?)

The use of this mark, too, should be easy. You use the question mark in only one place – after a *direct* question. In typing skip two spaces after the question mark at the end of a sentence.

`Can they deliver by May 15?  I doubt it.`

Note 1: Do *not* use a question mark after a command that is phrased in the form of a question for the sake of politeness. As you have just learned, such a command ends with a period.

Will you please let us hear from you in the very near future.

Won't you come in, please.

If you are uncertain as to whether a particular sentence is a question or a command, ask yourself, "Does the sentence really require an answer or is it merely a courteous command?" If the sentence requires an answer, use a question mark. If the sentence does not require an answer, use a period.

Note 2: Be wary of run-on sentences in your use of the question mark.

Right: Will you be at the banquet? We certainly hope so.

NOT: Will you be at the banquet, we certainly hope so.

Note 3: The question mark punctuates a *direct* question. Do not use a question mark at the end of a sentence that refers indirectly to a question; use a period.

Direct Question: **Do you know when the new models will be available?**

Indirect Question: **He wonders if you know when the new models will be available.**

Note 4: No matter how long a direct question may be, end it with a question mark. Don't let the length of a question deceive you.

Are you certain that we can expect delivery of the merchandise by January 14 despite the newspaper's report that a strike may be called by the union at midnight on December 31?

Note 5: The question mark usually *ends* a sentence. On infrequent occasions, however, the question mark may be used in the *middle* of a sentence that contains a series of closely related questions. After each such question mark, skip two spaces and start the next word with a lower-case letter.

```
Can you name four Presidents?
four Vice-Presidents?  four Chief
Justices?
What would be our unit price if
we purchase six gross?  twelve
gross?  twenty gross?
```

3. THE EXCLAMATION POINT (!)

Here's the mark of punctation that's simplest to use. *Use the exclamation point after an exclamation*—that is, after a word or words of strong feeling or emotion:

Hurrah!

No!

Wait until you test drive the new Ford!

That's life!

What a wonderful day!

The exclamation point is effective in creating emphasis provided it is not overused. Too often the inexperienced writer peppers the page with so many exclamation points that it loses all value as a mark of emphasis. Try to "hoard" your exclamation points and use them only for that infrequent thought that *really* commands special emphasis. Use your exclamation points sparingly!

Space twice after an exclamation point before starting the next sentence.

```
Alas!  Our time is up.
```

4. THE COMMA (,)

Do you use commas correctly at all times? About a hundred years ago the use of the comma was a great problem. You see, at that time there was almost a competition between authors to see who could write the most obscure sentences. The literary style of the day favored long, complicated, tedious sentences, bespattered with commas and semicolons. It was left to the poor reader to unravel this cobweb of confusion as best he could.

Thank heavens, times have changed. Today the tendency is toward short, simple sentences and easy-to-follow punctuation. Nowadays you commit a serious error if you use too many commas. You must have a *definite reason* for every comma you insert. If you don't have a reason, leave it out.

There really aren't many rules governing the use of the comma. In fact, we can break the use of the comma into only six easy-to-master rules.

RULE 1.

Use commas to separate words or phrases listed in a series. Each of the following sentences illustrates this use of the comma in a different instance.

1 **Our new offices are located in a towering, ultra-modern, air-conditioned skyscraper.**

2 **The Electrex Meter has been carefully, precisely, and painstakingly assembled for maximum sensitivity.**

3 **Wool, cotton, linen, or silk will be used in the manufacture of this dress.**

4 **The newly installed bookkeeping machine automatically bills, posts, and maintains an inventory control.**

5 **The Armed Forces are ever-alert on land, in the air, and on the sea.**

6 **In this course your objectives are to write, to speak, and to think clearly.**

7 **That our opponent is aggressive, that he is clever, and that he is ruthless must be recognized.**

8 **Turn the ignition key, gently press the gas pedal, and push the starter button.**

Note 1: Examine all of the sentences above. Notice that a comma has been placed *before* the conjunction when it precedes the last item in the series. This is the modern rule of punctuation.

Note 2: Often you may be undecided about whether or not to place a comma *after* the last item in a series. You can solve this problem by testing the last item as though it were alone in the sentence and not part of a series. For example:

1 **Our offices are located in a towering, ultra-modern, air-conditioned (, ?) skyscraper.**

TEST: *Our offices are located in an air-conditioned skyscraper.* (Needs no comma.)

THEREFORE: .... **a towering, ultra-modern, air-conditioned skyscraper.**

In technical terms, what this shows you is that when a series of adjectives modifies a noun, you should not put a comma after the last adjective. If you forget this technical explanation, no matter; the important thing is that you remember how to *test* your answer. Then you can never go wrong.

2 **The Electrex Meter has been carefully, precisely, and painstakingly (, ?) assembled.**

TEST: *The Electrex Meter has been painstakingly assembled.* (No comma)

THEREFORE: .... **carefully, precisely, and painstakingly assembled.** Technically: When a series of adverbs modifies a verb (or other part of speech), do not put a comma after the last adverb.

3 **Wool, cotton, linen, or silk (, ?) will be used in the manufacture of this dress.**

TEST: *Silk will be used* . . . (No comma)

THEREFORE: **Wool, cotton, linen, or silk will be used** . . . Technically: When you have a compound subject, do not use a comma to separate the last item in the subject from the predicate.

4 **Courage, fortitude, and wisdom (, ?) these are the strength of the nation.**

TEST: ... *wisdom, (this) is the strength of the nation.* (Needs a comma.)

THEREFORE: **Courage, fortitude, and wisdom, these are the strength of the nation.** Technically: Use a comma after the last word in a series if the series is followed by a *complete* sentence.

BUT: **Courage, fortitude, and wisdom are the strength of the nation.** (No comma)

Note 3: Occasionally a series will be written with correlative conjunctions between *all* items in the series. In this type of series omit the commas.

The Electrex Meter has been carefully and precisely and painstakingly assembled.

Wool or cotton or linen or silk will be used.

Note 4: Do you see why no comma is placed after *new* in the following sentence?

Try our new scouring powder.

New is an adjective and **scouring** is an adjective, but they are not in series. **New** modifies the word-group **scouring powder**, not just the noun **powder**. Here are other examples of the same situation:

We are looking for an intelligent, pleasant, enthusiastic young man. (*Young man* is treated as a word-group.)

The government's objectives are secure national defenses and rapid national growth. (*National defense* and *national growth* are treated as word-groups.)

Note 5: Sometimes *pairs* of words or phrases will be listed in series. In these instances, use commas to separate the *pairs* from one another.

To write and speak well, to think and act rigorously, and to live and fight courageously are your ideals.

Note 6: Many firm names are composed of a series of names of individuals. Be sure to separate the names with commas in precisely the format used on the firm's official letterhead. For example:

Merrill Lynch, Pierce, Fenner & Smith

Batten, Barton, Durstine & Osborne

As a general rule a comma is not placed before the ampersand (&) that often precedes the last name in a series.

Note 7: Frequently a long list will be ended with the abbreviation *etc.*, meaning *and others*. A comma should be placed before the *etc.* and should also be placed after the period unless it ends the sentence.

Never write *and etc.* since this would mean *and and others,* which is obviously redundant.

Generally, do not use the abbreviation *etc.* when you can find a more explicit, less vague ending for the series. Do not use the abbreviation *etc.* when the series has been begun with *for example* or a similar phrase setting forth the incomplete nature of the lists. Do you see why this too is redundant?

Permissible: **The candidate expressed his views on farm policy, foreign relations, fiscal management, labor relations, etc.**

Improved: **The candidate expressed his views on farm policy, foreign relations, fiscal management, labor relations, and other vital national issues.**

NEVER: **The candidate expressed his views on vital national issues such as farm policy, foreign relations, fiscal management, labor relations, etc.** (Omit the *etc.* and the sentence becomes correct; or omit the phrase *such as*. You can't have both.)

Note 8: When typing, allow a single space after the comma.

RULE. 2.

Use commas to set off expressions that if omitted would not destroy the sentence or change its meaning. This rule covers a great variety of situations. To make it easier for you to apply Rule 2, we shall break it down into individual parts. But don't forget, they are all part of the *one* overall rule.

PART A.

Use commas to set off the name of a person directly addressed.

Mr. Smith, we know that you will cooperate.

We can omit **Mr. Smith** and still have a complete sentence:

Omit: **Mr. Smith**

Remainder: **We know that you will cooperate.**

Therefore, we set off **Mr. Smith** with a comma.

Observe that the name of the person addressed is set off with commas no matter where it appears in the sentences

Mr. Smith, we know that you will cooperate.

We know, Mr. Smith, that you will cooperate.

We know that you will cooperate, Mr. Smith.

Note 1: When the name of the person addressed occurs in the middle of the sentence, place a comma *before and after* the name.

On your honor, John, did you do it?

With your help, Mr. Jones, we cannot fail.

Note 2: This rule applies only to the name of a person who is *directly* addressed. If you are talking *about* someone, you don't set off his name with commas.

Smith is a good man.

Smith, you are a good man.

Note 3: Use commas when you *directly* address someone with a term other than his name.

You, my friend, are in for a surprise.

Let me tell you, fellow alumni, what the committee has done.

Here's a little test of what you learned thus far. See how omitting a comma changes the meaning of these two sentences:

1. **Mr. Jones, our salesman, will see you.**
2. **Mr. Jones, our salesman will see you.**

Do you see the difference in meaning? In Sentence 1 the salesman, whose name is **Jones,** will see you. In Sentence 2 *your* name is **Jones** and you will be seen by a salesman whose name we don't know. Let this be an object lesson that you must place your commas carefully.

PART B.

Use commas to set off an expression that explains a preceding word.

1. **Mr. Jones, President of Acme Steel, is here.**

President of Acme Steel merely explains who **Mr. Jones** is. We could omit it and still have a full sentence unchanged in meaning.

Omit: **President of Acme Steel**

Remainder: **Mr. Jones is here.**

2. **The Pacific Ocean, the largest body of water on earth, must be protected by a vast naval system.**

Omit: **the largest body of water on earth.**

Remainder: **The Pacific Ocean must be protected by a vast naval system.**

3. **We will send Mr. Smith, our representative, to visit your office.**

Omit: **our representative**

Remainder: **We will send Mr. Smith to visit your office.**

4. **The company, having been dormant for years, is finally reawakening.**

Omit: **having been dormant for years**

Remainder: **The company is finally reawakening.**

5. **Our firm will show you how, merely by changing your circulars, you can double your business.**

Omit: **merely by changing your circulars**

Remainder: **Our firm will show you how you can double your business.**

6. **Butter that is rancid is sickening.**

Omit: **that is rancid**

Remainder: **Butter is sickening.**

Do we actually mean that **butter is sickening?** NO! Only certain butter—**rancid butter** —is sickening. Go back and look at Rule 2 again. It says that we use commas to set off expressions that if omitted would not destroy the sentence *nor change its meaning*. **That is rancid** is *essential* to the meaning of our sentence. Therefore, it should *not* be set off by commas.

Butter that is rancid is sickening.

7 **Butter, which is in great demand, is selling well.**

Omit: **which is in great demand**

Remainder: **Butter is selling well.**

Do we mean to say that **butter is selling well?** Yes. Therefore, the use of commas is proper since the expression **which is in great demand** is *not* necessary to the meaning of the sentence.

8 **Air that is polluted is bad for you.**

Omit: **that is polluted**

Remainder: **Air is bad for you.**

Do we mean that **air is bad for you?** NO! Only **polluted air** is bad for you. Therefore, **that is polluted** should not be set off with commas since it is essential to the meaning of the sentence.

9 **The men in our office, who won the prize, will get a bonus.**

Omit: **who won the prize**

Remainder: **The men in our office will get a bonus.**

The use of commas here is correct if *all* the men in the office won the prize. The Remainder tells us that *all* the men in the office will get bonuses. Suppose that the men in our office won a bowling contest against the men in another office. Then the use of commas in this sentence is correct.

Suppose, however, there was a bowling contest in which each man was on his own. Some men in the office won and others did not. In such a case we would not use commas.

The men in our office who won the prize will get a bonus.

In this case, **who won the prize** is essential to the meaning of the sentence since it tells us exactly which men get bonuses.

Now, let's get technical for a moment to analyze what you have been doing in the last few example-sentences:

Butter that is rancid is sickening.

Butter, which is in great demand, is selling well.

The men in our office who won the prize will get a bonus.

Do you notice that each of these sentences contains a clause that begins with a relative pronoun – *that, which,* or *who?* These clauses are known as *relative clauses.* It is around these clauses that we sometimes put commas and sometimes do not, depending upon our meaning.

When a relative clause is essential to our meaning, it is called a *restrictive clause.* For example, in the sentence **Butter that is rancid is sickening,** the clause **that is rancid** is a restrictive clause because it restricts the type of butter we are talking about to one type: **butter that is rancid.**

When a relative clause is not essential to our meaning, it is called a *nonrestrictive clause.* For example, in the sentence **Butter, which is in great demand, is selling well,** the clause **which is in great demand** is a nonrestrictive clause. It does not restrict our meaning to any one type of butter – *all* butter is selling well.

So what you have really learned in Sentences 6-9 is that *restrictive clauses* are not set off with commas because they are essential to the meaning of a sentence; *nonrestrictive clauses* are set off with commas because they are not essential to the meaning of a sentence.

Where does this information leave you? Right back with the necessity to *test* whether a clause is essential or not. Even if you forget the technical names for these clauses, the important point is that you remember how to test to see if a clause or phrase is essential to a sentence.

One fine point that you may want to remember is this: In choosing between *which* or *that* at the beginning of a relative clause, use *that* if the clause is restrictive; use *which* if the clause is nonrestrictive. Go back to Sentences 6-9 to see how this has been applied.

Now, on to a few more examples of using commas to set off explanatory matter.

10 **My son, Alan, is attending college.**

The commas around **Alan** lead to the inference that Alan is an only son. *Test it.*

Omit: **Alan**

Remainder: **My son is attending college.** (Correct if he is an only son.)

If Alan has any brothers, the commas should be omitted since we are restricting our meaning to this one son. His brothers may still be in kindergarten.

My son Alan is attending college.

11 **Jackson Polk, of Harvard, will address the meeting.**

If there is also a Jackson Polk at Yale, you would omit the commas to restrict your meaning to the Polk at Harvard. Do you see why? Similarly, do you see why commas are omitted from the following sentences?

My friend George has written of you often.

The philosopher Locke expressed the rights of man.

The year 1933 ushered in the New Deal.

The word togetherness is overused nowadays.

The candidate expressing his honest ideals despite wide-spread public disapproval of them will often win out.

Test each of the following sentences to see why various elements have been considered explanatory and have, therefore, been set off with commas. Can you omit each of these elements that have been set off with commas and still have a complete thought that is unchanged in meaning?

Automation, or the use of automatic controls, is a new science.

The new playwrights, such as Arthur Kopet and Edward Albee, have brought renewed vitality to the American theater.

Our organization, like any young business, is eager to explore new markets.

These figures, all of which have been carefully checked, point to a disastrous conclusion.

We discussed a number of possibilities, none of which proved workable.

The candidate, realizing that the election was lost, conceded defeat.

This last sentence could be written: **Realizing that the election was lost, the candidate conceded defeat.** It should never be written: **Realizing that the election was lost, defeat was conceded by the candidate.**

The latter sentence would imply that *defeat* realized the election was lost. Always place the subject of a sentence directly after the introductory phrase or clause that modifies it.

You have already met the participial phrase in the unit on *Dangling Participles.* For example, in the sentence **Walking down the street, I slipped,** the phrase **walking down the street** is a participial phrase. **Walking** is the present participle of the verb **to walk**; hence, the name *participial phrase.* Pick out the participial phrases in these sentences:

Fighting for his life, he lashed out viciously.

The architect, seeing the finished building, was elated.

We ordered rather late, counting on immediate service.

Do you notice how each of the participial phrases in these sentences could be omitted without changing the basic meaning of each sentence? Following our general rule, therefore, you know that you should set them off with commas because they are merely explanatory phrases.

Observe this sentence, however:

Prices rising at a rapid pace are a sure sign of inflation.

Here we have the participial phrase **rising at a rapid pace.** Can it be omitted from our sentence? No. This phrase is essential to the meaning of our sentence. It is acting like a restrictive clause and, therefore, should not be set off with commas. In fact, it really is a restrictive clause "in disguise." What this sentence really says is this:

Prices **that are rising at a rapid pace** are a sure sign of inflation.

So, remember, when you start a sentence with a participial phrase, be sure to follow it *immediately* with the subject to which it refers. Otherwise you will have a dangling participle.

Right: Checking our inventory, we noted a shortage.

Wrong: **Checking our inventory, a shortage was noted.**

At this point your mind may well be reeling from exposure to complex sentences, dependent clauses, restrictive clauses, nonrestrictive clauses, participial phrases (restrictive and nonrestrictive)—and so forth. We can't blame you if you're beginning to get confused, so let's simplify all this down to the key point of RULE 2: *Use commas to set off expressions that if omitted would not destroy the sentence or change its meaning.* If you just learn to use this rule, the rest will fall in place even if you forget all the technical terminology after this course. It's *usage,* not terminology, that counts.

PART C.

Use commas to set off a word, phrase, or clause that interrupts the natural flow of a sentence. By *interrupt* we mean that it forces you to pause. Here is a list of commonly used words, phrases, and clauses that should be set off with commas when they interrupt the natural flow of a sentence.

accordingly	**namely**
again	**naturally**
also	**next**
besides	**nevertheless**
consequently	**notwithstanding**
finally	**otherwise**
furthermore	**personally**
hence	**respectively**
however	**still**
indeed	**then**
meantime	**therefore**
moreover	**too**

as a rule	**in brief**
as you know	**in the first place**
at any rate	**in other words**
by the way	**of course**
I believe	**on the other hand**
for example	**on the contrary**
if any	**that is**
in fact	**to be sure**

Note 1: The expressions listed above are not *always* set off with commas. When such an expression is used in a sentence in a manner that does not interrupt the natural flow of the sentence, you do not set it off with commas. Notice how these expressions do not force you to pause as you read the following sentences aloud.

However expensive the remodeling, we will go through with it.

If he is otherwise occupied, we will return later.

We therefore feel that you must act with caution.

BUT: **We feel, therefore, that you must act with caution.** (Here the placement of **therefore** makes you pause.)

Note 2: Exclamations such as **oh, yes, no,** and **well** should be set off with commas when they are used in a conversational manner to start a sentence.

Oh, you don't say.

Yes, we will attend.

No, I cannot accept your offer.

Well, you are probably right.

PART D.

Use a comma to set off a question that is added to a statement.

1 **You sent the letter, did you not?**

Omit: **did you not?**

Remainder: **You sent the letter.**

2 **Lovely day, isn't it?**

Omit: **isn't it?**

Remainder: **Lovely day.**

3 **You will do as we ask, won't you?**

Omit: **won't you?**

Remainder: **You will do as we ask.**

PART E.

Use a comma to set off a contrasting expression within a sentence — an expression that usually starts with **not, seldom,** or **never.**

1 **Mr. Smith has gone to Chicago, not to St. Louis.**

Omit: **not to St. Louis.**

Remainder: **Mr. Smith has gone to Chicago.**

2 **Our Board meets often in private, seldom in public.**

Omit: **seldom in public.**

Remainder: **Our Board meets often in private.**

3 **We have always enjoyed high attendance, never low, during Easter.**

Omit: **never low.**

Remainder: **We have always enjoyed high attendance during Easter.**

PART F.

The abbreviation **Jr., Sr.,** *or* **Esq.** *(Esquire) at the end of a man's name is considered explanatory in nature. So too is* **Inc.** *and* **Ltd.** *at the end of a company name.* Always place a comma *before* each of these abbreviations. Always place a comma *after* each of these abbreviations unless it ends the sentence in which case one period is all you need.

George Henry Smathers, Jr., is our newly elected President.

Enclosed is a letter from Robert G. Cyrus, Esq., our attorney.

Johnson and Johnson, Inc., recently published its latest profit figures.

If you use the title *Esq.* after an attorney's name, do not write *Mr.* before the name. **Robert G. Cyrus, Esq.,** or **Mr. Robert G. Cyrus** is correct.

Never: Mr. Robert G. Cyrus, Esq.

College degrees or honorary awards listed after a person's name are similarly set off with commas.

Elizabeth C. Ramsey, LL.D., Ph.D., has joined our faculty.

Kent Smith, D.F.C., is your Flight Commander.

PART G.

RULE 1.

The year written after a month and a date should be set off with commas since it is in the nature of an explanation of which month and day. Frequently, the careless writer omits the second comma that should follow the year in the middle of a sentence.

The Declaration of July 4, 1776, is still our guiding beacon.

If the name of the day as well as the date is used, use commas to set off the explanatory material.

The meeting on Tuesday, August 18, is scheduled for noon.

The meeting on August 18, Tuesday, is scheduled for noon.

RULE 2.

The name of a state or country after a city should be set off with commas since it identifies the particular city. Again, don't forget the comma *after* the name of the state or country in the middle of a sentence.

When in Rome do as the Romans do – and this means Rome, Italy, and Rome, Georgia, too.

When a street address is written out in a sentence, use commas to separate the various elements. Note that a comma is placed *after* the Postal Zone number but not before it. If you use a Zip Code number, place it immediately after the name of the state without a comma and omit the zone number.

Mrs. Porter has lived at 2234 Peachtree Street, Atlanta 13, Georgia, for seven years. OR: **2234 Peachtree Street, Atlanta, Georgia 30013, for seven years.**

RULE 3.

Use a comma to set off a short quotation from the rest of the sentence.

He said, "I will not budge an inch."

"Do unto others as you would have others do unto you," is the Golden Rule.

"Send the bills at once," he threatened, "or there will be trouble around here."

Note 1: When the quotation is not direct and not in quotation marks, no comma is necessary.

He said that he would not budge.

The Golden Rule says that we should do unto others as we would have them do unto us.

Note 2: When the quotation is not a complete thought in itself but is a necessary part of the entire sentence, you omit the comma even though you use quotation marks.

He said he was "extremely humiliated."

The summer days are "dog days."

Note 3: When a comma ends a direct quotation, *always* place the final comma *inside* the final quotation marks.

Right: "Send your payment or suffer the consequences," he threatened.

NOT: "Send your payment or suffer the consequences", he threatened.

If the quoted material ends with a question mark or exclamation point, you use this mark inside the quotation marks and omit the comma.

"Who will help me?" he asked.

"Wow!" he exclaimed.

If the quoted material ends with a period, you substitute a comma for the period, as follows:

"We are pleased to submit our payment," the letter stated.

BUT: **The letter stated, "We are pleased to submit our payment."**

RULE 4.

Use a comma to separate two complete thoughts that are connected by a coordinate conjunction such as **but, and, or, nor, yet.** *In other words, in a compound sentence place commas between all independent clauses.*

Our offer was made in good faith, and we trust that you will give it full consideration.

We are not prepared to act now, nor will we be prepared for many months.

Note 1: Note that in each of the foregoing examples the comma comes *before* the conjunction. There is no comma after the conjunction. The reason for this is obvious if you realize that the conjunction is part of the final clause.

Note 2: In a short sentence composed of two independent clauses connected by *and* or *or*, you may omit the comma if the meaning of the sentence is clear. As a rule of thumb, you may omit the comma if either part of the sentence is composed of five words or fewer.

Your order arrived and we shipped it immediately.

Pay the bill or return the merchandise.

If the two thoughts are connected by **but** or **yet**, include the comma no matter how short the parts of the sentence.

We are ready to deal with you now, but we won't be forever.

They were not expected, yet they came.

Note 3: You should know what's wrong with the use of the comma in this sentence:

Wrong: **We must change our advertising appeal, we may lose a large part of our market.**

You should remember from your study of run-on sentences that a comma by itself is not a strong enough "glue" to weld two independent clauses into a compound sentence. To correct this error either use a semicolon or a comma plus a coordinate conjunction or make two separate sentences.

Right: We must change our advertising appeal; we may lose a large part of our market.

Right: We must change our advertising appeal, or we may lose a large part of our market.

Right: We must change our advertising appeal. We may lose a large part of our market.

Note 4: Three or more complete thoughts (independent clauses) may be joined in a series in a single compound sentence. Separate all independent clauses with commas. Don't forget the comma before the final coordinate conjunction.

He came, he saw, and he conquered.

Plan your campaign, put it into operation, and guide it to a successful conclusion.

Note 5: Don't confuse a compound sentence composed of *two or more complete thoughts* with a sentence that contains a compound predicate composed of two or more predicates. In this latter type of sentence, do not use commas to separate the parts of the compound predicate. Examine the following two sentences:

We carefully set up our booth at the fair and arranged the displays attractively. (One subject: *We*. Compound predicate: **set up . . . and arranged.**)

We carefully set up our booth at the fair, but the public did not attend in large numbers. (Two complete thoughts – **We set up. . . . The public did not attend.**)

RULE 5.

You have already learned about the dependent clause. This is the type of clause that contains a subject and a predicate but does not express a complete thought. For example: **Since the order arrived . . . .** Subject: **the order.** Predicate: **arrived.** Complete thought? No.

To complete the meaning of a dependent clause, you must attach it to an independent clause. Thus: **We have worked hard since the order arrived.** You have learned that this is called a *complex* sentence. You have also learned that the natural sequence of a complex sentence is for the independent clause to come first, followed by the dependent clause. To help you remember this, we described the analogy of the independent clause being like a dog, and the dependent clause being like its tail. The tail should follow the dog—that's the natural sequence. Here are examples of complex sentences in the natural sequence:

We have started retooling since the order arrived.

They ran to congratulate him as soon as they heard the news.

She left the theater because she failed to get the part.

Frequently, however, the sentence may be inverted and the dependent clause placed at the beginning to give it greater emphasis. *When a sentence begins with a dependent clause, you use a comma to separate the dependent clause from the independent clause.* This comma indicates the inverted nature of the sentence. This comma warns the reader that the tail is coming before the dog.

Since the order arrived, we have started retooling.

As soon as they heard the news, they ran to congratulate him.

Because she failed to get the part, she left the theater.

Here are other examples of dependent clauses in inverted sentences. In studying these sentences, first examine the dependent clause and ask yourself, "Why does this clause not qualify as a complete thought?" Then examine the independent clause and check to see why it *does* express a complete thought.

Although you agree, we cannot accept.

After hearing your reply, he reconsidered.

As I arrived, they left.

As long as you try, you are bound to succeed.

As soon as I hear from you, I will decide.

Before you leave, drop in.

However unhappy you may feel, don't despair.

If you have an extra catalog, please send it to me.

Note 1: Remember that a dependent clause always contains a verb. (Check each of the above examples.) Don't confuse a dependent clause with a prepositional phrase. If a sentence begins with a phrase that does *not* contain a verb, do not use a comma to separate the phrase from the sentence unless the phrase is very long. For example:

On June 27 we received your offer.

In our previous correspondence we thoroughly discussed the various proposals.

At the last meeting a new President was elected.

BUT: **At the last meeting that you attended, a new President was elected.**

To gain access to the hall, try the back door.

Note 2: When you invert the normal order of a person's name and put the last name first, separate the names with a comma.

Jones, John Paul BUT: **John Paul Jones**

RULE 6.

Use commas in special instances to avoid confusion within a sentence.

a. *Use a comma to separate words that otherwise might be misread.* Note how the comma helps the reader in the following sentences:

Ever since, we have been increasing sales.

On second thought, of all our employees he is the most ambitious.

Only three days before, he came to New York.

b. *Use a comma to separate a word that is repeated twice in succession or any two sets of figures in succession.*

It has been a long, long time.

Whatever happened, happened fast.

I bowled 123, 158, and 185 on successive evenings.

BUT NOTE: **I need two 5-cent stamps.**

c. *Use a comma to indicate the omission of a word or phrase.*

This election we polled 14,372 votes; last election, 12,991. (The words *we polled* are omitted from the second clause.)

America gained twelve gold medals; Sweden, six; Britain, four; France, two. (What word is omitted?)

d. *Use commas to separate a large number into units of three digits.*

The national debt is greater than $300,000,000,000.

e. Letters: *Use a comma after the complimentary close of a letter except when using open punctuation.*

Sincerely,
Very truly yours,
Respectfully,
Sincerely yours,
Cordially yours,

Note that you capitalize *only* the first word in the complimentary close.

REVIEW OF COMMON COMMA ERRORS TO AVOID

1. Do not separate a subject from its predicate-verb by a comma if the predicate comes immediately after the subject.

Wrong: An inefficient, unreliable worker, should be discharged.

Right: **An inefficient, unreliable worker should be discharged.**

2. Do not separate a predicate from its object by a comma if the object comes directly after the predicate.

Wrong: Dale Carnegie wrote, *How to Win Friends and Influence People.*

Right: **Dale Carnegie wrote How to Win Friends and Influence People.**

3. Do not write the comma *after* the conjunction **but, and,** or **or** when it joins clauses in a sentence. Always place the comma before the conjunction.

Wrong: He applied for the position but, he did not get it.

Right: **He applied for the position, but he did not get it.**

4. Do not use a comma to separate the two parts of a compound subject, a compound predicate, or a compound object when they are connected by **and, or,** or **but.**

Wrong: The men, and the women proved equally capable. (Compound subject)

Right: **The men and the women proved equally capable.**

Wrong: She typed, or filed from nine to five. (Compound predicate)

Right: **She typed or filed from nine to five.**

Wrong: They shipped autos, and tractors from the warehouse. (Compound object)

Right: **They shipped autos and tractors from the warehouse.**

5. Do not use a comma to set off a *reflexive* pronoun (a pronoun ending in *self*) used for emphasis.

Wrong: Mr. Jones, himself, will give the report.

Right: **Mr. Jones himself will give the report.**

6. Do not use a comma before **than** in a comparison.

Wrong: It is wiser to fail, than not to try at all.

Right: **It is wiser to fail than not to try at all.**

7. Do not use a comma after a prepositional phrase at the beginning of a sentence unless the phrase is very long.

Wrong: On June 15, our vacations will begin.

Right: On June 15 our vacations will begin.

Wrong: In the winter, business shows an improvement.

Right: In the winter business shows an improvement.

5. THE COLON (:)

The colon is an easy mark of punctuation. You use it in only four simple ways.

RULE 1.

Use the colon after the salutation of a business letter except when using open punctuation.

Dear Madam:
Gentlemen:

RULE 2.

Use the colon to introduce a quotation of one long sentence or of two or more sentences regardless of length. Use a comma to introduce a quotation of one short sentence or part of a sentence.

Senator Jones replied as follows: "I know the importance of this investigation, but I would be ill-advised to become party to such a circus."

He said simply, "I accept."

RULE 3.

Use the colon to formally introduce a list or idea. Generally, a formal introduction includes a word or phrase such as **as follows, the following, these, this, thus.**

Erect the desk as follows: Attach the legs to the side panels; then nail the side panels to the top.

The following invoices are unpaid: No. 3721, No. 3723, and No. 3746.

The real problems are these: the price in Britain, the shipping cost, and the tariff.

Note 1: Observe the examples above to see when the word following the colon is capitalized and when it is not. It is capitalized when a *complete* sentence follows the colon. It is not capitalized when less than a complete sentence follows the colon.

Note 2: Compare the following sentences. Do you see why a colon is used in the first sentence but not in the second? What word makes the first introduction "formal"?

These are the reasons he succeeded: his great initiative, his perseverance, and his cleverness.

The reasons he succeeded are his great initiative, perseverance, and cleverness.

Note 3: In some sentences the formal introductory expression (**as follows, namely,** etc.) is omitted, but clearly understood. In such a sentence use a colon or a dash.

We missed three trains: the 5:15, the 6:07, and the 7:03.

OR:

We missed three trains — the 5:15, the 6:07, and the 7:03.

Note 4: Space *twice* after a colon before starting the next word.

RULE 4.

Use the colon to separate hours from minutes when expressed in figures.

6:43 a.m. **5:06 p.m.**

Note 1: On a timetable the colon is often replaced with a period.

6.43 a.m. **5.06 p.m.**

Note 2: Do not space after the colon in numbers of this type.

6. THE SEMICOLON (;)

The semicolon is a useful mark of punctuation provided that you use it sparingly. Its function in a sentence is to indicate a major pause or break. It indicates a greater pause than a comma, though not quite so great a pause as a period. Some writers have a bad tendency to write long, complicated, tedious sentences, using semicolons to string separate thoughts together like linked frankfurters. No more than you can easily digest a long string of frankfurters, can the average reader digest such a long string of thoughts. A complicated sentence is far more easily read and understood if it is broken into two or more smaller sentences by the use of the period rather than the semicolon. The semicolon, however, has a very definite and useful function when properly employed. So learn these three basic rules for the *proper* use of the semicolon.

RULE 1.

Use the semicolon to separate two closely related complete thoughts that are not separated by a conjunction such as **and, but, for, or, nor.** In other words, as you have already learned, semicolons can be used to connect two or more independent clauses to create a compound sentence.

Prices rose; wages fell. (The semicolon implies a relationship between the two events.)

OR: **Prices rose, but wages fell.** (The conjunction *but* expresses the relationship.)

OR: **Prices rose. Wages fell.** (The period does not necessarily imply any relationship.)

NEVER: **Prices rose, wages fell.** (This is a run-on sentence.)

Right: **To err is human; to forgive, divine.**

Right: **Mail the enclosed card now; you will receive your gift by return mail.**

Note 1: How do you connect the two independent clauses in a compound sentence? You have already studied three ways that should be familiar by now:

1. Use a coordinate conjunction (*and, but, or, nor, yet*) preceded by a comma.
2. If one of the clauses is very short (five or fewer words), you may omit the comma and use a coordinate conjunction by itself.
3. You may omit the coordinate conjunction and use a semicolon by itself.

There is one more way to connect the clauses in a compound sentence:

4. If each clause is very long, and if one or more of the clauses contains commas within itself, then you may use a coordinate conjunction preceded by a *semicolon* instead of a comma. The semicolon used in this manner helps the reader follow a complicated sentence without confusion. For example:

Naturally, having heard of the offer, he rushed to the employment office; but, despite his haste, he found that the job had already been filled.

Employing every means at his disposal, the U.S. Ambassador, Gregory C. Wright, attempted to befriend the inhabitants of that small, underdeveloped nation; and his efforts were ultimately rewarded by success, which was justly earned.

The American is noted for friendliness and innocence; the Englishman, for formality and reserve; and the Frenchman, for explosiveness and warmth.

Note 2: You have already learned about the use of the comma to separate items listed in series. Observe how a semicolon should be used to separate items in series where commas would be confusing.

Our new Board of Directors is composed of Rodney G. Jones, President; Augustus E. Smythe, Vice-President; and Ormand Cole, Jr., Secretary-Treasurer.

The totals are 3,728; 2,142,607; and 42,429.

Note 3: When using the semicolon in a sentence, skip only one space before the next word.

RULE 2.

Use the semicolon to separate two complete thoughts (independent clauses) that are connected by a conjunctive such as **accordingly, also, consequently, further, hence, however, indeed, in fact, moreover, nevertheless, then, therefore, thus, whereas.**

The deadline has passed; accordingly we are canceling our order.

The odds were insurmountable; nevertheless he fought on.

Please give us your exact measurements; then we can tailor-fit the suit to your dimensions.

The doors open at seven; however, you will be admitted at six.

Note 1: Do you see why commas would have been incorrect where semicolons are used in the four sentences above? Only the coordinate conjunctions *and, but, or, nor,* and *yet* are strong enough "glue" to hold independent clauses together when used with a comma. For "weaker" conjunctions like those listed above, you need the strength of a semicolon, not a comma.

Note 2: Observe that a comma has been placed after the conjunction *however* in the fourth sentence but has not been placed after the conjunctions in the other three sentences. The word *however* in Sentence 4 is independent of the thought expressed by its clause; it almost *requires* a pause. This is not true of the other conjunctions as used here; hence they do not require commas.

RULE 3.

Use a semicolon to precede an expression such as **for example, e.g., namely, viz., that is, i.e., to wit,** *when this expression introduces a list or explanation.* A comma is *always* used immediately following each of the above expressions.

He had one credo; namely, do unto others as you would have them do unto you.

We can choose from among many fine potential locations for the convention; for example, New York, Chicago, Los Angeles, or Honolulu.

If the list or explanation occurs in the middle of the sentence rather than at the end, use dashes rather than semicolons.

Many fine potential locations — for example, New York, Chicago, Los Angeles, or Honolulu — are available for us to select for the convention.

7. QUOTATION MARKS (")

RULE 1.

Use quotation marks to enclose a direct quotation. A direct quotation repeats the *exact* words of what was originally said or written.

In your letter of July 9 you state: "Our records indicate that shipment was made on June 15 via Universal Shippers, Inc."

Do not use quotation marks around an indirect quotation. An indirect quotation is a *rewording* of the original statement. It is frequently introduced by the word **that.**

In your letter of July 9 you write that the shipment was sent via Universal Shippers on June 15.

Note 1: Use a colon to introduce a direct quotation of one *long* sentence or of two or more sentences regardless of length. Use a comma to introduce a direct quotation of one short sentence or of part of a sentence.

The President declared: "In a time of peril such as this we must jealously guard our liberties and defend our national integrity against all encroachments."

The President said, "I am confident of victory."

Note 2: When a complete statement is quoted and ends the sentence, the period is placed *inside* the final quotation marks.

Patrick Henry shouted, "Give me liberty or give me death."

When a complete statement is quoted but does not end the sentence, a *comma* is placed inside the final quotation mark.

"Give me liberty or give me death," shouted Patrick Henry.

When a complete statement being quoted is broken into more than one part, enclose each part in quotation marks. Do not start the second part with a capital letter. Note the use of commas.

"Send us the bill," he wrote, "and we will mail you a check by return mail."

Note 3: When recording the direct conversation of two or more persons, place the statements of each person in separate quotation marks and in separate paragraphs.

The chairman shouted, "Order! Order in the house!"

"I will not be silenced," answered Jones, jumping from his seat with arms waving wildly.

"Gentlemen," interrupted Brown, "let us look at this matter in a calmer frame of mind."

Note 4: If a quotation consists of more than one sentence, the quotation marks go at the beginning and at the end of the entire statement. If the single quotation consists of more than one paragraph, the quotation marks go at the *beginning* of *each* paragraph, but at the *end* of *only* the *last* paragraph.

The letter read: "We are making this offer just this week. Note that it is being made together with our sale of daytime dresses. We are sure you will like our selection.

"Any time during the morning that is best for you will be best for us. Will you come?"

Note 5: Use single quotation marks to indicate a quotation within a quotation.

He said, "I believe in the old saying, 'Haste makes waste.' "

Note 6: When typing quotation marks, do not skip a space after the beginning quotation mark or before the closing quotation mark.

RULE 2.

Use quotation marks around the title of an article or chapter in a magazine, newspaper, or book. The name of a magazine, newspaper, or book is usually written either in italics or in all capital letters rather than in quotation marks. To indicate italics, you underline the name.

This month's Scientific American includes Professor Anderson's fascinating article on "Solar Particles and Cosmic Rays."

LIFE is doing a series on "The Universe."

Note 1: If the article *A, An,* or *The* is a part of the title of an article, it should be capitalized and included within the quotation marks. If it is part of the name of a magazine, it should be included as part of the material that is italicized (or underlined) or written in all capital letters.

RULE 3.

Use the quotation marks around unusual words, coined phrases, or colloquial expressions.

Our sales staff must be "on-the-ball."

We feel that Mr. Jones is a "square-shooter."

The way to understand this problem is to "conceptualize" it in your mind.

RULE 4.

Quotation Marks and Other Punctuation – Here's where a great deal of trouble can arise unless you are careful. Study these simple rules and you'll easily master this trouble spot.

1. *Always place a final period or comma inside the quotation marks.*

He said, "Let the chips fall."

"Give me the statistics," Jones retorted, "and I'll have the answers in a minute."

2. *Always write a final colon or semicolon outside the quotation marks.*

Here is a partial list of causes cited in "The Rising Cost of Living": higher wages, increased tariffs, lower rates of productivity growth.

The encircled troops were told, "Surrender or die"; they chose to fight on.

3. *The question mark, exclamation point, and dash are placed inside the quotation marks when they relate specifically to the quoted material.*

"Will you join me?" he asked.

"Wow!" was all he could say.

"Our flight position is –" were the pilot's last recorded words.

4. *The question mark, exclamation point, and dash are placed outside the quotation marks if they relate to the entire sentence.*

Did you read our article, "The Higher Light"?

Congratulations on your latest article, "How To Invest"!

"To be or not to be . . ." – Shakespeare.

8. THE APOSTROPHE (')

RULE 1.

Use the apostrophe to indicate the omission of a letter or letters in a contraction. Do not place a period after a contraction as you would after an abbreviation. Note where the apostrophe goes and what letters it replaces in the following contractions:

aren't	**I'll**	**he's**	**Gen'l**
can't	**he'll**	**I'm**	**Gov't**
couldn't	**she'll**	**it's**	**Nat'l**
isn't	**they'll**	**they're**	**Rec't**
weren't	**we'll**	**we're**	**Sec'y**

RULE 2.

Use the apostrophe to form the possessive case of a noun. If the noun does not end in *s*, add apostrophe *s* ('s). If the noun ends in *s*, add an apostrophe only.

A teacher's success depends upon a student's efforts.

John's office called, but Charles' line was busy.

Stenographers' skills will determine their success.

Remember, the possessive form of a *pronoun* does not take an apostrophe: **hers, its, ours, yours, theirs.**

Is this book hers?

Yours truly,

The firm sent its representative.

It's is a contraction of **it is. Its** is a possessive pronoun.

It's a fine day.

We think it's not going to last.

The stock was put on its shelf.

RULE 3.

Use the apostrophe to form the plural of letters and numbers.

Mississippi has four i's, four s's, and two p's.

This month we ordered a new shipment of No. 105's.

The plural of words being used simply as words is usually formed by just adding *s*. If, however, a particular plural formed this way might appear confusing, apostrophe s (*'s*) is added.

We want no ifs, ands, or buts.

He uses six I's in his very first sentence.

9. THE HYPHEN (-)

RULE 1.

Use the hyphen to divide a word that cannot be completed at the end of a line.

He thought that it would be too dif-
ficult.

The trend in letter writing today is to avoid the use of word divisions whenever possible. Your guiding rule when typing copy, therefore, should be to divide words only when it is absolutely necessary to do so in order to maintain a *reasonably* straight margin. A line of type that is five spaces shorter than the margin or three spaces longer is acceptable in business practice.

Observe the following rules about word division:

a. When dividing a word, you type the hyphen at the end of the first line, not at the beginning of the second.

b. Divide words only between syllables. A one-syllable word, therefore, may not be divided. You should not divide a two-syllable word if it has five or fewer letters. For example, do not divide words like *talked, ago, through, elate.*

c. A two-syllable word may not be divided if one of the syllables consists of only one letter. The word *consists* may be divided into *con-sists*. The word *arouse* may not be divided into *a-rouse.*

d. When a medial (middle) syllable of a word is a single vowel, that single vowel should *end* the first line and not start the second. The word *hesitate* consists of the three syllables *hes-i-tate.* It should be divided as *hesi-tate,* NOT *hes-itate.*

e. Do not divide a proper noun, a contraction, an abbreviation, or a number if at all possible.

f. If possible, do not divide a word if it is the last word of a paragraph or a page.

g. Do not end more than two successive lines with a divided word.

h. Carry over at least three or more letters.

Correct:		*Incorrect:*
shortly		**short-ly**
lux-ury		**luxu-ry**
con-sumer		**consum-er**

i. Divide hyphenated compound words only at a point where a hyphen naturally occurs.

sister-in-law self-control above-mentioned

j. As a general rule, divide words between double letters unless the word is derived from one that ends in a double letter (sma*ll*). In the latter case, the word is divided after the root word.

small-est	**rub-ber**
woo-ing	**excel-lence**
stuff-ing	**win-ning**

RULE 2.

There are certain expressions that should *always* be hyphenated:

a. Compound words that begin with **self**, such as **self-conscious, self-evident, self-assurance, self-respect, self-confident.**

b. Compound words that begin with **ex, pro**, or **anti.**

For example: **ex-President, ex-Senator, pro-American, pro-United Nations, anti-Communist.**

RULE 3.

There are other expressions that are sometimes hyphenated and sometimes not – expressions such as **up to date, high class, first rate, high grade, well informed.** As a rule of thumb, follow this procedure: Whenever any such expression comes *directly before* the noun it modifies, it should be hyphenated.

We have an up-to-date system.

Our store caters to a high-class clientele.

We deal in first-rate goods.

We need a twelve-foot stepladder.

He competed in the hundred-yard dash.

When, however, the noun being modified does *not* follow directly, use *no* hyphens.

Our system is up to date.

Our clientele is high class.

Our goods are first rate.

He ran in a race of one hundred yards.

Note 1: Generally, do not use a hyphen after an adverb ending in *ly* even if it precedes the noun:

highly trained athlete

brightly decorated hall

widely heralded appearance

oddly strange mixture

Note 2: Observe this sentence: **We are short of ten- and twenty-dollar bills.**

Note the hyphen after *ten*. This sentence really says: **We are short of ten-dollar bills and twenty-dollar bills;** hence the use of the hyphen after *ten*. Here are similar examples:

They stock half-, three-quarter-, and seven-eighth-inch bolts.

He swam in the 50-, 100-, and 220-yard free-style races.

They produced 24-, 32-, 64-, and 128-page versions of the book.

Note 3: When writing out numbers, you hyphenate compound numbers from twenty-one through ninety-nine. You do not hyphenate hundreds, thousands, or millions unless the entire number is used as an adjective directly before a noun. Observe these examples:

thirty-seven

one hundred thirty-seven

thirty-seven thousand six hundred and forty-five

one hundred thirty-seven thousand six hundred and forty-five

BUT: **a one-hundred-thirty-seven-foot fall**

a six-hundred-dollar reduction

10. PARENTHESES ( )

RULE 1.

Use parentheses to enclose expressions that are completely incidental, explanatory, or supplementary to the main thought of a sentence.

There is no possibility (so I am told) that this deal will be consummated.

You have already learned (see Lesson 2) about nouns.

Note 1: When a sentence ends with an expression in parentheses, place the period after the parentheses. For example:

In full consideration for our claim, we hereby agree to accept as payment the amount of Eight Hundred Dollars ($800.00).

Note 2: When a complete sentence appears in parentheses as part of another sentence, it is not started with a capital letter nor finished with a period. See the first two examples above. When a sentence in parentheses is an independent thought, it is started with a capital letter and ended with appropriate punctuation *inside* the closing parenthesis mark:

I have told the Director that you will have the goods delivered by Tuesday. (John, please don't let us down.) He will accept shipment no later than then.

Note 3: Do you place punctuation *inside* or *outside* the final mark of parenthesis? If the punctuation relates only to the material in parenthesis, place the punctuation *inside.*

His latest article ("Lost Opportunities") is certain to receive an award.

When using a telescope, never (Never!) look directly at the sun.

If the punctuation relates to the whole sentence and not specifically to the material in parentheses, place the punctuation *outside* the closing parenthesis mark.

No matter where we have traveled (in the United States and Canada at least), we have never found a better hotel. Do you see why the comma is placed *outside* the parenthesis in this sentence?

Note 4: In some instances it is proper to use either dashes or parentheses, whichever you prefer:

Right: **This offer (and it is our final offer) is too good to be refused.**

Right: **This offer—and it is our final offer—is too good to be refused.**

RULE 2.

Parentheses are used to enclose numbers or letters that itemize a list which is part of running text.

Practice serves to (a) improve your coordination, (b) increase your speed, and (c) develop your strength.

Note 1: If you had tabulated this list, you would write it as follows:

Practice serves to accomplish the following:

a. improve your coordination
b. increase your speed
c. develop your strength

RULE 3.

In formal documents numbers are frequently written out both in words and figures. Parentheses are usually placed around the figures. For example:

The total fee for our service shall be Six Hundred Dollars ($600).

We acknowledge receipt of your order for six hundred (600) barrels of crude oil.

Note 1: In spelling out a dollar amount in a legal document, capitalize each word in the figure and capitalize the word *Dollar.* The figure in parentheses appears after the word *Dollar*: **Six Hundred Dollars ($600).**

Note 2: In spelling out a quantity of material, do not capitalize the numbers or the unit of measurement, and place the figures in parentheses *before* the name of the unit of measure: **six hundred (600) barrels.**

RULE 4.

Brackets [ ] *are frequently used in a printed direct quotation to indicate matter that is not part of the quotation but that has been inserted by the editor.*

The minister quoted the old adage: "The exception proves [tests] the rule."

11. THE DASH (–)

RULE 1.

Use the dash to indicate a major break in the continuity of thought.

The large house – and make no mistake, it was large – was completely demolished by the fire.

I know – or should I say, I feel – that you will do well.

RULE 2.

Use the dash to emphasize an explanatory phrase.

We want to tell you about our product – the Schenley car.

America – that bastion of democracy – has an obligation to all human beings.

Note 1: Properly used, the dash is an effective tool to catch the reader's eye and keep him alert. If you use the dash too often, however, you destroy its effectiveness and leave a sloppy, difficult-to-read page. The good writer uses the dash only occasionally when he wants extra *punch.* It is his *Sunday punch,* not his *left jab.*

Note 2: The dash is frequently used to set off an explanatory phrase that contains one or more commas.

The top-rated shows – Beverly Hillbillies, I Love Lucy, and Father Knows Best – have all been situation comedies.

Note 3: Don't omit the second dash. If an explanatory phrase starts with a dash, it should end with a dash too – not with a comma.

Wrong: The top rated shows – Beverly Hillbillies, I Love Lucy, and Father Knows Best, have all been situation comedies.

RULE 3.

Use the dash after an expression such as namely or that is when this expression introduces a list in tabulated form.

We are aware of three determining factors; namely –

1. **the bad weather**
2. **the rise in prices**
3. **a shortage of labor**

RULE 4.

Use a dash before the name of the author after a quotation.

Unbroken happiness is a bore; it should have ups and down. – Moliere

Note 1: In business the preferred way to make a dash on a typewriter is by striking the hyphen twice leaving no space before or after this dash.

An alternative, considered to be less formal, is to space once, strike the hyphen once, and space again.

Preferred: `The officers of the company--the President, Vice-President, and Secretary-Treasurer --have approved the plans for merger.`

Less Formal: `The officers of the company - the President, Vice-President', and Secretary-Treasurer - have approved the plan for merger.`

12. ELLIPSES (...)

Ellipses are a series of dots used in the midst of a direct quotation to indicate that part of the quotation at that point has been omitted. *Three* dots are used at the beginning of, or in the middle of, a quoted sentence. If the omitted material is at the end of sentence, a fourth dot representing the period is added. Do not use more or fewer dots than these.

If a man has freedom enough to live healthy . . . he has enough. – Goethe

According to Immanual Kant: "Freedom is that faculty which enlarges the usefulness of all other faculties. . . ."

13. CAPITALIZATION

1. Capitalize the first word of every sentence. (You should need no special examples of this.)

2. Capitalize the first word of a direct quotation that is a complete sentence.

He said, "This job must be improved upon."

"This job," he said, "must be improved upon."

Note, however, that if you are quoting an expression that is not a full sentence, you do not capitalize the first word.

He said that this job "must be improved upon."

3. Capitalize the first word of each line of poetry.

"What fairings will ye that I bring?
Said the King to his daughters three;
For I to Vanity Fair am bound,
Now say what shall they be?"

4. Capitalize each amount when spelled out in formal or legal documents, as follows:

Eighty-seven Dollars and Twenty-four Cents
Sixty-four Thousand Dollars

5. Capitalize the word *dear* in a salutation when it comes at the beginning. Do *not* capitalize *dear* when it is in the middle of the salutation.

Dear Sir:
My dear Sir:
Dear Mr. Jones:
My dear Mr. Jones:

6. Capitalize only the first word in the complimentary close of a letter.

Sincerely yours,
Yours sincerely,
Very truly yours,

7. Capitalize nouns or pronouns that refer to God or to holy books.

Please hand me the Bible on that shelf.

The Holy Scriptures tell us that God created the world in six days and that He rested on the seventh day.

8. Capitalize college degrees such as *M. D.*; radio stations such as *WQXR*; initials standing for proper names such as *F. D. R.*; abbreviations for proper nouns such as *D. C.* for *District of Columbia.*

John Grossman, Ph. D., will address us.

He announces for WNBC.

Headlines about F. D. R. dominated the news during the New Deal.

He lives in Brattleboro, Vt.

Note the proper capitalization of Ph. D. meaning Doctor of Philosophy.

9. Capitalize the first letter of each important word in the *title* of a work of art or literature. Do not capitalize unimportant words such as *to, and,* and *the,* which occur in the *middle* of the title.

Have you read "How to Win Friends and Influence People"?

Washington's "Farewell Address" was his greatest speech.

He entitled his talk, "Russia, the Modern Dilemma."

Have you ever seen the painting, "The Blue Boy"?

10. Capitalize proper nouns. A proper noun is a noun that refers to a specific person, place, or thing. For example:

John Jones America Corvair

A proper noun is always written with a capital letter. Do you realize how important proper nouns are to the American system of free enterprise? Every company name, every product name, and every trade name is a proper noun. The business correspondence you will handle on the job will be filled with proper nouns. So study the *Hints* listed below. They will help you solve the capitalization problems you may face when you are in the office.

HINTS ON CAPITALIZATION OF PROPER NOUNS

HINT 1.

Always capitalize the names of *months* of the year and *days* of the week.

Classes begin on the first Monday in February.

HINT 2.

Never capitalize the names of *seasons* except in the rare instance when the season is being *personified*; that is, referred to as though it were a living being.

Our fall order was not delivered until winter.

Old Man Winter won't stop our snow tires from giving you perfect traction.

HINT 3.

Should you capitalize the name of a *direction* such as *east* or *west?*

a. When the name of a direction refers to a *specific section* of the country or of the world, it then becomes a proper noun and it should be capitalized.

The West is solid in its opposition to Communism.

The Southwest is rapidly gaining in population and industry.

The Mississippi flows through the North and the South.

b. When the name of a direction is used to refer to a point on the compass, it should NOT be capitalized.

The plane circled twice, then headed west.

Philadelphia is southwest of New York.

The Mississippi flows from north to south.

c. *Eastern, Southern, Western,* and *Northern* are capitalized when used as part of the name of a *major* world division such as a hemisphere, a continent, or a nation. They are NOT capitalized when used as part of the name of a *minor* world division such as a state, a county, or a city.

During recent years considerable economic consolidation has occurred in Western Europe.

This particular sales territory includes eastern New York, northeastern Pennsylvania, and northern New Jersey.

d. Names derived from a particular geographical locality are capitalized.

Southerner **Northerner**

HINT 4.

Should you capitalize a geographic term such as *river, ocean, mountain,* or *valley?* The answer depends upon how you are using such a term. Learn these three simple rules.

a. Capitalize a geographic term such as *river* when you use it as part of the name of a *particular* river or other geographic designation:

Hudson River
Pacific Ocean
Bear Mountain
Death Valley

b. Do not capitalize a geographic term such as *river* when it is placed *before* the name of the river:

The river Jordan

The valley of the river Nile

EXCEPTION: The word *mount* is capitalized even when it precedes the name of the mountain.

Mount Everest

Mount Rainier

Mount Whitney

c. Do not capitalize a geographic term such as *river* when you use it in the plural.

Missouri and Mississippi rivers

Atlantic and Pacific oceans

Appalachian and Rocky mountains

d. Political designations such as *state, city,* or *country* are always capitalized when they are a part of the specific name of the area.

New York City

New York State

Bucks County

When a political designation such as *state, city,* or *county* is written before the *specific* name, it may or may not be capitalized, depending upon its particular meaning in the sentence.

The state of Nevada is famed for its scenic beauty.

The State of Nevada has concluded its appeal to the United States Supreme Court.

HINT 5.

Should you capitalize a word such as *hotel, highway, tunnel,* or *revolution*? The rules here are similar to those you have just studied. Generally, capitalize such a word when you are using it as *part* of a specific name.

New Yorker Hotel

Lincoln Highway

French Revolution

BUT: **French and American revolutions**

New Yorker and Pennsylvania hotels

HINT 6.

Are titles such as *president, treasurer,* or *director* capitalized? The rule preferred is this:

a. Always capitalize the title of a person when it appears *directly* before or *directly* after the name of the title-holder.

President Johnson will see you now.

Send the message to John Jones, President of Acme Steel Company.

We received the letter from James Roberts, Assistant Director of the Zenith Oil Company.

b. Generally, capitalize the title of a *high-ranking* officer even when his name does not appear in the sentence.

The Senator will return soon.

The President was not at the White House.

c. There is some disagreement about whether the title of a *less important* office holder should be capitalized when his name does not appear in a sentence. The preferred business practice is to *capitalize such titles.* After all, you express your respect for a person when you capitalize his title.

Will your Sales Manager please contact me by phone.

The letter is from the Superintendent of our Wyoming plant.

The Treasurer of our firm will be pleased to attend the dinner.

NOTE: *Vice-President* is the preferred spelling, but *Vice-president* and *Vice President* are also acceptable.

HINT 7.

Do you capitalize the name of an organization such as *company, association, commission,* or *department*?

a. These words are capitalized when they are part of the names of *specific* organizations:

American Steel Company
National Association of Manufacturers
Sales Department

b. These words are capitalized when they are used as *substitutes* for the complete names of specific organizations.

We in the Company take pride in our latest production record.

The Association welcomes you to its vast membership.

The Department has been awarded a trophy for outstanding employee cooperation.

BUT: **There is a company in Denver with a fine production record.**

A new association is being formed by lumber dealers across the continent.

Which department handles this problem?

HINT 8.

Capitalize the names of *specific* governmental agencies.

United States Senate Police Department
Court of Appeals Board of Elections
Air Force Council of Foreign Ministers

Capitalize the names of political parties. The word *party* itself may or may not be capitalized: *Democratic Party*; *Republican party.*

HINT 9.

Certain words are derived from proper nouns but are not capitalized because they are now used as common nouns or as other parts of speech. In fact, you can make a fascinating study of former trademarks that have been deprived of their "right" to a capital letter because the courts held that the words had become part of our everyday language. Here are a few examples:

aspirin cellophane escalator
shredded wheat thermos bottle

HINT 10.

Do not capitalize the name of any *school subject* or course of study except for a language or a specifically described course.

This year I am going to study shorthand and typing.

BUT: **I added Shorthand IV and Advanced Typing to my schedule.**

I am studying English, but not Spanish or mathematics.

NOTE: Capitalize the words *high school* and *college* only if the specific title of a particular school is used.

I went to Riverhead High School and then spent three years at college.

This finishes your study of the rules of punctuation and capitalization.

You have learned many rules, but they were not too difficult. Actually, almost all of these rules were merely a review for you.

You certainly knew that a period is placed at the end of a sentence that makes a statement, a question mark is placed after a question, and an exclamation point is placed after an exclamation. You know that the comma is used to separate items listed in a series, to set off introductory expressions such as *therefore,* and to set off certain explanatory expressions. You knew that quotation marks are placed before and after a direct quotation, and that the first letter of a sentence must be capitalized. You knew all this, and much more.

All in all, probably three-quarters of the rules in this lesson were completely familiar to you. You applied them automatically without a second thought. It is mastery of the other one-quarter of these rules, however, that often spells the difference between the average, run-of-the-mill office employee and the highly paid, top-notch secretary or executive.

Do you feel you have fully mastered all the rules of punctuation presented in this lesson?

Do you feel certain that every transcript you hand to your teacher and later to your employer will exhibit perfect punctuation?

Here is the turning point in your training. If you want to move up as a superior employee, make certain that you know the rules of punctuation thoroughly. Review this lesson. Then review it again if necessary. It won't take long, and it will be well worth the small effort.

EXERCISE 48 Using the Period

A. Cross out all incorrect punctuation in the following paragraphs and insert all necessary periods and capitals.

this morning we received a request to submit a bid on the equipment specifications for the new vocational school now being erected in Erie, Pa

it is our policy, as you know, to work only through our regular dealers, we suggest, therefore, that you send a representative to follow up this opportunity for some very good business

we can be very helpful to you in preparing your estimate on the list of hand tools, and we hope you will let us work with you the large machine equipment, of course, is out of our line because of your long experience in this field, we know you will have no trouble in submitting a complete bid

* * *

we appreciate the information that you gave us in your letter of October 17

the purchasing agent for the Board of Education in Erie has given us permission to submit a bid on the equipment list for the new school since the bid must be submitted on or before November 19, it is necessary for us to work rapidly

some time ago you stated that there might be price changes after November 1 while we understand that increasing demands are being placed on the tool industry, still we must request a definite guarantee from your company that the prices in effect now will apply to the Erie school contract if it is awarded to our company

EXERCISE 48 — The Period

B. This problem deals with the proper use of the period. Insert periods wherever necessary in the sentences below. Indicate a capital letter if a new sentence is to follow.

1. I will be there at eight o'clock I shall see you then
2. Step forward to volunteer that is the way to help
3. Will you open the door, please my hands are occupied
4. Work now go to lunch later
5. Mr M Franklin Smith, Jr, lives in Pittsburgh, Pa
6. Dr Frank R Jackson, DDS, ordered these drills to be sent c o d
7. John R Boyd, Esq, was officially listed as *Sup't of Arsenals* and later as *Sec'y of War*
8. He gained $245 on his first venture, but lost $15,324 later
9. Washington, DC, is north of Raleigh, NC
10. The merchandise went to Cap't Johnson of Wallace Lines, Inc
11. We stayed at the YMCA in St Louis, Mo
12. Mrs Johnson asked Miss Smith to visit at noon
13. Norman Wells III received his BA from Yale and his PhD from Harvard
14. Won't you please come in, Mr. Smith
15. The US 4th Army Brigade is being transferred from Ft Dix, NJ, to St. Johns, BWI, aboard the USS Enterprise

EXERCISE 49 — The Question Mark and Exclamation Point

A. At the end of each of the following sentences, place a question mark, an exclamation mark, or a period – whichever is correct.

1. Did you send the letter
2. Please mail it at once
3. Won't you come in, please
4. Why wasn't it filed at once
5. A fine idea
6. The director asked many questions
7. Who is there
8. I am not sure who filed the letter
9. Will you be kind enough to visit us
10. Why not take a chance
11. Why
12. Can we doubt his sincerity
13. That is the $64,000 question
14. Amazing
15. What an amazing discovery
16. Did you see the shipment
17. Have they acknowledged our order
18. Wonderful
19. Won't you please consider our offer
20. This is wonderful news, isn't it

EXERCISE 49 — The Question Mark and Period

B. **This problem deals with the correct use of the question mark. Put question marks or periods wherever you think necessary; indicate a capital if a new sentence is to follow.**

1. Can you be there this evening
2. Will you please allow me to pass
3. Are you able to complete the exercises
4. Why don't you use a carbon it will help
5. Since our last order, have prices risen
6. I wonder why he was discharged
7. Are you sure that all figures have been carefully examined and checked
8. He asked me where you are going tonight
9. Can you name three generals three admirals three air chiefs
10. Why is he doing this, I wonder

EXERCISE 49 — Using Punctuation

C. **Insert periods, question marks, and exclamation marks wherever appropriate in the following letter.**

Gentlemen:

Last May we ordered the new novel by George Wilson, Jr As yet we have not received it although it is already July 15 May we ask for an explanation

Is the book out of print or was our order simply misplaced If it is in stock, please ship it at once, cod If not, let us know when we can expect it

Rush

Very truly yours

EXERCISE 50 — Commas: Separating Items in a Series

This problem involves the use of commas to separate items listed in a series. Insert commas in the following sentences wherever necessary.

1. We will leave by car rail or plane on Friday.
2. The successful teacher is friendly alert interesting and self-confident.
3. Our store deals in radios TV sets refrigerators and similar products.
4. We have correspondence from you dated August 3 August 18 September 6 and October 15.
5. You will not be able to resist our newest model when you see its long low streamlined appearance.
6. Newspapers magazines books and periodicals all will be on sale this week.
7. Our rates are $8.00 for a room without bath $10.50 for a room with bath and $18.00 for a suite of two rooms.
8. We deal in state bonds municipal bonds industrial bonds and railroad bonds.
9. We deal in state municipal industrial and railroad bonds.
10. Thirty days hath September April June and November.
11. We sell the finest kerosene benzene and alcohol lamps on the market.
12. The properties available are in Detroit St. Louis Cleveland and New York.
13. For lunch we offer roast beef salad and bread and butter.
14. Our courses include shorthand business English typewriting and bookkeeping.
15. She gave a stately prim correct appearance.
16. Would you be willing to spend a few dollars for a chance to break into a fast-growing profitable interesting respected profession?
17. Fame fortune and esteem – these were his lot in life.
18. Their firm deals in the finest silks cottons and woolens.
19. The box is neither lightweight nor presentable.
20. I can see now the lovely green lawn the broad gravel walk the giant shade trees and the perfect model of a colonial walk.
21. The new skyscrapers have been luxuriously ornately and decoratively designed.
22. The efficient telephone operator answers pacifies informs and cajoles the caller.
23. I want you to learn to write to compose to correct and to dictate letters.
24. That a modern novelist is frank that he is imaginative and that he is perceptive are recognized facts.
25. Ask questions politely listen to details carefully and follow instructions intelligently.
26. Tact wisdom and diplomacy – these are necessities of an enlightened intelligent foreign policy.
27. Please try our new furniture polish.
28. To plan and design carefully to purchase and order wisely and to build and construct sturdily are necessary steps.
29. The firm of Webb Prince and Berman is well known.
30. He planned to invite workers farmers storekeepers salesmen etc.

EXERCISE 51 — Commas: Set off Name of Person Addressed

This problem involves the use of commas to set off the name of a person directly addressed. In some of the following sentences commas have been omitted. Fill in all missing commas.

1. Thank you Mr. Shaw for the prompt attention given to our questionnaire.
2. We have directed Mr. James King of our credit department to discuss terms of payment with you.
3. They are being shown this week Mrs. Watson.
4. Mr. Adams we have learned that you will soon enjoy delivery of your new car.
5. I have looked further Mr. Grover into the Gray lumber situation.
6. Mr. Martin says that economic conditions will continue to be thoroughly sound.
7. Madam does the approach of warm weather suggest sending your furs to storage?
8. Is it the fault of this store that your account remains inactive Mrs. Wright?
9. Mr. White's inspection of our floor equipment was very helpful.
10. The January sales now being held throughout the store offer you exceptional values Mrs. Hays.

EXERCISE 52 — Commas: Set off Explanatory Expressions

This problem deals with the use of commas to set off explanatory expressions. Insert commas wherever proper in the following sentences.

1. Our representative from New Orleans Mr. A. J. Johnson is in town.
2. Asia the largest of the continents is becoming a major focus of international relations.
3. Our new location the corner of Sixth Avenue and 42nd Street is ideal for our type of business.
4. Our attorney Mr. G. A. Blake will call at your office tomorrow.
5. B. H. Brown golf champion of the South won the cup handily.
6. It is my pleasure to introduce H. Colin Phillips our friend and leader.
7. Would you enjoy living in a residential park a veritable winter wonderland of over 500 acres of high healthy beautifully wooded fertile land Mr. Smith?
8. We advise you to see either Mr. R. J. Jones Director of the Bureau or Mr. P. T. Smith his assistant.
9. The speakers were H. George Brittingham Professor of Business English and John Rogers Jr. Professor of American History.
10. The Mississippi America's longest river flows into the Gulf of Mexico.

EXERCISE 53 — Nonrestrictive Clauses

A. **This problem involves the use of commas to set off explanatory expressions. Each of the following sentences involves a nonrestrictive clause — that is, a relative clause that should be set off with commas. Insert commas as necessary.**

1. This morning we received a report from Mr. Johnson who is our representative in New York.
2. Wellington chalk which is the best chalk you can get is the most economical for school use.
3. Mr. Howard Clark who is president of the National Savings Association sent a copy of his latest address.
4. Our customers all of whom have been most kind to us will be pleased to hear of our latest plans.
5. The manufacture of this equipment which is the finest ever made is a painstakingly exact process.
6. These lessons which you should study every day will provide fine background for your future work.
7. Our office furniture all of which we bought last year is of ultra-modern design.
8. The new secretary who was trained at business school is the best we've ever had.
9. The luggage which was engraved with his initials was presented to Mr. Phillips.
10. The park which is noted for its old trees was established in 1889.

EXERCISE 53 — Restrictive Clauses

B. **Each of the following sentences involves an explanatory expression that should NOT be set off with commas because to do so would change the meaning of the sentence. Underline each such restrictive clause.**

1. The man who does a poor job does not last long in business.
2. The advertisement that catches the eye is the one that has a certain "plus."
3. Medicine is a profession that satisfies a man's desire to serve others.
4. Water that is stagnant is putrid.
5. Anyone who works hard can succeed.
6. Only those who are geniuses gain acclaim as musicians.
7. A rumor that we heard yesterday is disturbing.
8. The ledger that is in Room 217 is the one I want.
9. The officer who leads his men bravely gains their respect.
10. We observed a downward trend that is most unsatisfactory.

EXERCISE 53 — Commas and Explanatory Expressions

C. **Each of the following sentences includes an explanatory expression. Some of these expressions should be set off with commas; some should not. Place commas around those expressions that should be set off; underline those expressions that should not.**

1. Water that does not run rapidly becomes stagnant.
2. Your fall order which we received last week has been filled.
3. The man who runs the fastest wins the race.
4. John Doe who was tried for larceny was acquitted.
5. Deliver only those posters that you consider best as soon as you can.
6. The letter that was sent to him came back unopened.
7. This work which I feel sure you will enjoy is not very difficult.
8. The dress that I think you will like best has not yet arrived.
9. Our book is printed in type that is easy on the eye.
10. That woman who spoke to you at such great length yesterday is back.
11. This business which you have merely sampled these past months can provide ample excitement for a lifetime.
12. A red-headed woman who does not have a fiery temper is a rarity.
13. Mr. Oglethorpe is a man who knows this business inside out.
14. The order which we have been awaiting for weeks was delayed again.
15. He is the man whom I would elect.
16. My teacher Frank C. Smith has been an inspiring influence.
17. I myself have much to study.
18. The poet Milton wrote about heaven.
19. Our business like any other new business will benefit from experience.
20. These data all of which are interesting do not change our business prediction.
21. Knowing that sales are the lifeblood of an organization we shall hire an alert salesman.
22. The new executives that lead our top organizations have youth and vitality.
23. They shipped the merchandise in May assuming you wanted it for June 15.
24. A sales letter that paints word pictures brings maximum results.
25. His brother Albert is brighter than his brothers John and Herman.

EXERCISE 54 — Commas and Conjunctions

A. **This problem deals with the use of commas to separate words such as therefore from the body of the sentence. Insert commas wherever proper in the following sentences.**

1. It is however unnecessary for you to reply at once.
2. Feel free of course to take as much time as you need.
3. Naturally we were shocked to hear of the delay.
4. It is nevertheless imperative that your representative contact us at once.
5. We feel on the other hand that your client is entitled to some minor sort of relief.
6. As we understand the situation the failure was entirely the fault of your agent.
7. To be very frank we were satisfied with neither the lamps the shades nor the fixtures.
8. It is in our opinion impossible to predict the outcome at this moment.
9. This class however is the best we have had.
10. No one naturally can be blamed for such an innocent mistake.
11. As a rule commas should set off nonessential information.
12. I believe for example that a brusque answer does much harm and little good.
13. We feel therefore that politeness is an exemplary quality.
14. No they did not report on time.
15. Well all of us make mistakes.

EXERCISE 54 — Commas and Questions Added to Statements

B. **This problem deals with the use of commas to set off questions that are added to statements and opposing ideas beginning with not. Insert commas wherever necessary in the following sentences.**

1. You received our catalogue didn't you?
2. We will send you east not west.
3. It's going to be a banner month isn't it?
4. We shall judge a man by his accomplishments not by his looks.
5. We offered you this line last year didn't we?
6. You can do the job can't you?
7. Look for facts not opinions.
8. In treating employees one should be kind and understanding not rude and impatient.
9. This is easy isn't it?
10. We hold most meetings in the morning few in the afternoon.

EXERCISE 54 — Commas: Miscellaneous Uses

C. **This problem deals with commas used in abbreviations and commas used with dates and geographical names. Insert commas and periods in the following sentences wherever necessary.**

1. Frank Henry James is our new President.
2. We have received a letter from Morris C. Cohen Esq our attorney.
3. Frances Kearney LL.D. Ph.D. will support our fund drive.
4. Jack Kent Inc well-known publishers will give a cocktail party at the St. Regis.
5. John C. Squires Ltd our Canadian firm is quite active.
6. September 3 1912 was the date of the founding of the company.
7. July 4 1776 was a red-letter day for the U.S.
8. The affair last Wednesday August 17 was a huge success.
9. The issue for July 1964 is a particularly interesting one.
10. John James III has lived at 373 Ocean Avenue San Francisco California for five years.

EXERCISE 55 — Commas: and Direct Quotations

This problem deals with the use of the comma to set off a short direct quotation. Insert commas in the following sentences wherever necessary.

1. He said "This is ridiculous."
2. "We shall not stop fighting" said he "nor shall we retreat an inch."
3. "Why" I asked "doesn't he admit he was wrong?"
4. "This is the worst job I have ever seen" was what he said.
5. I told him "Either you accept our offer or we shall deal elsewhere."
6. "Send the check to my office" he wrote.
7. "Who punched the clock at 5 P.M.?" he asked.
8. "Eureka!" he shouted at the top of his lungs "I have the solution."
9. General MacArthur swore that he would return.
10. He stated "I shall return!"

EXERCISE 56 — Sentence Errors

A. **This is a review problem on run-on sentences and sentence fragments. Proofread the following letter crossing out each error and writing in your correction. Review the material on run-on sentences and sentence fragments in Lesson 1.**

My dear Miss Green:

The Drake Hotel is a comfortable and well-managed manor. Situated on a beautiful piece of land in the hills of Bell Harbor. From the heart of Baltimore it can be reached by train or automobile. In less than an hour. Although it is near the city. It is far enough removed for rest and quiet.

Majestic old trees and attractive walks add to the beauty of the grounds the extensive lawns reach to the shore of Chesapeake Bay fishing and boating are always in season.

If you can possibly arrange your vacation to fall in August you will find the Drake Hotel at its most beautiful flowers are in bloom and the shade trees are at their lushest. Of course some of our regular guests prefer the fall when the trees are ablaze with color. And the ground is covered with a thick carpet of fallen leaves.

We extend to you and your friends. A cordial invitation to visit us.

EXERCISE 56 — Commas: Compound Sentences

B. **This problem deals with the use of the comma in compound sentences. Insert commas wherever necessary in the following sentences.**

1. Our letters haven't been very serious but underneath their semi-jesting tone runs the feeling that we will eventually get your business.
2. It was inspected it was tested it was tortured but it didn't fade or shrink.
3. Last year we had the pleasure of sending you one of our publications and we hope that it has proved of value.
4. Booklets and showroom demonstrations are interesting but actual performance on the job is convincing.
5. An excellent pool is available for those who like to swim and for those who like to play golf there is a beautiful 18-hole course.
6. Every lesson in the manual is easy and every principle is outlined in complete detail.
7. We tried and we succeeded.
8. Forgive our curiosity but why have we not heard from you?
9. Your offer was received and was carefully considered by the Board.
10. You have not written us for many weeks nor have you bothered to pay your bills.

EXERCISE 56 — Commas: Complex Sentences

C. **This problem deals with the use of the comma in complex sentences. In some of the following sentences commas are missing. Insert such commas wherever necessary.**

1. We have enjoyed full employment despite the world situation.
2. Despite the world situation we have enjoyed full employment.
3. Realizing his position John resigned.
4. John realizing his position resigned.
5. Mr. Smith despite his vast knowledge did not know the answer.
6. Despite our advice he accepted the offer.
7. Rushing to the rescue he was injured by a falling board.
8. Because of your fine past record we are keeping your account open one more week.
9. Forgetting all he had been told he stood before the audience dumbfounded.
10. While attending a convention last month I met an old friend.
11. We have accomplished much since we started.
12. As soon as the clock struck five the employees stopped working.
13. Because there were extended coffee breaks management was irritated.
14. After hearing the good news he sold his stock.
15. He will not bargain unless you do so in good faith.

EXERCISE 57 — Commas: Miscellaneous

This problem deals with the use of the comma in a variety of instances. Insert commas wherever necessary in the following sentences.

1. Last year our stockholders shared in profits of over $60000000.00.
2. On July 15 1964 the workers in our plants numbered 6475.
3. The contract dated August 4 1956 is still valid.
4. He has lived at 1220 Elm Avenue Springfield Illinois for eight years.
5. Despite poor January sales our overall net profit for the past year was over $250000.
6. We addressed the letter to Mrs. Robert Patterson 5202 South Spruce Avenue Madison Wisconsin.
7. Since our last visit in December 1963 we have reconsidered your $3000000 expansion plan.
8. We have reviewed your books for the month of July 1964 and we find a $3257.50 discrepancy with our figures.
9. On December 1 1964 we expect you to deliver 50000 tons of No. 10 steel to our warehouse at 1614 Bruce Avenue Pittsburgh Pennsylvania.
10. Please change my address in your listings from Polly Jones 616 Almond Street New Orleans Louisiana to Mrs. Robert Mayer 327 Elm Avenue Miami Beach Florida.
11. Ever since we have avoided telephoning.
12. Only three hours before we saw him alive.
13. It has been a long long process of waiting.
14. Whoever spoke spoke in vain.
15. Our arms budget exceeds $48000000000.

REVIEW EXERCISE — The Period, Question Mark, Comma

This is an overall problem dealing with the use of all the marks of punctuation you have already studied. Insert commas, periods, or question marks wherever necessary in the following letter.

Gentlemen:

Your letter and the booklet "Live Records" reach us at a time when our bookkeeping system is a matter of great concern This booklet therefore has received our careful attention

Since our office force was reduced last year the

(continued)

REVIEW EXERCISE (continued)

marked development of business during the past year has increased the urgency of our bookkeeping problem Though we have been considering the use of bookkeeping machines for a long time we are not yet convinced however that such a large outlay of money would result in a satisfactory return Nevertheless something must be done to relieve the pressure which is becoming great of our work

Will you have your representative Mr. Roberts call on Monday May 10 at ten o'clock to discuss arrangements

It is our intention to have Mr. Roberts examine our ordering billing and shipping procedures. Above all we want him to meet our bookkeepers and clerks and after he forms an impression of them we would like him to submit a written report of his recommendations with respect to personnel This would seem to be a reasonable approach wouldn't it

Are you aware of the many many new products that are being offered by our firm to customers throughout North America Central America and South America Since January 1963 we have been involved in a $3000000 expansion of our product line that has succeeded despite great odds Today we stand first in volume of sales in this field and we intend to maintain this position

Our problem is to handle the bookkeeping load and that I believe is exactly what your firm can help us achieve We look forward therefore to Mr. Roberts' visit

Sincerely

EXERCISE 58 — The Colon

A. **This problem involves the use of the colon. Insert a colon in each of the following sentences wherever proper. Add other punctuation where necessary.**

1. We have recorded your order as follows one wooden cabinet one chair three metal files one desk
2. He is quoted as saying "My only regret is that I have but one life to give for my country."
3. At precisely 456 P. M. our plane departs.
4. The following is stock on hand 3000 #10 envelopes, 2500 #13, and 1500 #17.
5. This is what he said "No amount of money could ever repay you for the fine unselfish job you did on behalf of your nation."
6. The letter began "Dear Sir I wish to thank you for your help."
7. The President stated "My fellow Americans I speak to you today on a matter of grave importance."
8. The problems we must face are these avoiding nuclear war upholding liberty developing free societies.
9. We listed three stock prices $5.52 $5.59 $6.01.
10. The following furniture was ordered three tables four chairs and four sofas.

EXERCISE 58 — The Semicolon

B. **This problem involves the use of the semicolon. Insert a semicolon in each of the following sentences wherever proper. Add other punctuation where necessary.**

1. We have not received your exam as yet consequently we have delayed sending your next lesson.
2. This is a fine surprise we were just thinking of you.
3. We have done our best the rest is up to you.
4. There are two reasons for our decision namely your determination and your doggedness.
5. To be perfectly frank I am sorry to see him go but I know that try as you might you had no alternative but to fire him.
6. The market went up for some stocks others, however, declined in value.
7. All of us were concerned about the employment picture for the year as presented by the government but following your advice we felt it our duty to remain calm.
8. Our Society includes James Brown the eminent painter Jack Jules the famous caricaturist and Cynthia Prince the well-known columnist.
9. He had one principle namely to do unto others before they did unto him.
10. The manager spoke to the staff about staying late however it was to no avail.

EXERCISE 58 — Punctuation Review

C. **This problem involves the use of the colon, semicolon, comma, and period. Insert these marks wherever proper in the following sentences.**

1. We offer a choice of three models the stately Classical the functional Colonial or the streamlined Modern.
2. Once again we are extending the time however in the future there will be no further extension
3. Standing up in the Assembly Patrick Henry shouted "Give me liberty or give me death"
4. Mrs. Housewife just mail the enclosed card postage is prepaid
5. The traits that I most admire in a man are these honesty wisdom and perseverance
6. During the past few months which have been especially hectic I inspected the following divisions the Tennessee factory the Missouri offices and the Louisiana warehouse
7. Therefore we are pleased to be able to extend this invitation but bear in mind that much as we would prefer that it be otherwise this must be our last offer
8. You Mr Smith have already received our final offer henceforth we shall not bother you again
9. To err is human to forgive divine.
10. Since our last report we have restudied the figures you submitted but despite our attempts to reconcile them the surplus figures do not coincide.

EXERCISE 59 — Quotation Marks and Other Punctuation

A. **This problem deals with the use of quotation marks and other marks of punctuation. Insert all necessary punctuation in each of the following sentences. Capitalize where necessary.**

1. he told his secretary Marie give your full attention to this purchase order.
2. do you manufacture these they asked
3. he spoke with authority saying you may be certain that our firm adheres only to the highest standards of business ethics
4. your article southeast asia has created a stir.
5. did you receive any compensation for writing the coming battle of congress
6. he asked the question how can we justify our own failure to help them
7. of all the men I know he said none compares with mr jones
8. try our new air conditioner the ad stated it will bring comfort to your home or office
9. the enclosed booklet make your own weather will show you how to maintain your volume of business during summer months
10. how are sales for your book make your own weather

(continued)

EXERCISE 59 (continued)

11. in your letter you write that the price of shipment will soon go up
12. Shakespeare wrote the evil that men do lives after them the good is oft interred with their bones
13. Nathan Hale shouted my only regret is that I have but one life to give for my country
14. don't give up the ship the commander bellowed.
15. let us know by return mail he wrote whether you will accept the offer.
16. he accused his competitor of being a blind pig-headed mule.
17. rush help or – were the last words we heard
18. Great was all he could shout.
19. Did you read the article can you diet
20. tomorrow and tomorrow and tomorrow – Shakespeare

EXERCISE 59 Using Quotation Marks

B. Properly punctuate the following:

Memorandum to J P Roberts

We received a letter from Modern Offices Inc that reads as follows

Gentlemen We have your letter of June 15 in which you enclosed the specifications for the safe equipment to be installed in the new offices of the Martin Manufacturing Company

We shall be glad to send you pictures and details of Western safes that meet these requirements

It would be more convincing however to have you and your customer visit us in Cleveland May we therefore extend an invitation to you and your customer to come to Cleveland at our expense

Please let us know when it will be most convenient for you and we shall make the necessary hotel reservations

Cordially yours

In view of the invitation extended to us in this letter I think we should very seriously consider sending a representative to inspect the Western safes in Cleveland

EXERCISE 60	The Apostrophe

A. **This problem deals with the proper use of the apostrophe. Choose the correct word.**

1. (It's, Its) a wonderful opportunity for you. 1. ________
2. Can this be (yours, your's)? 2. ________
3. (Your, You're) offer is most interesting. 3. ________
4. The (women's, womens') coats are in here. 4. ________
5. (There, They're) are three reasons for this decision. 5. ________
6. Give them (their, they're) due. 6. ________
7. (They're, Their) fed up with this type of bickering. 7. ________
8. Send us a gross of (No. 10s, No. 10's) and a hundred (No. 17s, No. 17's). 8. ________
9. A (mans, man's) success is measured in terms other than money. 9. ________
10. The company sent (its, it's) form letter. 10. ________

EXERCISE 60	Possessives and Contractions

B. **This problem deals with the use of the apostrophe in forming possessives and contractions. In the following letter insert apostrophes and other punctuation wherever necessary.**

Dear Miss Roberts:

We cant understand the failure of your firms representative to visit any of our shops during his two-week visit to our city. Its apparent to us that your sales staff misunderstands our companys position in this city. Were not a small chain of widely separated stores. Ours is a

(continued)

EXERCISE B. (continued)

large organization with no two stores more than ten blocks apart and none of them more than a few minutes walk from the center of town.

Our figures for the past half years sales reflect this concentration in our citys prime market area. These sales figures show that ours is a very profitable operation. Ones personal tastes shouldnt influence his decisions in business matters. Hard facts and figures should be the businessmans only criteria.

Well be very much pleased to open our books and records to your firm at your representatives convenience. Wouldnt you be foolish to let this opportunity go by unnoticed? Its not too late to change your mind.

Each of our shops has its own individual management and its own individual personality. All of them are famous for their consistently fine goods -- the best in mens womens and childrens clothing.

Were justly proud of the reputation weve established among our towns most respected people. Wont you please accept this invitation to send one of your representatives to inspect our stores and our books. Were looking forward to your reply within a few days time.

Sincerely,

EXERCISE 61 — The Hyphen

A. **This problem involves the use of the hyphen to divide words at the end of a line. Assume that each of the following words comes at the end of a line. In the spaces provided, write the two parts into which the word should be divided. Consult your dictionary if necessary.**

1. problem ____________ ____________
2. narrate ____________ ____________
3. amount ____________ ____________
4. hopeful ____________ ____________
5. message ____________ ____________
6. natural ____________ ____________
7. question ____________ ____________
8. inert ____________ ____________
9. innate ____________ ____________
10. legible ____________ ____________

EXERCISE 61 — Compound Words

B. **This problem deals with compound words. Some compound words are written as one word. Others are hyphenated. Still others are written as two separate words. Below is a list of compound words written separately. In the space provided, write them properly.**

1. self evident — 1. ____________
2. letter head — 2. ____________
3. ex President — 3. ____________
4. self control — 4. ____________
5. vice chairman — 5. ____________
6. father in law — 6. ____________
7. all right — 7. ____________
8. can not — 8. ____________
9. not withstanding — 9. ____________
10. real estate — 10. ____________

(continued)

EXERCISE B. (continued)

11. ex governor	11. ______________
12. type written	12. ______________
13. editors in chief	13. ______________
14. over due	14. ______________
15. post card	15. ______________
16. self conscious	16. ______________
17. any body	17. ______________
18. vice president	18. ______________
19. no one	19. ______________
20. some thing	20. ______________

EXERCISE 62 — Parentheses, Dash, and Hyphen

This problem involves the use of the parentheses, the dash, and the hyphen. Insert all necessary punctuation in the following sentences.

1. It is self evident at least it should be so to a reasonable man that our economic outlook is brightening.
2. Please look at our advertisement you can find one in this month's issue of the New Era to see what we mean by vibrant layout.
3. You should be able to collect the facts and we mean all the facts with little trouble if you are willing to apply yourself.
4. And the Licensee hereby agrees to pay Licensor on the first day of each month commencing on January the first Nineteen hundred and sixty five the sum of one hundred dollars $100.00.
5. As you have already learned see Lesson XIV a pronoun should agree in person and number with its antecedent.
6. We are interested I might say extremely interested in the report of those men who attended your factory demonstration.
7. As a result of our long experience never forget we have been in business for over a hundred years we feel it our duty to urge you to reconsider your decision.
8. Our representative Mr. Fred Perry didn't you meet him at our last convention will be glad to assist you in any way possible.
9. This chance and it's your very last chance is a fine opportunity.
10. Practice to a listen carefully b speak clearly c make your point.

EXERCISE 63 — Proper Nouns

A. **This problem involves capitalization of proper nouns. Some words that should be capitalized are not capitalized. Other words that should not be capitalized are capitalized. Cross out all incorrect letters and write the correct form above each.**

1. The Medlock tool co. appreciates the Information it received from you on october 17.
2. Our Local board of education requests bids on the new School
3. The Boardman vocational institute has a new superintendent, samuel Jones.
4. Allen and white, inc., received your Order for the Fall line early in September.
5. Mr. Robert c. Phillips, chairman of the Firm of Phillips and sons, intends to open up the west as its newest market.
6. the Carlsbad hotel is located South of Main street.
7. The Advertising Agency of Bemis, Baumer, and Beard offers exceptional coverage throughout the northwest.
8. We have inquired of our Attorney, mr. john I. dowings, to ascertain our Rights against the Omega insurance co.
9. The assistant director of The Lakeland hotel is john doe, jr.
10. The president left the white house by Limousine at Noon and rushed to the airport.
11. The Bookkeeper passed his c. p. a. Examination.
12. Our vice-president went south for the Winter.
13. The u. s. s. president Pierce is in its Berth in liverpool, england, ready for a difficult crossing of the atlantic ocean.
14. The american society for the prevention of cruelty to animals is known as the a. s. p. c. a.
15. According to mr. James a. Downing, secretary of the american association of manufacturers, the northwest is a fertile field for expansion; however, secretary Downing warns against too great reliance upon the federal government. He feels that congress will not make any substantial Appropriations during its Spring session.

EXERCISE 63 — Capitalization of Proper Nouns

B. **This problem involves capitalization of proper nouns. In the sentences below, some words that should be capitalized are not capitalized. Other words that should not be capitalized are capitalized. Cross out all incorrect letters and write the correct form above each.**

1. The chevrolet is a popular car in the south.
2. The first monday of each Month is a good time for a Meeting.
3. Our fall styles are put into production in the Spring.
4. The Southern part of texas is hottest in the Summer.
5. The ohio river flows from East to West.
6. Every person of spanish descent should know some latin.
7. Our Employer had a british accent.
8. The united nations building is near the east river.
9. The River Nile is longer than the hudson river.
10. The united states supreme court is our highest tribunal.
11. The meeting was addressed by frank James, president of neon, inc.
12. The american medical association claims to speak for most Doctors.
13. The department Supervisor of stern's department store spoke yesterday.
14. It is sometimes wise to italicize words like platonic or pasteurize.
15. He was graduated from High School and went to Yale university.

EXERCISE 64 — Capitalization

A. **The following paragraph is written without any capital letters. Cross out each small letter that should be capitalized. Write the capital letter above it.**

on wednesday, january 17, president james jackson delivered his winter message to stockholders of the apex screen co. in a speech entitled, "meeting the mosquito menace," he explained the firm's expansion into the northwest as part of man's never-ending struggle against the insect kingdom. calling for "a screen on every window," he demanded greater efforts in southern parts of the united states, where the mosquito problem was most biting.

EXERCISE 64 Capitalization Review

B. **The following letter is written without any capital letters. Cross out each small letter that should be capitalized. Write the capital letter above it.**

mr. john murphy
17 lexington avenue
new york, new york

my dear mr. murphy:

are you one of the many new york city businessmen who would like to spend a few days or a few weeks in the country, but whose business interests demand that you not venture far from manhattan? the hotel gramatan in the hills of westchester county, midway between the scenic hudson river and long island sound, offers you a most inviting home 28 minutes from grand central terminal, the heart of the shopping and theater district.

the hotel is of moorish design, and the wide spanish balconies encircling it are literally "among the tree tops."

Accommodations are on the american plan, and the rates are considerably less than the cost of equivalent accommodations in town: single room and board, $50 per week and upward; large room and private bath with board for two people, $90 per week and upward.

an excellent golf course, eight of the best tennis courts in westchester county, a string of fine saddle horses, good roads for motoring and driving are offered.

walter e. gibson, drama critic of the new york times, visited the hotel gramatan in july of last year. upon his return to new york, he wrote the following in his column, going on in new york: "the hotel gramatan is one of the finest hotels i have ever visited. its european cooking is tops."

why don't you take a drive up the scenic hutchinson river parkway and visit the gramatan some time this fall?

very respectfully yours,

REVIEW EXERCISE | Capitalization and Punctuation

This problem deals with capitalization and punctuation. The following letter is written with no punctuation marks and no capital letters. Insert all punctuation marks. Where a letter should be capitalized, cross out that letter and write the capital letter above it.

randall and peck inc.
35 draper avenue
rochester 10 new york

gentlemen

the enclosed booklet make your own weather will show you how to maintain your volume of business through the hot summer months read about our new scott portable cooler that will bring summer comfort to homes offices hospitals and hotels in your city it is an air conditioning unit that is both quiet and beautiful it is almost as easy to install as a radio and it can be moved from room to room and from building to building you cannot afford to overlook this opportunity

one large industrial user of the scott portable cooler wrote us as follows

our plant is located in the south where we face tremendous heat problems during most of the year we had considered installing other air conditioning units but all of them were too expensive then we learned about the scott cooler last spring we ordered one of the scott air conditioners for our executive office and were so satisfied with its superb performance that our purchasing manager was instructed to order scott coolers for the entire plant. I can't recommend the scott cooler too highly

take the advice of this successful businessman and the thousands like him try the scott cooler

to help our dealers we have arranged a demonstration at the factory on april 8 and 9 we invite your sales and service managers to attend this meeting at our expense.

very truly yours

REVIEW EXERCISE — Punctuation

This is a review problem on punctuation. Insert all omitted punctuation marks in the following passage.

HOW BANKS OPERATE

The ordinary idea of a bank is of an institution where one deposits money for safekeeping and withdraws it as it is needed There are many people who think of a bank in no other terms who give no thought to the manner in which a bank profits by these operations

The two fundamental concerns of a bank are borrowing and lending money When you deposit money in a bank whether it is in a checking or a saving account you are lending it money The bank in turn lends this money or a part of it to others at a rate of interest that is higher than that which you receive The difference is the profit made by the bank Such an institution must keep a surplus on hand with which to accommodate your withdrawals or the checks that you issue

As a general rule a checking account balance draws no interest The depositor receives service for the use of his money A savings account however draws a small rate of interest and the bank profits by lending your money at a higher rate than it pays

Another commonly used service of a bank is provision of storage facilities for money securities important papers jewels and other valuables These are guarded in what is known as a safe deposit vault a place that is rented for a certain sum per year for this purpose

Banks sell service They hire borrow money and they rent lend money When one hires money he has to pay the rent which is interest He also has to provide collateral or security which may be sold in case the money is not repaid

In addition the banks offer many other services to their clients or customers They collect drafts checks and coupons from bonds they pay checks issued by depositors they extend credit and they act as trustees administrators executors and guardians They advise clients with regard to the investment of money in securities land or business of any kind They are usually able to advise and assist in all kinds of financial transactions

COMMON ABBREVIATIONS

1. States and Territories:

Alabama	Ala.	Kentucky	Ky.	Oklahoma	Okla.
Alaska	Alaska	Louisiana	La.	Oregon	Oreg.
Arizona	Ariz.	Maine	Maine	Pennsylvania	Pa.
Arkansas	Ark.	Maryland	Md.	Puerto Rico	P. R.
California	Calif.	Massachusetts	Mass.	Rhode Island	R. I.
Colorado	Colo.	Michigan	Mich.	Samoa	Samoa
Connecticut	Conn.	Minnesota	Minn.	South Carolina	S. C.
Delaware	Del.	Mississippi	Miss.	South Dakota	S. Dak.
District of Columbia	D. C.	Missouri	Mo.	Tennessee	Tenn.
Florida	Fla.	Montana	Mont.	Texas	Tex.
Georgia	Ga.	Nebraska	Nebr.	Utah	Utah
Guam	Guam	Nevada	Nev.	Vermont	Vt.
Hawaii	Hawaii	New Hampshire	N. H.	Virginia	Va.
Idaho	Idaho	New Jersey	N. J.	Virgin Islands	V. I.
Illinois	Ill.	New Mexico	N. Mex.	Washington	Wash.
Indiana	Ind.	New York	N. Y.	West Virginia	W. Va.
Iowa	Iowa	North Carolina	N. C.	Wisconsin	Wis.
Kansas	Kans.	North Dakota	N. Dak.	Wyoming	Wyo.
		Ohio	Ohio		

2. Canadian Provinces:

Alberta	Alta.	New Brunswick	N.B.	Prince Edward Island	P.E.I.
British Columbia	B.C.	Newfoundland	Nfld.	Quebec	Que.
Manitoba	Man.	Nova Scotia	N.S.	Saskatchewan	Sask.
		Ontario	Ont.		

3. Months of the Year:

Jan.	January	May	May	Sept.	September
Feb.	February	June	June	Oct.	October
Mar.	March	July	July	Nov.	November
Apr.	April	Aug.	August	Dec.	December

4. Compass Directions:

E.	East	N.W.	Northwest	S.W.	Southwest
N.	North	S.	South	W.	West
N.E.	Northeast	S.E.	Southeast		

5. Units of Measure:

Length		Weight		Time		Electronic	
cm.	centimeter	cg.	centigram	d.	day	a.	ampere
ft.	foot, feet	gm.	gram	hr.	hour	c.	cycle
in.	inch	gr.	grain	min.	minute	kc.	kilocycle
m.	meter	kg.	kilogram	mo.	month	kv.	kilovolt
mi.	mile	lb.	pound	sec.	second	kw.	kilowatt
mm.	millimeter	mg.	milligram	yr.	year	mc.	megacycle
yd.	yard	oz.	ounce	a.m.	before noon	v.	volt
				M.	noon	w.	watt
				p.m.	afternoon		

6. Standard Business Terms:

abbreviated, abbreviation	abbr.
absolute	abs.
acknowledged	ack'd
acre	A
adjective	adj.
ad libitum (at pleasure)	ad lib.
administration	assn.
Administrator	Admr.
Administratrix	Admx.
adverb	adv.
advertise	adv.
affidavit	afft.
against	vs.
agent	agt.
agreement	agmt.
America, American	Am.
American Automobile Association	A.A.A.
American Bankers Association	A.B.A.
amount	amt.
and	&
and others	et al.
and the following pages	ff.
Anno Domini (in the year of our Lord)	A.D.
anonymous	anon.
answer	ans., A.
apartment	apt.
approximate	approx., ap.
article	art.
Associated Press	AP
association	assn.
at	@
attention	attn., atten.
Attorney	Att., Atty.
Avenue	Av., Ave.
average	av., avg.
Bachelor of Arts	A.B., B.A.
Bachelor of Science	B.S.
balance	bal.
bank	bk.
banking	bkg.
barrel	bbl.
Before Christ	B.C.
board	bd.
bill of lading	B/L
bills payable	B.P.
bills receivable	B.R.
bill of sale	B/S
Boulevard	Blvd.
branch office	B.O.
brother	Bro.
brothers	Bros.
brought forward	b.f.
building	bldg.
bulletin	bul.
bureau	Bu., Bur.
bushel	bu.
box	bx.
by authorization	P.P.
by way of	via
capital	cap.
Captain	Capt.
carbon copy	c.c., cc
care of	c/o
catalog	cat.

Centigrade	C.
cents	c., cts.
certificate	cert., ct., ctf.
certificate of deposit	C/D
Certified Professional Secretary	C.P.S.
Certified Public Accountant	C.P.A.
chapter	chap., ch., C.
charge	chg.
Christmas	Xms., Xmas.
collect, or cash, on delivery	C.O.D., c.o.d.
company	co.
collection	coll.
Colonel	Col.
commerce	com.
commission	comm.
compare	cf.
continued	contd., cont., con.
copyright	©
Corporation	Corp.
correct	OK
credit	cr.
creditor	Cr.
degree	deg.,°
deliver	del.
department	dpt., dept.
dictionary	dict.
Director	Dir.
discount	dis.
district	dist.
division	div.
direct current	d.c., dc
ditto, the same	do.
dollar(s)	d., dls., dols.
dozen	doz.
Doctor	Dr.
Doctor of Philosophy	Ph.D.
Doctor of Dental Surgery	D.D.S.
Doctor of Divinity	D.D.
Doctor of Laws	LL.D.
Doctor of Medicine	M.D.
each	ea.
Editor	Ed.
electric	elec.
employment	empl.
enclosure	enc., encl.
end of month	e.o.m.
envelope	env.
equal	eq.
errors and omissions excepted	E. & O.E.
establish	est.
Esquire	Esq.
et cetera, and so forth	etc.
example	ex.
exchange	exc., exch.
Executor	Exec.
Executrix	Execx.
expense, express	exp.
extension	ext.
Fahrenheit	F., Fahr.
Federal	Fed.
Federal Bureau of Investigation	FBI

Federal Communications Commission	FCC	Journal	J., Jr., Joun.
Federal Deposit Insurance Corporation	FDIC	Junior	Jr.
Federal Reserve Board	FRB	Justice of the Peace	J.P.
Federal Trade Commission	FTC	karat	K., kt.
feminine	fem., f.	laboratory	lab.
figure	fig.	language	lang.
first	1st (no period)	large	la., lge.
first class	A-1	latitude	lat.
folio	fo., fol., f.	leave	lv.
footnote	fn., ftnt.	Ledger folio	L.f.
for example	e.g.	Legislature	Leg.
Fort	Ft.	lesson	Les.
forward	fwd.	let it stand	stet
fourth	4th (no period)	letter	ltr.
free on board	f.o.b.	letter of credit	L/C
freight	frt., fgt.	library	lib.
from	fr., fm.	Lieutenant	Lieut., Lt.
		limited	Ltd.
gallon	gal.	line	l.
General	Gen., Gen'l	list price	L.P.
General Headquarters	GHQ	literature	lit.
general mortgage	gm	location, local	loc.
goods	gds.	longitude	long.
Governor	Gov.	lumber	lbr.
government	gov't		
gram	g.	machine	mch., mach.
gross	gr.	Madam	Mme.
guaranteed	gtd.	Mademoiselle	Mlle.
		magazine	mag.
half	hf.	Major	Maj.
hardware	hdw.	Manager	Mgr.
Headquarters	Hq.	manufactured	mfd.
height	ht.	manufacturing	mfg.
Highway	Hwy., Hy.	manufacture	mfr.
history	hist.	manuscript	ms., MS.
Honorable	Hon.	mark	mk.
horsepower	hp., hp	market	mkt., mar.
hospital	Hosp.	masculine	m., mas., masc.
hundred	C	Master of Arts	M.A.
hundredweight	cwt.	Master of Ceremonies	M.C.
		maturity	mat.
I owe you	IOU	mathematics	math.
illustration, illustrated	ill., illus.	maximum	max.
improvement	imp., impr.	medium	med.
in the place cited	i.c.	memorandum	memo.
in the same place	ib. ibid.	merchandise	mdse.
in the word cited	op. cit.	Mesdames	Mmes.
inches	in.	Messieurs	Messrs., MM.
inclusive	incl.	metropolitan	met.
Incorporated	Inc.	midnight	mid., mdnt.
industrial, independent	ind.	military	mil.
inferior	inf.	miscellaneous	misc.
initial	init.	Mister	Mr.
in regard to	re	Mistress	Mrs.
insurance	ins.	money order	m.o.
intelligence quotient	I. Q.	Monsieur	M.
interest	int.	mortgage	mtg.
International	Int.,	mount	Mt.
International Business Machine	I. B. M.	municipal	mun.
Interstate Commerce Commission	ICC	namely	viz.
inventory	invt.	namely or to wit	sc., scil., sct.
invoice, investment	inv.	national	Nat., Natl.
Invoice Book	I.B.	no good	n.g.
Island, Isle	I.	not sufficient funds	N.S.F., N/S
italics	ital.	Notary Public	N.P.
		note well	n.b., N.B.
joint	jt.	number	no., #

obituary	obit.
obsolete	obs.
opened	opd.
opposite	opp.
optional	opt.
ordinance	ord.
organization	org.
original	orig.
Pacific	Pac.
package	pkg.
page	p.
pages	pp.
paid	pd.
pair	pr.
pamphlet	pam.
paragraph	¶, par.
parcel post	p.p.
parenthesis	paren., par.
parkway	Pkwy.
part	pt.
patent	pat.
payment	payt.
per annum	per an.
per cent	%, pct.
piece	pc.
pint	pt.
place	pl.
place of the seal	L.S.
Plaintiff	Plf.
population	pop.
Post Exchange	PX
Postmaster	PM.
Post Office	P.O.
postpaid	ppd.
postscript	P.S.
pound sterling	£
pound, shilling, pence	£, s., d.
power of attorney	P/A
preferred	pfd.
premium	pm., prem.
President	Pres., P.
price	pr.
principal	prin.
private branch exchange	PBX
problem	prob.
Professor	Prof.
Profit and Loss	P & L, P/L
pronoun	pron.
public	pub.
Publishing, Publisher	Pub.
quality	qly.
quantity	qty.
quart	qt.
quarter, quire	qr.
question	Q.
railroad	R.R.
railway	Ry.
ream, room	rm.
receipt	rec't
receivable	rec.
received	recd., rcd.
reference	ref.
Registered	®, rg., reg.
Registered Nurse	R.N.
regular	reg.
Reply, if you please	R.S.V.P.
report	rep't
returned	rtd.
Reverend	Rev.
right	rt.
road	rd.
route	Rt.
rural free delivery	R.F.D.
rural route	R.R.
Sainte	Ste
Savings	Sav.
section	sec.
Senate, Senator	Sen.
Secretary	Sec., Secy.
Securities Exchange Commission	SEC
Senior	Sr.
school	sch.
shipment	shpt.
signature	sig.
signed	/S/
singular	sing.
so, thus	sic
square	sq.
standard	std.
steamship	SS.
stock	stk.
Street	St.
subsidiary	subs.
Superintendent	Supt.
supplement	supp.
syndicate	synd.
table	tab.
tablespoon	tbsp., T.
teaspoon	tsp., t.
telephone	tel.
temporarily	pro tem.
Territory	Ter.
that is	i.e.
the following	seq.
the same	id.
thousand	M
township	Twp.
trial balance	T/B
Treasurer	Treas.
Trust, Trustee	Tr.
United Nations	U.N., UN
United Press International	UPI
University	Univ.
very important person	VIP
volume	vol.
warehouse receipt	W.R.
waybill	W/B
week	wk.
weight	wt.
which was to be proved	Q.E.D.
wholesale	whsle.
work	wk.

INDEX